AF615954

KP

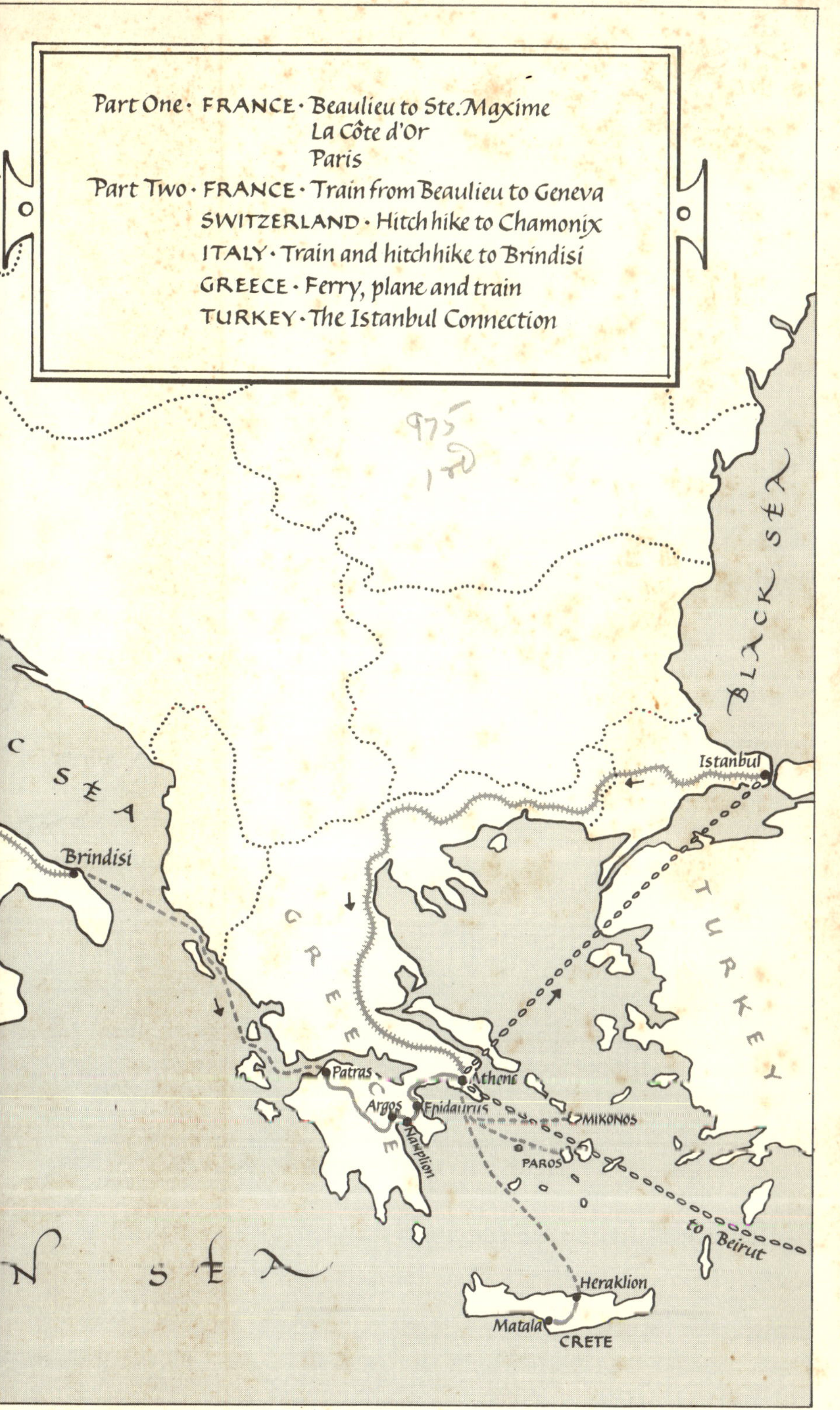

Part One · FRANCE · Beaulieu to Ste. Maxime
La Côte d'Or
Paris
Part Two · FRANCE · Train from Beaulieu to Geneva
SWITZERLAND · Hitchhike to Chamonix
ITALY · Train and hitchhike to Brindisi
GREECE · Ferry, plane and train
TURKEY · The Istanbul Connection
BLACK SEA
Istanbul
C SEA
Brindisi
GREECE
TURKEY
Patras
Athens
Argos
Epidaurus
Nauplion
MIKONOS
PAROS
to Beirut
N SEA
Heraklion
Matala
CRETE

LESSONS OF THE ROAD

AN OVERLAND JOURNEY TO THE EAST

Michael Schiffer

KENAN PRESS · NEW YORK

PUBLISHED BY KENAN PRESS, A SIMON & SCHUSTER DIVISION OF GULF & WESTERN CORPORATION.
SIMON & SCHUSTER BUILDING, ROCKEFELLER CENTER, 1230 AVENUE OF THE AMERICAS, NEW YORK, NEW YORK 10020.
KENAN PRESS AND COLOPHON ARE TRADEMARKS OF SIMON & SCHUSTER.

DESIGNED BY EVE METZ
MANUFACTURED IN THE UNITED STATES OF AMERICA

1 3 5 7 9 10 8 6 4 2

LIBRARY OF CONGRESS CATALOGING IN PUBLICATION DATA

SCHIFFER, MICHAEL.
LESSONS OF THE ROAD.

1. NEAR EAST—DESCRIPTION AND TRAVEL. 2. SOUTH ASIA—DESCRIPTION AND TRAVEL. 3. SCHIFFER, MICHAEL. I. TITLE.
DS49.7.S25 914'.0455 80-18110
ISBN 0-671-25380-8

I would like to express my appreciation for permission to quote from the following: Henry Miller, *The Colossus of Maroussi,* © 1941 by Henry Miller, reprinted by permission of New Directions; Plutarch, *The Age of Alexander,* Ian Scott-Kilvert translator, translation © 1973 by Ian Scott-Kilvert, reprinted by permission of Penguin Books Ltd.; Thucydides, *The Peloponnesian War,* Rex Warner translator, translation © 1954 by Rex Warner, reprinted by permission of Penguin Books Ltd.; Alexandra David Neel, *Magic and Mystery in Tibet,* © 1965 by University Books, Inc., published by arrangement with Lyle Stuart; Thubten Jigme Norbu and Colin M. Turnbull, *Tibet,* © 1968 by Thubten Jigme Norbu and Colin M. Turnbull, reprinted by permission of Simon & Schuster, a Division of Gulf & Western Corporation; John F. Avedon, "In Exile from the Land of Snows," from *Rolling Stone Magazine,* © 1979 by Straight Arrow Publishing, Inc. All rights reserved. Reprinted by permission.

I offer my personal thanks to Cheryl; Richard; Marie and her family; Joan Raines; Dan Green; Ralph Gutlohn; Jerry Roberts; David Austin; Lawrence Lasker; Linda Kiefer; John Franchot; Maureen Strange; Frederic D. Kent; Laelah Verot; Alex Vertikoff; Jacques and Mimi Canonici; Herbert and Elizabeth Cutler; and my parents.

To Cheryl, Richard and Michèle

CONTENTS

VOYAGE, noun masculine (from Latin, *viaticum*, silver, money for a journey). Act of going from one place to another fairly far away. *Slang*. Hallucinatory trip provoked by a drug. *Les gens du voyage*, the artists of the circus.

—*Petit Larousse Illustré*, 1974.

PART ONE

FRANCE

1973

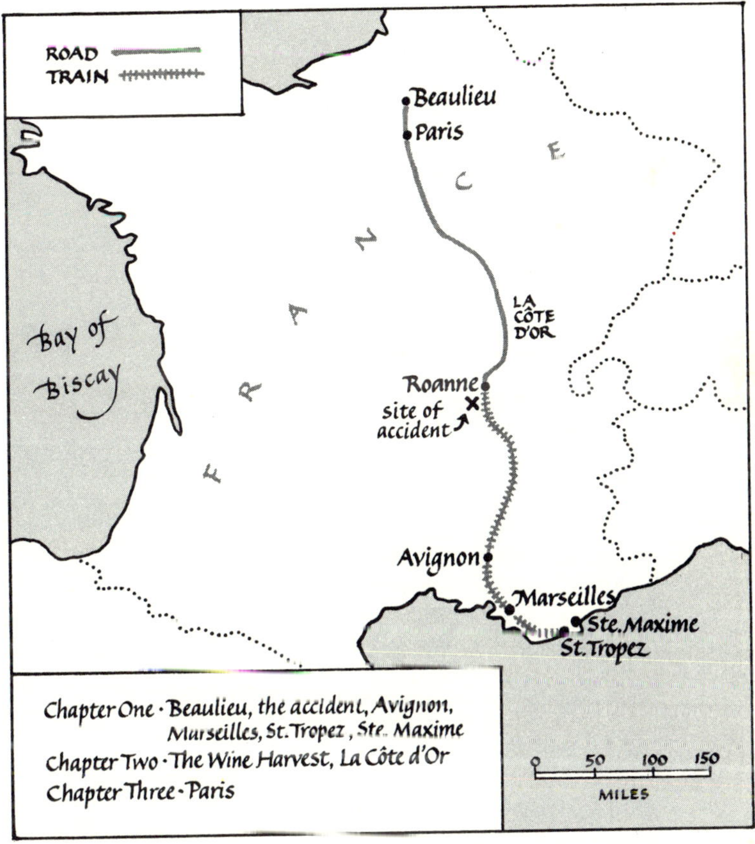

I'M A GUEST HERE in a large mansion in a small village in France. Maids attend my every need. They watch in horror as I lean back in antique chairs that shatter and crack. They iron my clothes. The gossip stops when I walk by, but it doesn't really matter, I can't understand a word. Even the children talk down to me, my five years of French, a waste.

"In my own country," I tell them, "I am a writer," but no one seems to care. They wonder about my intelligence, my powers of comprehension. Even Rudi, the cocker spaniel, responds with greater alacrity to their suggestions. We take long walks through the orchards and plowed fields. Rudi lies down, flat out in large mud puddles and drinks without lifting his head. He bounds through the wheat.

I've learned to remove my shoes before entering the house. Prior to that there were sandy tracks along routes I must have traveled and I'd taken to carrying a large towel, which I swept behind me like a tail. Upstairs are hardwood floors and red carpet runners. The boards creak on every step. The only way to go unnoticed is to lie still in my room, which I try most every night, at least until morning comes and the smell of coffee drifts under the door.

One month ago I was in San Francisco, selling handmade jewelry at Fisherman's Wharf, when Marie, the youngest daughter of a large French family, arrived with her boyfriend, saw the setup and invited me back to the tiny village of Beaulieu to instruct her. Tired of the fog and the cold summer nights, I accepted, but instead of the little farm I had envisioned, I feel like I've wandered into a Tolstoyan novel.

Marie's family has three maids, a gardener, and twenty full-time field hands. Papa, the patriarch, a wry old Catholic with a shrewd eye, inherited his land and turned it into one of the first modern farms in all of France. At one point he owned nearly the entire village, but he's sold it off bit by bit to the men and women who work for him. Of all the people out here I get along with him best. Having retired from actively running his operation (although he still handles the paper work), he takes time and delight in explaining things that the rest of the family have long since taken for granted.

Maman, his wife, is a warm, funny, unbelievably energetic woman from a family of old North African colonials, called *pieds noirs* (black feet) by the natives for the shoes they wore into the desert. She's in constant motion, fussing with the maids or clucking over her grandchildren. At Sunday lunch we rarely number fewer than fourteen. On holidays the brood may swell to more than thirty.

Dinner is at seven-thirty sharp. When Maman is ready she rings a cast-brass bell in the shape of a little serving girl. The first time she did that and Arlette popped through the door I nearly flipped, but all that passes my lips now is, "*Le beurre, s'il vous plait.*"

The soup is good, the bread fresh, the salad perfect. I am seduced. I work even harder to justify my presence. Marie and I pound *bijoux* (pronounced *bee-joo*, meaning jewelry) all day, and show up at mealtimes looking like chimney sweeps.

We are a source of high humor for the family, who, not surprisingly, are among our best customers. The eldest son runs the farm and heads the local growers' cooperative. The second son, in the time-honored tradition of second sons, joined the Army and worked his way up to be aide-de-camp to a high-ranking French official; while the third son, Henri, manages the wine estate of which Marie's parents are one-fourth owners.

The eldest daughter, a weekend regular, is a Paris schoolteacher. The second sister, recently returned from six years of self-imposed exile (about which she says nothing) has gone in less than a decade from being a Girl Scout leader to an activist nun to an anarchist revolutionary. The third daughter, with the face and figure of a Rubens nymph, married an art dealer of aristocratic background and bore him three gorgeous daughters, perfect soft-skinned beauties; while the youngest son is a Communist, who lost one position as a result of his political leanings, then injured his back on an assembly line and returned to work on the farm.

That brings us to Marie, the baby of the family, twenty-two years old, but twenty years younger than her oldest brother, Alain. Marie has had to struggle all her life against the pecking order in this barnyard of brothers and sisters, each of whom, regardless of his or her political leanings, has taken some solace in the fact that there was always someone (baby Marie) who had a harder time doing things than they.

Frustrated trying to get explanations for things which had already been explained at least seven times, once to each of her siblings, Marie learned to clown; then at sixteen she bloomed, charming and funny, a beauty in her own right, with dark-brown hair and flawless olive skin. She led a gang of kids on vacation in the south of France, grew tired of the nuns at school, then took off at the first opportunity for Spain to learn Spanish, then to England, where she began speaking American with the first of her foreign boyfriends.

By the time I've met her, Marie speaks English with almost no accent, although in the course of her recent amours her command of her native tongue has slipped considerably. When I first arrived in France and we stopped for some pastry, the lady complimented her on her French, and wouldn't believe Marie when she protested that she *was* French.

Before I got here I imagined that we'd wind up as lovers, but refusing to mix business with pleasure (or perhaps she has other, better reasons), Marie keeps putting me off, and as time goes by I find I'm becoming a parody of myself, "Capitaine Bijoux" they call me, a comic-strip hero serving time, chained to the stake in the little house Marie's Papa has given us to use as a workshop.

Even with the two of us working as one (I'm undeclared, technically just an adviser, like the U.S. military in Vietnam), we'd be strapped without the help of Marie's parents, who are glad to see her learning a skill, even if it is just *bijoux*. Survival for an independent artisan in France can be extremely tough. You have to pay a stiff tax whether you show any profit or not, twenty percent is added onto materials and tools, while an incredible thirty-three percent is levied on items classified as deluxe.

It's hard enough to make it in the States, but with taxes so high and so much of the French worker's income eaten up in food and rent, our market is minuscule. The government in Paris doesn't like marginals. They'd just as soon squeeze them out.

Today is my birthday. I'm the same age as my father in that old Army Air Force photograph. He was handsome and radiant back then, but I feel burnt out, nostalgic for his past. He grew up in the Depression, left home when he was fifteen and wound up in a war, but although he hated it, never said one good word about it, I'm stupid, I've never believed him.

I figure he was lucky, that at least he got to see the world (bombing runs over Burma) and had the chance to confront his fears firsthand. That's what we (and I use the term loosely) hated most about Vietnam. My friends and I were closet heroes; we could have used that war, but wound up getting student deferments, or paying good money to have our half-truths spun into madness by Park Avenue psychiatrists.

We fought the good fight, or the good non-fight, non-fighting being the aim of that ground swell, and took consolation from being right—easy enough back then. I was at Harvard during Vietnam. Our faculty was doing such a good job justifying that war, they made it sound so downright attractive, that we tried to bring it home.

When busloads of cops pulled into Harvard Yard one fine April morning before dawn, we were packed inside an occupied building, arms linked, chanting "Solidarity Forever." I must confess I didn't know the words. I was there because my friends were there. People were drawing lines in those days and one felt obliged to step to either side. Besides, my girlfriend was there.

We sang some more and had the whole building rocking, when suddenly the fence sitters on the steps outside shrieked and the singing stopped. Glass from the foyer doors, which had been chained shut, hit the floor and the cops rushed in, reaching out with riot clubs. Feet shuffled and people cried as the police pressed forward in gas masks and shields, swinging harder now, busting heads. You could hear them go *pop, pop, pop.*

That was enough. I jumped out a window, dragging my girlfriend with me. It was a smart move, but an act of cowardice nonetheless. She would have stayed, but getting beaten with a nightstick was not my idea of valor. I walked around the Yard, screaming at the deans, trying to air out my insides, and in one sense have been running from that moment ever since.

Now I'm in France, cut off in this idyllic village, so peaceful I'm about to go nuts. Unfortunately, I'm stuck, because as soon as I arrived we invested all my funds in silver, to transform into baubles to dangle before the eyes of jaded tourists on the Mediterranean coast. I shouldn't complain; even the most mundane chores, like buying bread, can be an adventure out here, but I'm looking forward to the time when Marie has learned the basics and we can finally hit the road to sell.

I wake after seven to the sound of tractors—Massey-Fergusons, rattling their teeth in the courtyard. There's a bomb under the lawn somewhere, left by Germans in the First World War. None too eager to find out where (precisely) it lay, the family constructed a wall around it and planted grass. The gardener holds his breath and mows lightly. The dogs don't give a yip.

After breakfast I got roped into a shopping trip with Marie.

We hop in her brand-new Volkswagen bus (she's just talked her Papa into freeing up part of her dowry) and descend from the farm (built on the bones of a fifteenth-century monastery) down the one main street of Beaulieu, past the church and out into the rolling hills.

Fifteen minutes later we reach the next town. Marie heads down to the druggist, leaving me in line with an armful of yogurt, when one of those impossible French schoolgirls walks in, having just braved the gauntlet of young toughs, sitting outside in a bored circle on their motorbikes. The poor girl hikes her skirt, trips on shoes three inches off the ground, then retreats into her angry little pout when the boys stare. Of course, the boys would gawk even if she were covered up in a blanket or a sack, so who's to blame? No one. No blame. Why can't I get that through my head?

We climb back into the bus to retrace our route on the narrow country road. The fields have already undergone a subtle transformation since I first arrived in early June. The basic progression is God-given, but out here in farm country man orchestrates the changes, conducts a symphony of corn and wheat. Seedlings shimmer, they turn dark green and swell, everything yellows, the baton drops and—Chop!—the whole thing is laid bare. Sugar beets simmer, the fruit trees are stripped, the ground's plowed under and the cycle starts again. I can see it all before me, almost hear it.

It's raining. Cold flowers push forth in bunches and shiver in the mist. Madame Dubonnet, our next-door neighbor, is waiting for the meat truck to pass, standing in a little shawl on the half-paved road that runs past our workshop into the fields.

"*Il fait froid, eh?*" she says, shivering. "What deplorable weather!"

Last year there was no rain at all and everyone was miserable, but now when it rains, it's too wet. Dubonnet stares across the road at the Party poster she put up. I still can't get used to the fact that the lady next door is a leftist. I thought it was illegal.

Soon the meat truck pulls up, driven by a woman in a spotted smock—the butcher, La Bouchère. She throws open her side window, revealing trays of beefsteak, cutlets, chicken and sausage. Dubonnet looks them over, spots the pork and says, "That's pork? It's lean. Last week I bought a whole one, but it was fatty."

"Really?"

"Yes, I assure you it was." Madame Dubonnet's been picking pork for forty years. Today she can tell a lean one, but when she took one last week she couldn't. She goes on, "Can I pay you next week? This week I have bills . . . and taxes . . . ah, these taxes! *Là, alors* . . ."

"I know, my taxes are due the fifteenth."

"And the electricity!" says Dubonnet, trumping.

"Oh, my electricity's not too bad . . ."

"But you must pay it, eh?"

"I suppose," says La Bouchère, sadly. "Maybe one day we won't have all these taxes. *That* will be the revolution."

"It's coming," says Dubonnet, "Friday the strike, then the general strike on the nineteenth . . . then we'll see something, eh?"

"Oh, the general strike . . . I'm not so—"

"No, it's coming!"

"Listen, what difference will it make?" La Bouchère is frozen in her truck. She drives five hours to get to Beaulieu by noon on a route covering twenty-five villages a week.

Dubonnet shifts her tack. "*Ah, oui,* what'll we have then? We'd best watch out, eh? We'll wind up with a civil war—one group knocking on another . . . *ah, oui,* then it will be hard! *Merci, Madame. Au revoir.*"

She takes her cutlets and poulet and pads back to her faded pink and pastel-yellow door. La Bouchère rolls her eyes and turns to my ground beef, perfectly lean, what the French call *viande hachée.* We listen to Dubonnet inside complaining about the grandchildren who get in her way, the son-in-law who ran off and then had the gall to come back, her husband's boss, the price of meat and always the weather.

Madame Dubonnet is a satisfied woman, with her house, her family and her garden, but one day—*là alors* . . . then she will be truly happy. I can hear her through the walls—"Look where you walk on my flowers, children . . . look where the dog went, eh? Eh? I ask you . . ."

The weather warms. There's nothing much to do between now and September but spray for bugs and pray for rain, so Marie's family takes off for Nice, leaving us alone in the big house. One night after supper an old drifter stops by, looking for work. Marie is at a loss. Even if there were work, there's no one here right now to hire him.

"How about some food?" she asks. "Are you hungry?"

"Yes, Miss, I'm very hungry."

She invites him in and checks the pot for leftovers—artichoke hearts in a thick onion sauce. "No," he says, "I can't eat that, not with my stomach."

"How about fish?"

"I don't like fish," he says, "make me an omelette," and when Marie asks him how many eggs, he says, "Four."

"Four?"

"I could say five. I haven't eaten in two days."

Marie's eyes flicker with grief at the sight of this cantankerous old man, left to wander out his days pushing around a little two-wheeled cart (parked outside) half leaning on it to hold himself up, going from door to door, farm to farm and region to region, staying alive as best he can. The sudden light and prolonged exposure have him dazed, so Marie leads him to the sink, then sits him down and starts fluttering around, getting his meal together.

Her reaction is showing me a side of her I've never seen. She puts more empathy into this guy's omelette than I've got in my whole body. Marie may have been born into luxury, but her roots are in the soil and she knows what it's like to be without. I suspect her mother's been feeding strangers this way for years, through a couple of wars.

The old guy warns her not to cook the eggs too long, then

talks as he eats. "Time between jobs used to be nothin'. Used to get there in no time, now it takes all my time. This is good. Good eggs."

"My brother's away," says Marie, "I'll ask around tomorrow. I'm not sure there's any work."

"That's OK, there's plenty a' farms." He tears off a piece of bread and starts into the Camembert, emptying the decanter of wine. "I worked two weeks last month with a young fella, treated me just fine. Had me eat right there with him, family and everything. Had a nice bed, worked hard, pulled my weight . . . I'd a' stayed forever, but the work got done. Two weeks 'll seem like a year when you get right down into it. I was sorry to leave that place." His eyes cloud up. "You two married?"

"No," says Marie.

"We're working on it," I grin.

"What are you, German or something?"

"No, American."

"You speak good French. Just stay with it and just like that, nobody'll know. I mean it. He speaks good French, eh?"

"Not bad," says Marie.

"Well—" he pushes back from the table—"that was good. Can I sleep somewhere? Out in the barn?"

"Of course," says Marie, "I'll get some blankets."

She runs off, leaving the two of us alone.

"No kidding," he says, "your accent's good. It's just a little off, that's all. Stay with it. How long you been here? A month? Three more weeks, that's all you need. You'll sound like a regular Frenchman."

Marie returns with the blankets and hands them over as he heads out the door. That pained look is back in her eyes and I can see the wheels turning. She'd like to put him up, but it's really not her house. What if something happened? Where would he sleep?

"All right," he says, "thanks a lot. Is that the barn over there? Thanks. Thanks for the eggs. I'll ask around in the morning."

"I'll talk to the foreman," says Marie.

"Good. You take care of her now," he says to me, then, "*Bon soir.*" He walks off with the blankets balanced on his little cart and that's the last we see of him. When morning comes the blankets are folded up by the kitchen window and the drifter is gone.

Somehow his going and my staying marks a change in the order. I'm a member of the household now, I've been accepted, but I'm relieved to see, judging by her response last night, that no matter how I might have wound up here, Marie would not send me away hungry.

August 1—We're driving south in Marie's beautiful new bus, heading to the Mediterranean to sell, when, looking back to talk to the two German hitchhikers she's just picked up, Marie takes her eyes off the road, and before she knows it the bus itself is off the road and the windshield is totally green, hissing, sliding sideways through the tall weeds. I get bounced around to the rear for a surreal view of the two Germans dropping slowly, suspended like cosmonauts in a space capsule as the white VW rotates around them. Three quarters of the way through the first roll we slam into a phone pole, by a train track, down a steep hill.

The funny thing is that right before the accident I had a premonition. We had just come from Marie's brother's wine estate in Burgundy, where for two days we ate like kings, drank the finest wines, sipped Armagnac from '42 and smoked Havana cigars until our heads were spinning. The domain is housed in a château built during the reign of Napoleon III. Dining-room doors open onto a balcony overlooking an unequaled vista of dark-green vines bearing hard little grapes. Stone walls break up the fields, ordering the landscape, giving it form, giving one's eyes a place to rest as they move across the mountain.

Every square inch of land in Burgundy is treasured. They savor every fossilized stone in the lime-rich soil that gives the wine its character. Looking out across the fields that first evening, I was easily overwhelmed. I'm just a kid from Philly, after all. I went to Harvard, sure, but only with loans that I'm still paying off at $33.23 a shot.

Marie's brother and sister-in-law were casual about all this wealth and before long I too was at ease, flirting shamelessly with their daughters, picking them up and swinging them about my head. On the third morning we said goodbye and started south again, then two hours down the road a thought came into my brain, fully formed like a proverb, "*Il faut savoir tomber, et puis monter,*" which means, You have to know how to fall, and then get back up.

It was an odd little notion (I usually don't think in either proverbs or French), having to do with the heights where we'd just sojourned. I worked it around in my head, remarking on its curious gloom, then ten minutes later Marie had us down in that ditch . . .

I step out through the place where the windshield used to be, see the wheels spinning and the phone line dangling, then head back in for the hitchhikers. The guy has lost his glasses and is very agitated. I'm pretty damned agitated myself, but I find his specs, take his arm and lead him out, explaining in French, which he speaks even less than I, that everything will be all right.

The hitchhikers take off to avoid the cops, as Marie and I go back to assess the mess. The interior of the car is coated with boiled eggs, fruit cake and homemade jam. All our tools are under the plywood bed. If we hadn't bolted it down as an afterthought, the Germans would have been crushed.

We wind up camping in a field of nettles, go back the next day to oversee the extraction of our mangled bus from the hole, then drive it with a peaked roof, *sans* windshield, some fifty miles to a VW dealer in Roanne. Marie's brother arrives a day later from Burgundy to cart off the bulk of our stuff (everything we owned was in that truck, we had planned to live and work on the road, like Gypsies), then we move on to Plan B, in which I get to lug our backpacks, tent, table, two chairs and jewelry to the railroad, so that Marie can save a few bucks hitching.

I barely have time to wave goodbye before she sticks out a hip and flags down the first of her Porsches. Clad in cutoffs and a T-shirt, Marie is one of the finest hitchhikers, fictional or otherwise, ever to thumb her way down the pike. I have a vivid picture of her riding in air-conditioned comfort, while I, heaped with junk, struggle to the station to wait two hours for the Mistral, headed south. I can just see Marie fighting off the advances of Italian counts and ski bums, who beg her to pass a few days, hours, minutes even ("How about here in the front seat, while I drive?") with them in passionate intimacy ("*Mi amore . . .*"), as I push my way onto a train to Marseille packed asshole to elbow with French sausage salesmen and vacationing nymphs.

How coolly these French girls see themselves in men's eyes. How coldly they practice cruelties unheard of in less civilized climes. I sit on our satchels, keeping hold of my senses, as odors of armpit and desire rise and mingle in the heat. The window is slashed with phone poles passing at an even clip. I shut my eyes, but the clatter continues.

I pass the time this way, thinking back to those quiet days in Beaulieu, watching the young girls with their bare arms, thinking how much better things might be, but on the other hand, how much better they are than what might have been. We might have been killed in that car crash. I could be back in Philly, for Chris'sake.

So what if our car wound up in a ditch? So what if Fate took a half gainer with a three-quarter twist? It's still the best and worst of all possible worlds, there's nothing new about the situation, I'm just going to have to start paying more attention to those little premonitions of mine. A simple "Be careful" to Marie on the drive down from Burgundy would have saved us a lot of trouble.

The upshot of all this is that our selling trip to the south of France is a bust. We would have done fine at Avignon, but the theater festival was closing by the time we arrived, so we sold a few things, then pushed down to a campground halfway between St. Tropez and Ste. Maxime, where we lie in our tent, surrounded by vacation vehicles that blot out the sun.

Television aerials jut into the sky. The dulcet tones of tight-lipped lady announcers with rock crystal hairdos filter through the curtains. While the men are out fishing or drinking in the local bars, their wives work, scrubbing and cooking. Women don't go on vacation in France. They do not have August off. They spend their time trying to fulfill the pledges of recreational-vehicle salesmen who promised their spouses all the comforts of home.

Our first day in Ste. Maxime we learn that street sales have just been prohibited. We try to ignore that fact, but buyers are wary and our jewelry tarnishes quickly in the heat. Down the road in St. Tropez our luck just gets worse. The only legal place to sell is in the morning market, and the cops are quite adamant about keeping the riffraff off the streets.

Marie and I get up at dawn and hike six miles with our folding tables and chairs to squeeze in between the carrots and cheese. Still waiting for our first sale at noon, we wind up trading earrings for lunch, then Marie has to restrain me from giving away a necklace for a sponge mop. I can't help myself. The guy's got a great rap.

Things pick up just enough for us to stretch out our stay on the fabulous Riviera to one month, then we head back north to sell a few more *bijoux* to some stores in Paris. We spend the next thirty days shuttling back and forth by train from the city to the farm, waiting for our badly bent VW to be repaired, and by the time that's done it's late September, time for the wine harvest.

The Wine Harvest (Les Vendanges)

SEPTEMBER 29, 1973, Burgundy—Rain falls, battering the fruit. Rows and rows of little beads are worked into a lather in the chapel down the hill, but the gods have had their say. The slowly ripening grapes are suddenly bloated. No matter what we do, nineteen seventy-three will remain a "little year."

The quiet château where we had sojourned earlier is awash with activity. People have streamed in from all over Europe. The Spaniards have come en masse with their wives and cousins. For the beautiful Angelina, this is a honeymoon, the consummation of her marriage the subject of snide jokes behind her husband Pépé's back. The German students are here for the third year. They've got something to prove and are off to the races this morning before my feet are wet. Beginners (like myself) cut one bunch at a time, as if we're making wine by the glass.

Before long there's blood. I grab the grapes, turn my head, slash, and the soft pad of my left hand is dripping crimson into the pail. This is the true transubstantiation, the blood of the worker turned into wine. It is the secret something extra that will raise this Burgundy to the lips of kings at Maxim's, La Tour d'Argent—blood, my blood, fermented, cured.

While standing around waxing rhapsodic this way, I'm falling way behind. The German student (Dieter) and a host of

Spaniards are cutting two to my one. I crawl on my knees, pulling myself down the wires of the vine until *casse-croûte,* brunch, the breaking of the crust. We tear into loaves of fresh bread, cheese, salami and table wine from the Midi, then start again, slogging through the first morning, then riding back from the fields in an old panel truck for lunch.

Cutting grapes is hard work. Picking apples, which I did in Washington State, is a picnic compared to the wine harvest, where we're constantly bent over or kneeling down to the bottom rows, where the good grapes grow. The top grapes are sour, they're called conscripts and are left on the vine. Good wine is made from the swollen clusters underneath, where we grope as for the udders of a cow.

We push forward screaming "*Panier!*" (Basket!) each time our plastic pails are full, taking a breather while our field chief, René, hustles across the rows to hand over the empties and haul our loaded buckets back to the bins. After one day I'm coated in blood and mud, so tired that I turn in immediately after dinner to sleep.

Next day there's hot coffee and more of the same, except that the sun is breaking through the clouds and people are starting to joke around. I'm still back in the pack, in my typical American fashion looking for some new way to do this thing, some system. Thousands of years they've been making wine, but I, like Ford, have a better idea.

We work until seven, then gather around the fire after dinner. To my left is Roger, a young Breton, puffing contentedly on his leprechaun's pipe. The Bretons (from Brittany) insist to their credit that they are not French, but descendants of a Gaelic race that erected monoliths along the coast at Carnak. Spiritual heirs of the Druids and probable next of kin to whoever built Stonehenge, they're highly politicized these days, organized in a movement to establish greater autonomy from the central government in Paris and recognition of their true heritage. Things have been so bad that for many years it was illegal to give a child a Breton name or to teach the traditional language.

Roger and I sit by the stone hearth, playing guitar, singing Dylan tunes and irritating the French students, who want to sing fight songs from their local rugby clubs. They're a jolly lot, the French, but they have an almost genetic insensitivity to the blues. At best they turn everything into *Le Jazz Hot*, but tonight they just want a *bagarre*—that's a brawl—and it looks like they might get one, until a crew from another estate shows up and starts griping about how bad they've got it, and everyone cools out and starts singing peasant songs.

Yes, we're back to the land, although most of us have seen more land in the past two days than in the previous six months. The Spaniards and Bourgignons, of course, are right at home. They work at a steady clip through the second day as their women fill the rows with old favorites from Catalonia; but there is no joy in Mudville until the third morning, when we move into the best fields of the domain, the bonds fall off, the effects of his sedentary life are forgotten and Capitaine Bijoux, unshackled at long last, jumps out ahead. There is a frantic reassessment. Dieter, the young German, has pulled up lame. A squad of *gung-ho*'s sets out to catch the maniacal Bijoux, but by the time they overtake him he's cut his way into their hearts.

We're all in this together now, racing forward, pelting each other across the rows, bound by oath to bellow the Alleluia chorus from Handel's *Messiah* each time the grapes thin out and we're able to scramble ahead without effort. Our cadre is led by Michel, a squat fireplug from Le Havre; next there's Pasquale (one deepens his tone and gestures with his hands when speaking of the sultry Pasquale, a Parisienne with a wine-dark whisper, her lips swollen full as the rain-soaked grapes); then Jean-Pierre, the loveliest boy in France (the young girls follow him about and wring his gloves into their hair); and not last in the least, Jacques Cano (pronounced *can-o,* like "can o' worms"), the mad genius Corsican sculptor.

Cano is about average height, with coal-black eyes, coal-black hair and eyebrows raised at either side. His blood is

Mediterranean, but his skin is translucent and pale, like northern light in a Paris window. He wears an ascot, dangles a smoke and sings as he works, "*Sans culottes, sans pantalons, nous allons danser* . . ." (No shorts, no pants, we're gonna dance), twirling his big mustache and duck-walking up the rows, sketching the beautiful bottoms in his mind.

Jacques is living out a lifelong dream working this *vendanges*. After dinner he gets out his note pad and starts in on a set of faces straight out of Brueghel. I sit at his shoulder, laughing, and wind up as a satyr on his page, tongue lolling, the horns of Moses growing from my curls, condemned to eternal lust. I'm not alone. Satyrs abound. Hoofs beat the floor boards, flanks steam in the evening's cold. The women are giddy. Mad laughter from the corner, where the boss's wife is cloistered with the virgins from Spain.

On the seventh day Cano and I get the call to work in the factory, a small warehouse adjacent to the workers' quarters, where the boss spends all day and much of the night tending to the vats. Marie's brother Henri is a scrupulous *viticulteur*. He oversees the process whereby the grapes are loaded into a grinder, where two people try to pick out the rotten clusters without getting their fingers crushed. From there the grapes are carried up by a conveyer belt to glazed tanks 10′ x 10′ x 10′, to which Henri adds a scoop of sugar and yeast to start the fermentation. Cano and I work all morning, throwing out the bad grapes, doing the small things that help make the difference between our wine and the wine down the road, then after lunch it's time to *piger*.

Red wine is made by leaving the seeds, stems and skins in the juice for ten days (to make white wine, one separates the clear juice from the skins immediately, to make a true rosé, you leave them together for a few days). What happens, however, is that CO_2 formed in the fermentation process rises and packs the solid particles three feet thick at the top. The only way to bring the skins back into the juice so they can lend their full flavor and color is to jump on top and keep on jumping until the crust breaks through, then grab onto a board and pump for all you're worth until three hundred cubic feet of solid matter have been thrust underneath.

The traditional woodcut of the wine harvest shows a barefoot peasant in an oaken tub, crushing grapes between his toes. One might expect that wine-making as an art had progressed beyond this primitive state, but the fact is that twice a day someone must take off his clothes—"*Sans culottes, sans pantalons* . . ." sings Cano, delirious with joy—and dance on top until the grapes give way and he's neck deep in the bubbly brine.

I say *he*, because women are not permitted in the wine. An ancient superstition warns that the menstrual cycle may interfere with the cycle of fermentation. Marie ridicules this sexist malarkey, but Henri and his wife ignore her. They might be wrong, but they don't want to be the ones to find out.

I keep my mouth shut and it's a damned good thing, because otherwise I might drown—but what a way to go. One of the great wines of France, one of the finest in the world and I'm swimming in the stuff. Little bubbles kiss my genitals. Vapors fill my brain.

I move on to the next vat and jump up and down some more until the warm juice oozes through and I'm sunk again, up to my neck in Cano's hysterical laughter. Baptism in wine, deep communion with the grape. I emerge whole, this is my body, bless my soul . . . drunken in the eyes of the Lord.

We work nine long days, but on the ninth night we party. Someone snips the last bunch in the field by the side of the house, then we gather for snapshots and a short ceremony, anointing ourselves with wine, grabbing at the sweet young things like Sophie and holding them down, watching them writhe as we cram handfuls of grapes between their legs and down their breasts.

We hurry in to shower, then pile into cars to ride down to Beaune, the central town of Burgundy, where workers from all over the region are celebrating the end of the harvest.

The *vendanges* here is brief, but critical. A day too soon or too late followed by a change in the weather can make or break a vintage, but now the wine is in. The boss will tend it, taste it and test it twice a day for the next two years, but that's his business. We're done.

One advantage of doing the *vendanges* in a place like Burgundy, where crews are small and the wine commands a high price, is that the owners can afford to treat you well, if they're so inclined. Too often in modern France it's business as usual, but Henri prides himself on maintaining the old tradition of treating his workers like family. He and his wife have been feeding us royally from the start, but tonight will be something else entirely.

I see that right away when we get back to the estate and Jean-Pierre (the prettiest boy in France) comes out in an evening gown belonging to a rather large Englishwoman named Julie. He's escorted by dumpy Michel, who lays his head on Jean-Pierre's breast, while reaching in for Kleenex to blow his nose.

There are fifty people at this party, with women in various stages of ripeness and desirability, but Jean-Pierre puts them all to shame. He and Michel stage a full-fledged farce at the head table, pounding each other with pocketbooks and vamping on the boss. Everyone is drooling over Jean-Pierre, but he's engaged to a girl back home, who must rate three stars in *Michelin,* judging by what he's turned down all week, so he works out his frustrations by tantalizing us, pouting and throwing kisses at the Spaniards.

Meanwhile, La Patronne, the boss's wife, is running around embracing her boys while overseeing the serving of a dozen legs of lamb which have been roasted for this spread. The cooks, who have worked harder than anyone this past week, heap the table one last time with *crudités,* oddities and plain old good food, but all anyone will ever remember from this night is the wine.

We start out with a Meursault, a white from a nearby village. It's dry, perfectly balanced, exquisite with the soup. Next Henri produces one of his own wines, a full-bodied 1970 from the first fields we cut. It's excellent, robust and heady. We're just warming up on the *gigot* (lamb roasted with garlic), the green beans and the crisp fried potatoes when the boss slips into his cellar again and steps out bearing bottles of '66.

Henri's got nine different *cru,* nine distinct wines from the scattered fields that make up his domain. The very best is a '64 from the field that gives his estate its name, but it's too young, so powerful that even nine years later it still needs more time. The best wine ready to drink, therefore, is his '66, bottles of which have been open and breathing for hours.

The first taste stuns us into silence. One has the impression of pouring rubies down his throat. Few of us have ever experienced anything like it. There's a look of utter bliss on the faces of the wine-savvy Bourgignons who make up the regular crew. They stand and give the boss the Burgundy salute, a little hummed chorus and hand-clapping routine, then they drain their glasses and chant, "*Pépé, une chanson,*" until Pépé, the proud bridegroom, rises and sings a song in Spanish. All his buddies join in at the end, then we all confer the Burgundy salute again and call out, "*Françoise, une chanson,*" until Françoise sings and we drain our glasses once more and continue around the room this way until everyone has sung, drunk and been toasted.

Cano is beside himself. He considers it sacrilege to guzzle the wine this way. "Outrage!" he thunders. "You might as well pour it down the drain. You have to savor it, sip! Ah," he mutters, "you're just a bunch of peasants."

The bedlam ceases for an instant as Angelina rises to break our hearts with an aria, then I get the call and win many friends with a crisp rendition of "Frère Jacques." This is some fine wine. We drink on and on and get higher and higher, but no one's drunk and no one staggers. It's a different kind of intoxication. We push back the tables and take over the center of the room as Henri breaks out the champagne. Someone produces a turntable with a few 45's, and soon American rock 'n' roll blares out over a scene from an old Grecian urn. Weather-beaten field hands grab the young girls away from their duennas and spin them round. The circles get tighter and faster. The women never touch the floor. With the front door open wide and spare glasses all around, one has the feeling that Zeus himself (in any form) might drop in for a taste.

Paris

FALL IS IN a frenzy. Leaves are leaping from the trees. Cano races along, dodging traffic, practicing his American.

"Superwow, man . . . yes? Far out. My uncle's tailor is rich . . . you like?"

"Terrific."

"Ah, putain, cet Americain, c'est pas la peine." He barks at the women, who walk away. Cano's taste is quite refined. He likes big bottoms and signs of life. I stop when he does, trying to pick out the thousand small details of cornice work and bas-relief that light him up and drive him on.

Across the foot bridge from the Louvre to the Left Bank, *en route aux Beaux Arts,* Bonnard and a little Japanese painter elbow peacefully for position on the quay. The seedy splendor of antique shops in the quarter, polished and opulent brass and glass, reflections convex, concave, all free, stomping grounds on the way to the galleries. Paint dances on the shoulders of satyrs. All the women are undone, the statues come to life, rutting. "The little bronze—" Cano leers—"I want one like that."

We ride the Métro to see a piece he has just completed, a large sculpture on the soft rock wall of the wine cellar of a Paris merchant. A standing figure of a male nude bears aloft a bowl, while female figures recede on both sides, growing more abstract through stages until they suggest both the broad planes of a Gauguin woodcut and the squat solidity of carved pre-Columbian rock. The work is magnificent, lighted like an altarpiece behind oak tables where the tasting is done, but I can't help thinking it a shame that it's down here, underground on the outskirts of Paris, instead of in a museum. Cano says he doesn't care. What matters to him is the work.

At one point in our wanderings I make the mistake of mentioning the counterculture. "Counterculture?" he rails; "you talk about a counterculture? That's because you have no culture! How can we have a counterculture here? We have Rubens, Rembrandt, Michelangelo—" he waves his hands as if the masters were working in the apartments just above our heads—"it's all we can do to live up to them, we'll never even come close! We're not looking to throw this over. *Au contraire, mon vieux*, we fight to go on. The barbarians [that's us, the Americans] are howling at the door."

Cano grows long in the tooth. The streets infect him, they fill his brain with energies far too explosive to keep inside. We walk for miles, stop for a carafe of wine, then sweep out onto the street to pick up where we left off, with me at his shoulder, straining to catch his lingering Corsican brogue. I'm too easy, too enthralled, an American in Paris.

We step up to the bar of Au Pied du Cochon ("At the Pig's Foot"), famed for its onion soup, across from Les Halles. Cano buys a pack of smokes from the bartender, winks at the waitress, then leads the way past the restrooms into the dingy stairway leading up to his flat.

Les Halles (pronounced *lay ahll*) was the open-air market of Paris. Butchers still cross the square with bloody carcasses over their shoulders, but the lacy wrought-iron superstructure is half down, on its way to being demolished. Coming soon: big office buildings and high rent. The whole district is doomed. Poor Irma La Douce.

The fall is chronicled in a series of canvases painted from Cano's third-story window. Good art, but poignant. By the time the series is done, he'll be forced to leave. So what? There'll be nothing more to paint.

Jacques' wife, Mimi, makes coffee. She's a sweet, solid woman who helps support his habit by working for the welfare department. Cano has her in stitches, talking about our morning. We slice some cheese and fruit and look out the window across the empty lot, past the hole where Les Halles should be, at the truncated city walls stopping at the cyclone fence. This part of Paris is dangling by a tendon. It will soon be severed, leaving only a phantom memory of the vitality and life that were cut off, like the hands of a man falsely accused of being a thief.

Cano insists that I paint, he has no faith in words, so I dip a brush in black and stack a few chimneys which water to gray, wash across windows and run down gutters into the street. He praises my feeble efforts ("Hey, Mimi, this cunt knows how to draw"), dangles a smoke and laughs as he sketches my face.

After hanging our work on the wall, he drags me across town to meet his old friend and mentor Piller, a great bear of a Swiss painter and sculptor. Like sea air, the scent of earth and oils in Piller's atelier opens the nostrils and cleanses the mind. Jacques and Piller rant and rave. They stroke Piller's muscular bronzes with their eyes, their lips foaming at the mere mention of form. They're mad, both of them. A little laughter here, a little wine and it's 1881, there's mat knives and razors everywhere, a guy could lose an ear.

This morning I woke late, banged open the shutters and swore I saw Henry Miller passing below, a baguette over his shoulder, keeping an eye on things until someone arrived to relieve him.

For one brief moment it was just like old times. The ghosts of Paris came parading behind. Out of closed windows, through the grillwork they streamed, laughing, to take their places among the rhythmic masses of Moufetarde. Miller waved his arms and called them by name—"Rimbaud, Baudelaire . . ." he cried, while they all murmured, "He's back."

I rushed down to join them, but when I reached the street the laughter was gone. The ghosts were lonely. They swept the sidewalks in gentle gusts of wind, blowing hair across the faces of occasional lovers, longing for the poets who partied with them nightly and poured the extra rounds where they drank their fill.

Back in my room after a short walk through the market, I looked down and Miller returned, heading the other way across the page, muttering under his breath. Latching onto him this time I listened as he read out road signs, store windows, key words to some hieroglyph I've yet to decipher. His grammar was impeccable, his accent atrocious, but he didn't seem to care. I was wrong. He's not gone and he's not waiting for replacements. The old guard's been out there a long time, but I'm the one who's relieved.

CRISE DE FOIE

The most important thing, whether one is on the road or sitting home, boring people to death with the slides, is one's health. Mine had been pretty good, with the exception of a few head colds and mornings after, at least until this morning when, while walking in Montmartre, a blinding flash of fever struck me in my tracks.

For a time my only recollection was the smell of burning cement, which the Gypsies call Lucifer's ash, and a pulsating chaotic rumbling of the blood in my gut. "That éclair," I moaned, "that damned éclair . . ."

Groping my way into the Metro, my innards burning hotter and hotter, I realized to my horror that I could no longer control the slow molelike progress of a fart. There was no putting this one down. It eased out silently as the doors of the second class Metro car closed on some twenty-odd people. (Odd? They were downright strange.) I saw the look of disbelief on their faces as they clutched their throats and fell. Would the neutron bomb be like this? The windows were intact.

I myself then passed out, regaining consciousness only at Republique, beside the legendary maze of Le Marais (the swamp). Mythological creatures bellowed underneath. Days, weeks, months passed and all the things I'd never done flashed before my eyes.

I went sailing in the Bahamas. I pinch-hit for Rod Carew. I was about to begin my poetry reading at Carnegie Hall, when without warning the darkness emptied, my brain drained and I found myself standing, brightly lit if not illuminated, on a naked plateau. I felt no fear at being lost, but rather a dizzying rush, like the whoosh of the Metro taking off, at being found out.

The smell of burning gypsum thickened. Django Reinhardt played background from the grave. I could just barely make out the face of the old man, half Indian, half Arab, who beckoned with a bent finger, glommed a cigarette and cackled, "The French have a name for it."

They call it *crise de foie*, crisis of the liver. Not to be confused with *crise de la foi* (no *e*, crisis of faith), or *mauvaise foi* (bad faith), which are every bit as common, but seldom as serious. In all my years of acid indigestion and heartburn I've never felt anything like it. Leave it to the French. I'm positive I was poisoned. Ptomaine—that damned éclair—surely the creme custard was sour.

"No," they tell me, "just a *crise de foie*. Overindulgence. Lie still. It will pass."

"Oh, my liver," I groan, catching on.

"You'll live."

"*Ma foie . . . ma foie . . .*" They shut the door.

Things are not going well. My resistance is low, my sex drive diminished and my social life, a disappointment. Perhaps that's why I'm not too upset at the thought of returning to the States to work the Christmas season for my old buddy John in Boston.

Outside of Jacques and Mimi and a pair of potters named Suzette and Michel, I've made few friends. We've been shuttling back and forth between the apartments of Marie's two sisters in Paris; but despite their hospitality, I've never been in one place long enough to really feel at home.

I'm getting along fine with the family, but sense a growing estrangement between myself and some of the young people I've met. We don't seem to operate on the same level. At one point Marie and I took a trip to Belgium to see the Rolling Stones when Keith Richard was still wanted in France on one of his numerous drug charges. A Paris radio station chartered a train that ran from Gare du Nord across the border, fully equipped with piped-in music and wall-to-wall dope. As soon as the train stopped in Brussels, an army of long-hairs raced uphill to the stadium, past Belgian bankers and bakers huddled on their stoops, wondering if this were a new invasion of degenerate Huns.

We reached the arena, stampeded inside and found a large open floor in front of the stage. The French hippies ran for the seats, while Marie and I moved down to the dancing floor, close enough to watch The Mick and far enough away to get a good sound mix. Only after the last rows of the stadium were filled did the French audience spill reluctantly down around us.

The lights dimmed and the crowd grew quiet. Suddenly Billy Preston came on with his warm-up band in outrageous purple-sequined jumpsuits and two-foot Afro wigs, playing "Dance to the Music." I started to twitch, but the French hippies behind me were chanting,

"*Assis . . . assis,*" which means "sit down."

"Wait a minute," I shouted, "he's—"

"*Assis . . . assis.*"

My man Billy, meanwhile, was crooning, "Dance . . . dance . . . dance to the music," boogying across the stage like a bear on roller skates, trying to get a rise out of this stoned-out crowd, who grew more and more obnoxious until they threatened to drown out the music altogether.

Eventually the message got through and we wound up in the usual orgiastic mass, but the whole thing was so ridiculous it reminded me of a story I heard at the *vendanges* to the effect that God put so much physical beauty into France that all the other countries of the world were jealous, so to even things up, he invented the French.

Rock concerts are hardly important in the greater scheme of things, but when we get around to politics, it just gets worse. I would have expected to find something in common with the young French left, 1968 and all that, but as soon as I open my mouth they have me pegged. Marie says that I'm too thin-skinned, that they're only baiting me because they see that it works, but the fact that it may be more personal than political doesn't make it any easier.

Identify with the folks back home in any way and I become the enemy, the Yankee liberal imperialist. I feel a great self-loathing at the posture I'm forced to maintain. I've been through all these late-night arguments before, and I know full well that there's a kind of irreducible logic to Marxism, but logic is still a tool and what it accomplishes depends on whose hands it's in. When logic begins to imperiously dictate choice, like the wrench saying, "Use me, revisionist idiot!" I tend to turn my back.

My French is pretty good by now, but communications are failing. I struggle through their well-rehearsed traps, trying to ignore their smirks. Their eyes laugh at the stupid American. Jesus Christ, gimme a gun, we'll see who's violent!

This John Wayne imitation elicits the first signs of respect, but I'll have to be careful not to abuse it, not to lean too far the other way. I've always been a borderline case, it seems to run in the family. My grandfather left Russia after the pogroms to avoid fighting for the Tsar, and he would have done the same thing for the Reds. He was no pacifist, either. He wrestled in the pro ring up in Buffalo for five bucks a throw, and had to earn the right to stay on his first job in the States by straightening out an Irishman who thought that quiet was dumb. Morris knew from experience that some people face trouble all their lives. He believed in democracy, but had little faith in the mass. They had come at him before, they could change their hats and come at him again.

I'm all for social change and against Vietnam, but I need a break. That's why I don't feel so bad about climbing on the Air France jetliner for the ride west. I'll be back. It's just that my fuse is running as short as my cash, and it's time to replenish both.

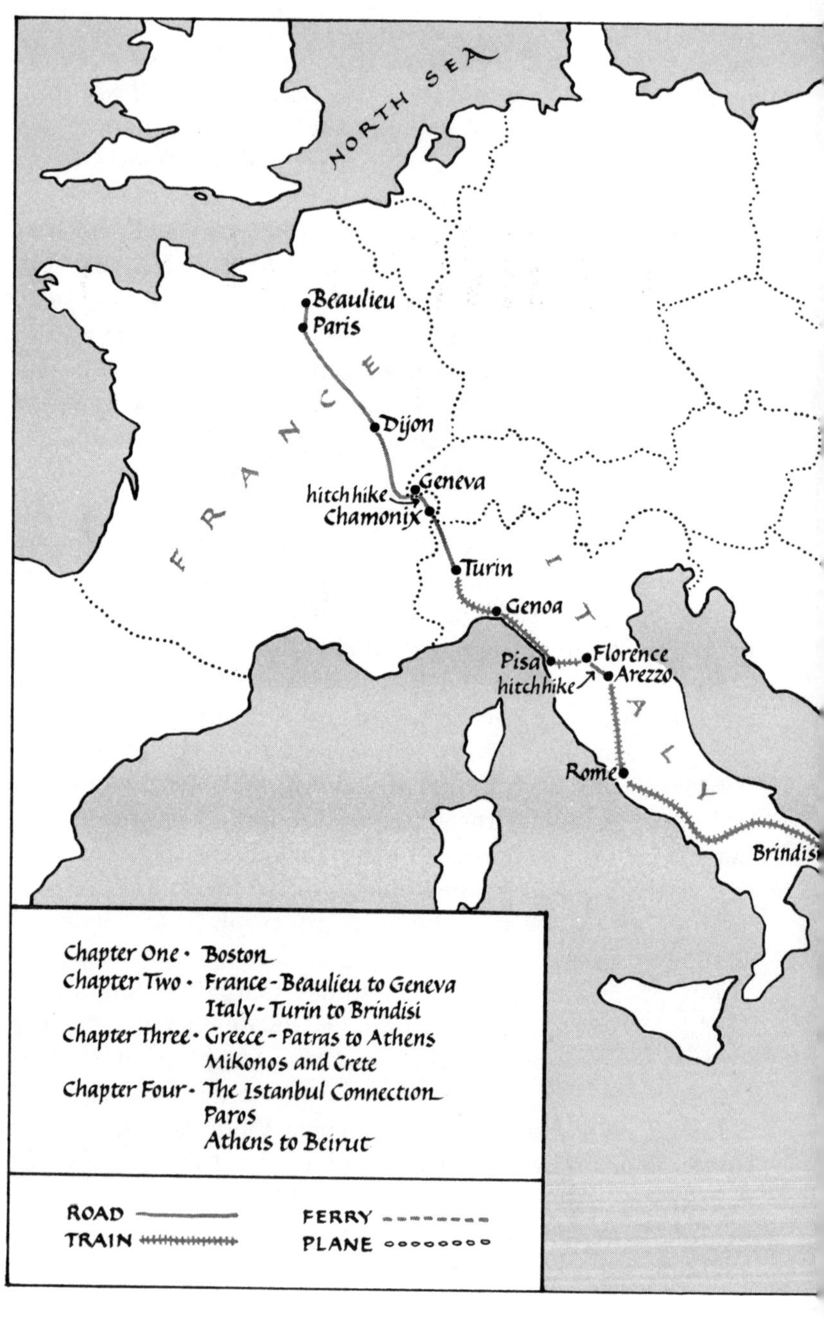
NORTH SEA
FRANCE
ITALY
Beaulieu
Paris
Dijon
Geneva
hitch hike
Chamonix
Turin
Genoa
Pisa
Florence
hitch hike
Arezzo
Rome
Brindisi
Chapter One · Boston
Chapter Two · France - Beaulieu to Geneva
Italy - Turin to Brindisi
Chapter Three · Greece - Patras to Athens
Mikonos and Crete
Chapter Four - The Istanbul Connection
Paros
Athens to Beirut
ROAD
TRAIN
FERRY
PLANE

PART TWO

CHRISTMAS

1973

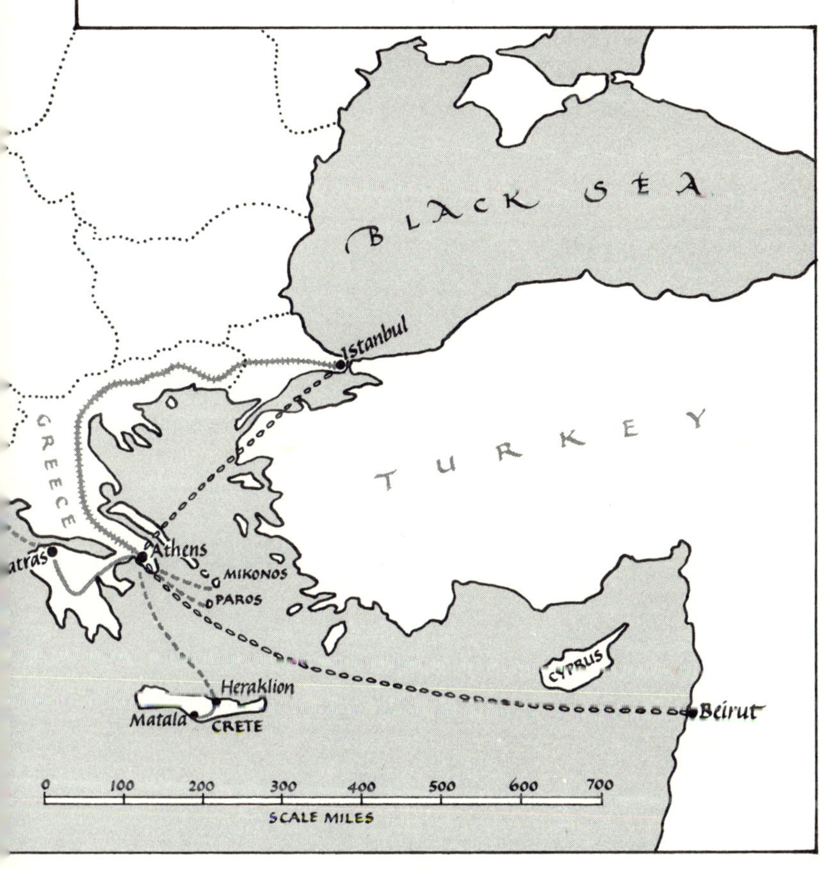

I ARRIVE IN Boston late in November to begin working for my old friend and mentor, John, the zen jeweler, who first took me on when I was six months out of Harvard and reeling from my rejection at the local burger emporium, where I was deemed unfit to wash dishes. Master John, who had just returned from California to set up a workshop, took one look in my eyes and decided he could use an apprentice.

He had no idea what he was in for. After sixteen years of schooling I had no connection with my hands. The training, combined as it was with yoga and meditation, began to take on some of the aspects of one of those emotional rehabilitation programs where they reteach you first to crawl, then walk. After eight months I was able to support myself, so I moved out to Berkeley to enter law school at the University of California.

Law school was like intellectual boot camp after the chaos of Vietnam at Harvard. We were told to mean what we said, or at least to know what it was we were saying, and to see things from more than one perspective. It was soon apparent, however, that I was working nights and selling jewelry each weekend on the street, to get another job, law, that I really didn't want.

I enjoyed law school—there's nothing boring about case histories of families tearing each other up and guys building walls for spite—but after several run-ins with the celebrated decisions of Brandeis and Cardoza, I decided that if I was going to fill my head with language, it might as well be my own. I quit after one year, figuring that at least now if I got into trouble, I'd have some friends who could bail me out.

At that point I moved across the bay to San Francisco and began the yearly ritual of returning at Christmas to work for John. I still feel a little awkward sitting in his fancy store behind the glass we trashed in the riots of '69, but when I nod to the cops, they nod right back, because here I'm no hippie bum out on the street, but a trusted employee, working insane hours with John in his North Cambridge studio, trying to produce half a year's merchandise in five weeks.

My partner up at the old sweatshop is Don, another college friend of John's from Harvard. When Don was a freshman he got caught walking a woman out of his dorm ten minutes after curfew and was suspended for the year. Don argued that he had only been talking and had lost track of time, but he must not have been their type, because they tossed him out anyway.

That was the climate when we first arrived at school. We had to wear coats and ties to every meal, including breakfast. Women were allowed in the dorms just three nights a year, and all of us lived in mortal fear of getting caught with the same women we were trying to satisfy while avoiding getting pregnant. It was, in short, the same repressed life style that characterized the fifties.

One of my old roommates once suggested that the Vietnam protest had as much to do with sex as with politics, and that the moment Harvard's deans abolished parietal hours and permitted women not only to visit, but to live in the dorms, they bought themselves a peace that will reign independent of the vagaries of foreign policy.

John, Don and I are soon joined by Cheryl, a roommate of my sister's one summer when I dropped in from a disastrous trip out West with nowhere to go. Cheryl was just seventeen when I met her, shy, wild and stiff. We wound up together whenever she wasn't hitching off somewhere (this was the summer of Woodstock) and we've been that way, on and off, ever since.

Cheryl visited me one time during my senior year (over the objections of her parents), then we traveled that summer in a Volkswagen bus with a friend named Danny, after which I went back East and she took off again for Europe, or Venezuela, or the Yucatan, or some place every time she could. She works, saves her money and goes.

Cheryl's effects are subtle. Her mind is elsewhere part of the time and she's been around, so what she says is not always coming from the same old place. She's self-effacing to a fault, but that just makes it harder to pick up on that dogged insistence of hers, a trait I will not fully appreciate until she has me halfway around the world. We begin by discussing the possibility of her returning with me to France, and before I know it she's talking about Nepal. I cut her off, telling her to stop pressuring me and go hammer some hoops, which she does, but there's a funny little smile on her face that scares me.

Usually I'm in the workshop, since Cheryl's much more decorous and a better salesperson to boot, but every so often I pull a shift in John's small store, where shoppers are crowding in from the cold, reminding me of Sunday morning in a good Jewish delicatessen. We need one of those Take-A-Ticket machines they use in the bakeries.

"Next! Number 163 . . . 164 . . ."

"Wait! I've got 163."

"OK, lady, what'll it be?"

"I'd like something in a little emerald."

"Fine. Two carats? How about a little over?" I love it when it gets like this, I pretend I'm a counterman, one of those guys who can break four eggs up at one time, two in each hand . . .

"All right, next! Number one six five . . . one six six." Like a veteran pinch hitter, a Manny Mota or a Dusty Rhodes, you could wake me up in the middle of the night with a sale on the line and I'd drive it home. If a customer's hesitating over a necklace, I help her on with it. Insisting how lovely it looks, I run a finger sloping across her chest, drop an aside about how nicely it falls that way, and it, she's in the bag.

Married women, ingenues, it doesn't matter. Mothers and daughters, beware. I'm allowed to handle the women, I'm a jeweler and this, for all its limitations, is an intimate business. When they ask me how it looks, I gaze into their eyes. Fiddling with those maddening little clasps, I breathe hot air down their necks as their boyfriends and husbands look on helplessly.

I realize it's crass, but it works. I don't like this business, it brings out the worst in me, that old avaricious instinct I would have liked to have renounced when I quit law school and gave up the chance to get really rich. This *bijoux* stuff is nickel and dime. The only good thing about it is that the coins all roll at the same time. Aside from that, women are the only perk; and now that Cheryl's here, that's out, so it's fortunate for my peace of mind and good for business too, that I'm generally back in the workshop, out of harm's way, miles from that intoxicating mix of perfumes with the perspiration of faculty wives in wool coats.

It's almost Christmas and brother John is in heaven. He stands by the counter going *ho-ho-ho* as the cash register rings like a sleigh bell. Tapping his foot lightly, he keeps time with shoppers humming Yuletide carols picked up like so many communicable diseases from record stores blaring Ray Coniff into the innocent streets.

France February 1974

CHERYL DOES DECIDE to come back with me and is accepted right into the family. Actually, she is family. It was her brother whom Marie was seeing when she first came to the States. Everyone likes Cheryl—so much that very quickly it seems as if she's been here the whole time and I'm the stranger. She takes over the instructional chores, freeing me to start spending more time upstairs at my little desk, writing.

Some Parisian friends of the family lend us a cottage, where we set up house. Our second-story window overlooks the southwest side of town down to the fifteenth-century church. The wall around our yard is hundreds of years old, lined with velvet moss and tiny blossoming flowers. The three of us start to fend for ourselves, cooking our own meals, although we continue to draw heavily on the big house for fresh eggs and last summer's fruit and potatoes. The two women, Cheryl tall, blond and fair, Marie short and sultry with long brown hair, walk each night to the kitchen of the lady with the dairy cows (and four broad-backed daughters) to get our liter of milk. We boil it before bed, leaving it to cool on the stove, then wake and skim the rich butter-cream into a jar in the fridge. When a month's worth has accumulated, we run, do not walk it up to Angel, the pastry cook, who routinely turns out the most insanely rich cakes and cookies imaginable.

We take our main meal in the afternoon, like proper French, lingering over table wine, Camembert and hard cider from Normandy. I'm getting bossed around a bit, outnumbered by females two-to-one, but it has its rewards. I set a few stones and try my hand at etching, then Marie's brother-in-law, the art connoisseur, bravely commissions me to make a massive bracelet in eighteen-karat gold to house a pale flawed emerald the size of a walnut. I go to Paris, buy a rod of gold the thickness of a fountain pen, thirteen inches long, then take it home and work it for three days, popping the tendons in my hands. This experience, as much as any other, convinces me that I'm wasting my time working metal. I hand the bracelet over to him, squinting to avoid seeing its problems, relieved that I've done no damage to the stone and determined to find some other way to make a living.

The weather warms, tractors take to the muddy fields and buds swell the branches of the fruit trees. Marie's sisters and cousins start showing up for weekend bike hikes and mushroom-hunting forays into the forests. The nicest thing about the French countryside is that each municipality maintains its own woods. The landscape passes from timberland to field with none of the monotony that can characterize farm country in the States. Everyone puts in his two *sous* at the town council to determine how much wood to cut and how to protect the local game, and as a result France is like a miniature world, lovingly arranged, as if God were a retired hobbyist with an inordinate amount of time on His hands.

The plan was to stay with Marie for two months, then to take off while she attempts to sell her jewelry one more time in the south of France, so late in April Cheryl and I pack one small backpack each, wave goodbye and hop a train to Paris. I've got a sleeping bag, a down jacket, a pair of shorts, two pair of underwear, one T-shirt in addition to the one I'm wearing, a flannel shirt and three pairs of socks. This wardrobe will serve me for seven months. On my feet, a pair of Clark Treks, a flat-bottomed, nondescript all-purpose shoe offering little style and no support, that will carry me eight thousand miles and thirteen thousand feet into the Himalayas. So much for being prepared.

We ride by train to Dijon, then transfer onto another line headed for Switzerland. Imagine foothills rolling up into the mountains. Now imagine falling asleep and missing the whole thing. When I wake it's late in the day and we're in Geneva. Encumbered by our backpacks, we settle for a hotel by the station, five dollars a night for two.

One enters through a dark hallway beside a bar. The air is stale with tobacco, booze and urine. The walls are flecked with chipped paint and old plaster. Wooden steps lead up two flights of stairs to a thin door with a flimsy lock. We step inside, bounce the bed, then take off to sightsee among the gold Bulovas, the Longines-Wittnauers, the felt bourse bulletin-boards with their white stick-on letters indicating current rates of exchange.

Nowhere does one have a stronger sense of his place (whatever it may be) in a capitalist world than in Geneva. Its peaceful avenues and lakeside vistas suggest a health spa or an old-age resort; but underneath one can feel the drone of commerce, the steady click of adding machines tallying up the take from drug smugglers and military strongmen actually looking forward to the coup so they can get on with the business of being rich, the digital hum of interest accumulating in gold-lined underground vaults. Geneva is ancient, but not out of time. It keeps time, perfectly modern and sedate. It's charming, yet arid and cold, like the frosty accents of German homelanders who speak their impeccable French without a trace of Mediterranean *joie de vivre.*

Back at our dingy Hôtel du Gare, motorbikes whine down the street. Trains will be coming and going all through the night. Every so often a bus takes off, an altercation arises.

We're finally asleep when a clamor starts up in the hallway and someone begins banging on our door, mumbling something in French about a key. Pulling on my pants, I shout, "*Allez-vous en, monsieur,*" which means, Get out of here, sir!

"What is it, Michael?" Cheryl's awake now, but not too alarmed.

"I don't know." Crossing the room one foot at a time (how else?), I draw and open my Swiss Army knife. A Swiss Army knife is the last thing you'd want in your hands in a fight. It would just as likely fold up and lop off your own fingers as draw enemy blood, but who wants blood? I advance to the door, my puny blade gleaming in the moonlight. The drunk continues to bang on the wood.

"Allez vous-en, monsieur. Allez, allez." Still using the formal *you,* polite, but menacing, I take another step.

"Michael, will you put that thing down and come to bed? He's just crazy. Forget it."

"I know," I say, "that's just it, be still." Some people never get it straight. It's the crazy ones who scare you.

Chamonix. Even in the off season hotels aren't cheap, so we camp in the woods and make love under the stars in our left-right, male-female sleeping bags, hers purple, mine sky blue. The next morning we ride to the cloud-capped Needle of the Midi, a spire beside Mont Blanc, the highest mountain in Europe, in a cable car, which sounds more appropriately terrifying in its French variation, *téléphérique.*

The fact that hundreds of thousands have taken this ride before us offers little comfort as the car pitches and sways on its slender braid, making as if to dive like a great metal dodo into the valleys below. Up top, where the peak has been appropriated for a communications post, the architecture is early Maginot Line or World War II pillbox. Nothing is especially steady in the wind. It's beautiful, very cold, and no less scary on the ride down.

From Chamonix we hitch with a trucker through the tunnel to Italy, then pick up with an Italian cop in a Fiat, on his way down from the mountain outpost to visit his wife. Bit by bit we hitchhike out of the Alps into the lowlands, then catch a train that takes us through the belt of the Apennines to Genoa, or Genova, or, as the French say—and one must wonder why they feel compelled to change every name to suit themselves —Gênes.

We rest a night along the coast, then ride the train the next morning to Pisa, to check out the famous tower. You've seen the pictures, heard the hype, now stand in the presence of the magnificent Campanile, its shadow bearing down upon you. Wonder at the Renaissance majesty of the Pisa Cathedral and Baptistery, which are, if anything, more impressive, if straight.

It's hot in Pisa in early May. I eat an ice cream, then lie down in the cool grass while Cheryl takes her photographs. After a short nap I wake and try to stand, navigating by the stacked tiers of the thirteenth-century marvel dominating the sky, but I tip sideways, listing badly, my inner ear confused.

"Listen to it," I tell myself, lying down again, looking down the length of my body at that tower, 180 feet high and 14 feet out of whack. Clouds scudding by add to the illusion. It's falling. It, like the civilization which produced it, must one day lie in rubble. But the tower pitches headlong and will continue to do so, disregarding what we feel is logical or right, as it has ever since Galileo dropped his balls of unequal mass over the edge. He taught the world a lesson that day, just as I'm learning one now.

There's no substitute for the real thing. You can see the photos and read the books, but you'll never gauge beforehand the effect upon your senses of wonders such as this. They outdo your imagination and restore your faith in the amazing. Samuel Johnson once claimed that "all wonder is the effect of novelty upon ignorance." That may be so, but I can't help feeling that the gout-ridden pundit of eighteenth-century England was somehow missing the point.

Florence. That Renaissance one reads about elsewhere, whose landscapes loom darkly in the backgrounds of famous portraits, here surrounds one in mosaic tiled splendor of family crests and tabletop seascapes of lapis lazuli, marble and carnelian. Michelangelo's *David*, arrogant, yet shy, defends one aesthetic ideal, while reclining nudes guard sepulchers and hairs grow from the bones of saints in jewel-encrusted reliquaries only the faithful could adore.

The entire city of Florence is a museum, of which the halls, palaces and cathedrals are merely wings, extensions of the minds of Renaissance men like Da Vinci, who would have sold his soul to fly. Outside in the piazzas, pigeons puff up and stalk each other in fine feathered parody of the tight-booted young men cooing at the fair-haired girls from England and America. The city is bustling in early May, filled with the smell of pizza by the slice, but we're able to secure a place in a family-run *Pensione* (several steps down from the hotels and inns) for just six dollars a night. The room is remarkably large, with two double beds, glazed terra cotta floors and a cool breeze from the windows overlooking a church across the way.

We tour the art treasures by day and the back streets at night, looking for restaurants filled with Italian workers where we know we'll get our money's worth. Our second afternoon we hook up with a sallow young Norwegian poet, sort of a Scandinavian Lawrence Durrell, who drinks large quantities of chianti while discoursing with a passionate gaiety that cannot mask his melancholy. We take him for a poet because he says he is. One bears no bound volumes on the road. One's poetry is inscribed in the air, its flavor warm, drunken and slightly sour. Like the wine, it's cheap, but it flows.

For one magnificent week we stuff ourselves wtih culture, *cappuccino* and sunsets on the Ponte Vecchio. Our last day Cheryl and I cross the Arno River and hike up a hill past villas plush with unruffable calm, the villas of Henry James in exile, up to Fort Belvedere, erected by Giovanni de' Medici in the 1590s. We stroll around the courtyard, watching the kids playing soccer, then sit down on a grassy knoll (will that phrase ever be free of the taint of John Kennedy's death?) overlooking the entire valley.

Cheryl and I are starting to feel some of the pull and tug that comes from traveling together, some of the mutual exhaustion of constant contact, but the scene before us erases all that. Florence at our feet, we lie on our backs, watching the sky, falling into each other's arms, then rolling down the cool lawn. We turn slowly at first, then faster and faster until a woman gasps and we stop. When I look over my shoulder my heart freezes and the blood drains straight from my head. That hill we've so innocently rolled down has just ended without so much as a warning bump at the fortress wall, which drops off some eighty feet, straight down. If that woman's gasp had come a half second slower, it would have been too late.

Cheryl and I pick ourselves up and race down to the lowest part of the river valley, eat dinner, then pack our bags to hitch out the next morning toward Arezzo, southeast of Florence, where Alice, the Swarthmore roommate and best friend of an old college flame of mine, lives with her husband, Aurelio, an Italian duke who won her heart during a wine-selling trip to the States. Alice comes from a family of Wall Street stockbrokers, self-styled aristocrats, who had their hands full when the authentically credentialed Aurelio flew in to obtain the legal rights, with all appurtenances thereto, to their daughter.

The affair began well enough the night before the wedding with an informal party at a fancy East Side townhouse where we frolicked under the banner of the Porcellian Pig, ironic symbol of Harvard's most exclusive "final club," a term that in and of itself conveys that precious sense that its members have truly arrived. When I first arrived on campus and learned what those fancy red brick buildings were, I saw Red; but, of course, I was much younger then and am better able to deal with people who exclude me now.

Aurelio thrilled the women that night, pressing his lips to their Camay soft hands while chilling their husbands with his studied indifference. The next morning I attended an all-male prenuptial luncheon, featuring the most inane speeches, toasts and dedications to be found anywhere outside a Rotarian's hell, then the couple got married in a picturesque Protestant ceremony (the intricacies of whose denominations, like so many foreign currencies, are lost on me) and we all adjourned to the reception hall of a fancy downtown club.

It was only then that I was able to fully appreciate how truly good-looking this family was. They were so scrubbed, shining and toothsome that I half expected Ted Kennedy to walk in and annex the whole clan, declaring it his by right of eminent domain. I draped a napkin over my arm and got through the afternoon posing as a busboy, while a combo of violin, clarinet and upright bass wandered from table to table, their leaden melodies undanced to.

The dining done and the formalities over, Alice assembled her cousins, said a few parting words, then tossed the bridal bouquet right at my girlfriend, who caught it and burst into tears. It was quite touching. We were breaking up at the time and we both knew it wouldn't help.

The newlyweds ran down the red carpet into their rented Ford, although it was obvious he would have been more at home in a Ferrari, then Aurelio hit the starter, spun the wheels and tore away from the curb, spattering gravel into the shocked faces of her family, whose jaws dropped at the sight of their lovely daughter disappearing forever into the clutches of the swarthy, albeit titled stranger.

That was the last I saw of Alice, but knowing she's in Arezzo and doubting that she has an excess of visitors, we decide to stop by. We're having trouble getting a ride when two young men pull up on motorbikes, offering to convey us to the autoroute on-ramp. As soon as we climb on, the two men split up and I lose sight of Cheryl. It looks like a setup—the old get-the-girl-and-dump-the-guy-in-the-boondocks routine—and nothing I've seen of the Italian male reassures me. The courts here are still debating whether rape is to be construed as a crime.

My only collateral is the guy in front of me. I'm holding on, trying to figure out how to strangle him without getting killed myself, when Cheryl reappears in the distance, waving frantically. We get down at the turnpike and thank the guys for the ride, which probably saved us hours, but instead of being grateful, we are completely unnerved.

Now we move up to the on-ramp to watch the Italians careen by in their matchbox autos, rubbernecking at Cheryl in her tight dungarees. An old lady slows up to scold us. Moments later a young male driver spins around to gape (he won't pick us up, of course), then slams into the rear end of the old bitch, who was so preoccupied with us that she forgot to pull out onto the road.

The two of them get out of their cars and start shaking their fists as a big semi enters the on-ramp, sees the crack-up and slows. Cheryl and I wave it to a halt and hop on, then settle back into the soft seats to ride on the left past the two hapless motorists, still down there screaming.

Our driver, a quiet type, slowly works up the nerve to ask, via sign language involving the ring on his finger, whether Cheryl and I are married. That's the first thing any Italian will want to know. He shakes his head sadly when we answer no, then begins sneaking glances at Cheryl, who responds with a smile. He turns his eyes back to the road.

Outside of Arezzo we get down at a café to enlist the aid of a waiter, who makes a few phone calls for us, then twenty minutes later Alice appears, looking more sophisticated than I remember her in an elegant silver Mercedes, to convey us to her hillside estate. We catch up on a few friends, then Alice describes the life she's been living since her marriage, in which she's expected to socialize with old Italian women of acceptable ancestry, playing cards at afternoon teas, while her husband goes out shooting pigeons. His counterparts, the young aristocratic sportsmen, take turns cornering her whenever he's not around, trying to convince her to make love to them. Although she's been living near Arezzo for four years, speaks excellent Italian and is married to a person of the highest standing, Alice has a reputation to live down. American girls are easy.

She takes us on a tour of her wine estate, explaining that she and the Duke are in a squeeze. The young people are moving to the cities to earn cash and live the fast life. Operational costs are rising faster than the price of their wine (which doesn't command the premium of a good French wine) and as a result, she and Aurelio are having trouble making ends meet and are in danger of losing valuable acreage to real-estate speculators who want to build apartments on the lower forty.

Alice lives in a beautiful villa, but the downstairs is closed off and she does most of the daily chores herself. It's hard to bear the thought of her lovely vines being sacrificed to high-rise prefab concrete, a blight anywhere, but just as hard to imagine any young worker wanting to stay on to help support Aurelio's aristocratic life style. He appears at the door and shakes our hands, a bit more warmly than I remember from the wedding, but despite that fact that we're thousands of miles from home, we are not invited for dinner.

Aurelio's hospitality, of course, is hardly the issue. There are more serious problems in Italy. The upper classes are land poor and the workers are cynical. The upper classes are arrogant and the workers are lazy, take your pick, it depends on who's talking. Alice described how the local post office went on strike recently for five weeks. When they came back, instead of catching up on their work, they simply threw all the old mail away. The left's extreme and the right's corrupt. The lira is overblown.

Italy has seen better days. Not recently, perhaps, for it hasn't been all that long since Mussolini, but it does have a glorious past, without which I suspect there'd be nothing to hang onto. While Red Brigades kneecap robber barons and madmen strike the heads off *Pietà*s, Italy survives. One gets a sense of how and why while walking the streets among cathedrals and statuary blind to the passions of the age.

On the other hand, the current turmoil is really no worse than during that so-called golden age when Florence fought Milan and Genoa fought Florence and cities of like blood, language and destiny conducted the warfare that the classes continue today. Are the mistakes of ancient cultures justified by their achievements? Will ours be? Is there another, truly golden age ahead of us, or is it really as it was in the beginning, is now, and ever shall be? Who knows? The only way to cover your bets is to be prepared to give thanks either way.

• • •

Rome. We would probably have seen more of the eternal city had we been on a packaged tour. We did not eat spaghetti with Fellini or party into the night with redheaded whores. We did not have an audience with the Pope. We were in a hurry, the town was hot and our money was going fast.

We stayed in a cramped *pensione*-cum-restaurant managed by a little round Italian named Emilio, who professed a great love for Richard Nixon and tried to charge me for a dozen bottles of gaseous mineral water we did not consume. Our brief stay hardly qualifies me to expound at length, but a few things deserve mention: the gaudy excess of the Vatican; the matchless beauty of the Sistine Chapel, marred by authoritarian announcements in five languages telling people to be quiet, which were far more annoying themselves than the whispered conversations of awe-struck visitors; the Pantheon with its grand rotunda; the Coliseum and the cats.

Where once the mighty lions roared, mangy felines now breed and feed among the fallen columns of ruins. They bring life to the dead stones, perhaps even bearing the reincarnated souls of gladiators and emperors, or of those poor Christians who succumbed to their cousins. The cats are aloof. They've got better things to do than speculate. When not engaged in the rigors of the hunt or the public agony of their sexual arousal, they enjoy. They know how to yawn, to stretch, to scratch with class. They know what to do with an afternoon of warm sun.

Exhausted after a hard week of big-city tourism, we catch a train to Brindisi for the ferry to Greece. As far as I'm concerned, my travels are nearly over. We plan to visit Athens, see the museums, then head down to an island to cool out. Our tour of Europe has been of the whirlwind variety, but even so our cash is dwindling. There are many places we'd like to visit, but won't. Greece is farther east than I'd ever hoped to be. It will bring a well-earned rest and an end to our season on the road.

Greece

In Paris one roams from quarter to quarter through imperceptible transitions, as if moving through invisible beaded curtains. In Greece the changes are sharp, almost painful. In some places you can pass through all the changes of fifty centuries in the space of five minutes. Everything is delineated, sculptured, etched. Even the waste lands have an eternal cast about them. You see everything in its uniqueness—*a* man sitting on *a* road under *a* tree; *a* donkey climbing *a* path near *a* mountain; *a* ship in *a* harbor in *a* sea of tourquoise; *a* table on *a* terrace beneath *a* cloud. And so on. Whatever you look at you see as if for the first time; it won't run away, it won't be demolished overnight; it won't disintegrate or dissolve or revolutionize itself. Every individual thing that exists, whether made by God or man, whether fortuitous or planned, stands out like a nut in an aureole of light, of time and space. The shrub is the equal of the donkey; a wall is as valid as a belfry; a melon is as good as a man. Nothing is continued or perpetuated beyond its natural time; there is no iron will wreaking its hideous path of power.

—HENRY MILLER, *waiting for the war to sweep down through Europe,* The Colossus of Maroussi, *1941.*

For if we except the victory at Marathon, the sea-fight at Salamis, the battles at Plataea and Thermopylae and Cimon's exploits at Eurymedon . . . Greece fought all her battles against and to enslave herself. Every one of her trophies stands as a memorial to her own shame and misfortune, and she owed her ruin above all to the misdeeds and rivalries of her leaders.

—PLUTARCH, Life of Flamininus.

It's been a long time, but the lessons of the classics haven't changed. They all too beautifully articulate the language of strife, the poetry of domination. We're still moved by the individual act of personal honor, but then the ancients could make them come alive. The *Iliad*, the *Odyssey*, one need merely raise his eyes from the page to leap the rail, measuring the self against remote possibilities of Homeric swims to islands near and far. How far? The sea is littered with light. The islands alight in the deep.

We land at dusk at Patras and step unsteadily onto the dock. The writing on the signposts is all funny, upside down and sideways. In Italy I could understand the headlines, they said I had a good accent from eating Italian food, but Greek? The only Greek I ever heard was from guys making pizzas with thick crusts. They had travel posters on the walls. They don't teach Greek in the public schools, not even in translation. In the early sixties we still had Latin, but now? Visual ed., and that's just in the suburbs. We miss quite a bit taking our history from religion and our culture from the tube.

Greece. The air is different, the light is different, the streets are flat, the buildings white. We walk around town, find a cheap hotel (it says HOTEL and looks cheap), order dinner (the kind of desultory fare one always gets when he doesn't know what he's doing), then walk back to the sea.

All roads led to Rome, but now they have a different source. This civilization is ancient, eastern, it seems to have bubbled up from a crack in the mountains, it spills over in strange sounds in the mouths of old men. Is the earth moving, or is it just another ferry pulling out? The sun is fierce, a red ball of fire dropping into the waves; one waits for the hiss and the rising cloud of steam.

Cramped by lack of funds, we make a few mistakes on our tour of the Peloponnesus, miss Mycenae and waste a day at Argos, then we climb the fort at Nauplion and ride north to the pine hills of Epidaurus, to that one place selected by the world-tuned ancient Greeks for their holy amphitheater. The site is peaceful, calm and conscient. We stand in the back row as a tour guide whispers on the theater floor, his every syllable audible. He scratches a match and more than two hundred feet away we hear it burst into flame, then he leads his busload of tourists on and there's silence. Even the wind holds its breath. Everything is still as the hills attend the further convocation of powers in prayer, the healing laughter, the visionary remembrance.

Athens. First the foothills leading in, over which the Spartan armies marched, laying waste, then the city itself, dense, modern-white, fast and dirty. Someone directs us to the old district, called the Plaka. Its narrow walkways are festooned with violet and magenta bells of bougainvillaea, while down below one can find some of the cheapest student hotels in Europe, one in particular, noted for its student roof, where for thirty cents one can crash in the company of thirty perfect strangers. My habit of sleeping lightly derives from this period. If you can sleep while all about you are losing their wallets, having their passports slipped through slits cut in the bottoms of sleeping bags with their owners still in them, you deserve your rest. Fortunately one takes long siestas in Athens, resting up on park benches while the city closes tight from two to five.

High above, looking out in all directions, stands the Parthenon. It's easy to see, from the center of this wide valley fringed with hills, why the Athenians postulated themselves at the center of the universe. Atop the Acropolis, their natural rock fortress, they built a marble shrine whose truth emerges as a moment's beauty: a frieze, a beam and the pillars they rest upon. You're afforded just a glimpse, no more. You can't take it with you no matter who you are or how long you look, although the little man with the walrus mustache will be happy to take both your photo and your dollar.

Four days we tour the town and museums, then we hop a bus to Piraeus for the ferry to Mikonos. Mikonos has a reputation as a jet-set hangout, but it's still pre-season by a week or two, so we're able to find a room in a private home for three dollars and prepare to unravel from all our travels.

We take half-hour bus rides to fishing boats which convey us to Paradise and Super-Paradise, nude beaches on the island's unprotected rear, or hike out across the hills, through empty fields broken by rock walls piled up over the centuries. The walls are everywhere, even on the most remote ridges and bluffs. The hills are dry, the sea is clear and cold.

Back in town, the whitewashed walls of Mikonos form a maze seen best at twilight when the sky's blue descends in iridescence. Flowers spill from patios painted weekly by women who make the upkeep of this porcelain setting their lifework. At night the lights of tourist ships string out across the harbor. Mikonos' famed windmills spin silently above alleyways throbbing with music and the dark luster of people seeking love.

Cheryl and I were befriended on the way over by a bank clerk and his lover, a frail Dali-esque artist who makes his living painting men. He took an immediate liking to my profile and even admired my watercolors, calling them "vulnerable." When Cheryl retires early one evening, I happen to bump into him down by the bay. His lover discreetly leaves us alone, listening to the water lapping up his moonlit enticements. He promises much. He promises everything. "When in Rome . . ." is one thing. "When in Greece . . ." quite another.

At the end of our week, we meet up with a character named Lee, a British hippie who's been wandering back and forth from India for nine years, making his living buying goods in the east and selling them to tourists on the islands. Cheryl takes every opportunity to get him talking, and soon I find myself falling under the spell of the possible. India's a lot closer in Greece than it was in Paris. Cheryl's low-key strategy is beginning to pay off. She very shrewdly keeps quiet and gets Lee to describe the mountains of Nepal, the dirt roads of Afghanistan. There's plenty of time to decide, he tells us. Summer is monsoon season, so we wouldn't want to leave before August. The next day we push on from the packaged charms of Mikonos to return by ferry to Piraeus for a ship to Crete. Crete promises wild shores and adventures. In one sense, it's on the island of Crete that this story begins.

> Greece is what everybody knows, even in *absentia,* even as a child or as an idiot or as a not-yet-born. It is what you expect the earth to look like given a fair chance.
>
> —HENRY MILLER, *The Colossus of Maroussi*

The ferry is filled with islanders, dancing on the lower decks to music played on a *bouzouki* and an ancient Cretan *lyra,* and called by a dirty old man whose lyrics draw laughter on every verse. A gorgeous dark-haired Cretan woman, lithe and voluptuous, takes on the men, matching their hip gyrations, dancing them down one by one. The woman's face grows flush as the music plays on. Her satisfaction deepens, suffusing the room.

I wander onto the top deck, listening to the engines' hum and watching our wake, trailing off into darkness. Cheryl and

I sleep in each other's arms outside the smoke-filled passenger lounge, then get up as the boat is pulling into its slip and race down the gangplank, across town to the bus station. Told that the next bus south doesn't leave until two, we check our packs and walk back to the Herakleion museum, which turns out to house one of the finest collections of the folk art of a single culture in the world.

The imperial art of Greece is housed in Athens, in the National Museum, but this museum in Herakleion maintains a continuity, offering a broad range of daily objects from one people, the Minoans, whose legendary king Minos ruled over a civilization credited with the invention of one of the first forms of written Greek.

From the years 3000 B.C. to 1600 B.C., Crete was the light of the world. Cut off from the mainland and unconcerned with the threat of invasion, since seafaring had yet to be turned to warlike aims, the Minoan society, cross-fertilized by the early dynasties of Egypt, flowered. Later it was supplanted by more aggressive cultures, but the legacy of the Minoans lives on in frescoes from the palace at Knossos featuring dolphins, dancing girls and acrobats participating in the rites of the local bull cult.

Cheryl and I, having both made our living working silver and gold, are amazed at the simplicity and grace of the Minoan art, the humor of their pottery, the elegance of beads put together by craftsmen who sat cross-legged on dirt floors, directing flames onto solder joints by blowing through long reeds.

As we leave the museum to go back to the bus, we find ourselves with another young couple, unusually sullen and silent, who've been more or less trailing us ever since the ferry. The guy is about six feet tall with brown hair, average good looks and a great tan. The woman is six-one with blond hair, trim tanned legs and the biggest breasts I've ever seen. No wonder they're sullen. They're obviously tired of being gawked at. I look. I look again. Unbelievable.

We board the cramped bus together and ride south, bumping over roads whose quality rises and falls with the terrain, then get down late in the day at a seedy little south-coast town called Matala. Although a perfect cove on the map, Matala's been overrun lately by the backpack brigade. Roman caves carved in the soft rock along the water's edge are fouled with piss and debris. Music from the beach-front café pollutes the calm. Rooms are expensive and the bus is already gone, so I approach the couple with the good tans and big breasts to casually suggest that it might be to our advantage to throw in together to see if we can find a place for four that we couldn't afford on our own.

The young man is a Canadian named Larry, and the woman (slightly older than he) a Dane named Jan. Once the ice is broken they turn out to be extremely friendly. The women start talking as Larry and I take off on an exploratory hike over a ridge to the west, agreeing that anything, even nothing would be better than Matala.

An hour later we scramble down a cliff to the tideline, which stretches several miles in a barren arc. Everything is silent and gray as we trudge on to a second set of cliffs, beyond which the coast is impassable, then turn back, discouraged. Halfway down the beach we come upon an old man who hadn't been there before. He waves us over.

As we pull up beside him, he holds up a pack of cigarettes, which I decline with a sanctimonious wave of my hand. The old guy gets angry. "Whaddya mean, 'None for me'?" he grumbles. "Whattsa matter? Too good to smoke with me? Too good to share my filthy habit?"

"OK, OK," I say, sitting down and taking a smoke.

"Light?" he asks, still in Greek, of course.

"Thanks." The old guy smiles and I inhale, grateful for the excuse. Don't bother to give up tobacco if you're heading out on the road; you'll spend all your time alone. What do Larry and I have in common with the old Greek without the cigarette? He holds it sideways, admiring it as if it were a woman, shaking it with appreciation like an Italian saying, "*Bella, bella*" with his hands. I shake my own and nod. It's quite a fag. Larry too, he's of the same mind. We have nothing to fear from this conversation, there's no possibility of offending each other's politics or religion, we are all one, part of the universal lung, engrossed, enraptured with the sight of bluish smoke being expelled in white clouds from our nostrils.

Remembering the purpose of our mission, Larry asks in the only word of Greek he knows, "*S'piti?*" pointing to it written down on a scrap of paper under a pathetic kindergarten drawing of a house.

"*S'piti?*" says the old Greek. "*S'piti?*" And then, in a short burst of what could only be "What, are you blind?" he points to a cluster of cinder-block structures just visible over the crest of sand. Down where we'd been before, in the gray tunnel of sea and sky, they'd been hidden. Larry and I shake hands with the old guy, then run over to find a young Englishman named Geoffrey, who tells us we may be able to rent a place in the town of Pitsidia from a man named Kostas. The Surgeon General can keep his warnings. Without that smoke it would have been close, but no cigar.

We head back to Matala, tell Cheryl and Jan the news, then hike over to Pitsidia, where we catch our man Kostas in his Kaféneon (coffee house) of the same name. He rents us a two-room cinder-block beach house for a total of thirty dollars, fifteen dollars per couple for a whole month. I don't care how bad the inflation's been (thirty-three per cent in the last year by some accounts) Crete is cheap. We hitchhike to market on weekends to buy tomatoes for six cents a kilo. We eat homemade cheese and carry thick sweet wine from a barrel to our campsite in plastic jugs.

We breakfast each morning on bread and jam, heating water for instant Nescafé on fires of driftwood and old fence posts, then ease ourselves over the slippery rocks to swim the half mile to the little beach behind the far cliffs, where the Greeks can't see us go nude. We lie on the beach all afternoon, basting and turning like spitted pigs, diving every few minutes into the sea. The water is just cool enough that ten minutes later we're out again, shivering, squatting in the sand among the rounded rocks, constructing elaborate forts against the water's siege.

In addition to Larry and Jan, our beach mates include Geoffrey, the erudite son of a miner in the English midlands, who quotes D. H. Lawrence, sketches figs, and courts the mysterious Dutch girl Anika; two Australian women on their way to England in no great hurry; a German girl named Jeannette; two French hippies who've left their baby in the south of France with friends; and a mad Kraut named Otto, with a shaved skull, who scares us half to death when we gather in his digs to drink his hot mulled grog. We pass the nights singing tunes by Dylan, the Beatles and the Rolling Stones, although Otto prefers to make up his own lyrics and does so at will.

A few days after arriving I take out a student composition book and begin to write. I had done some sketches in France, but this is my first attempt at fiction, the loosely disguised chronicles of a high-school kid named Richardson, who just happens to have had my old coaches, my bad dreams and my hard luck (in those last long days before the Pill) with girls.

Richardson—bless his soul—may never make it into print, but he answers, among other things, the age-old question of what to do with mornings in a near-ideal state. In Greece, one gives them to the Muse. She holds them in trust, feeling no compulsion to judge. All sorts of voices are heard for the first time as the quiet words flow. Occasionally a thought will rise in a line of surprising beauty. When that happens I have to learn to accept it, to put aside my *pudeur* and resist the urge to scratch it out. Like one of three moral monkeys in Paradise, I'm suddenly free to see, hear and speak. "See here! A speech!" Here, here . . . order in the court.

The month unrolls like a rug. Our rooms are the summer homes of nearby villagers, still tending their fields through June, so we have just a limited amount of time, but no one is concerned. We dive for mussels, bake bread in outdoor ovens and work on our tans. Larry's got two shades on me from his bare-backed trek through the mountains of Algeria that I'll never make up. When threatened with boredom, we hike three or four miles for provisions to one of two nearby towns. Twice we hike ten miles each way to an orange and lemon grove, to stock up on free fruit. Eden must have been like this. The Greek farmers around Eden were growing vines of *karpusis* (melons) that were not quite ripe when Adam and Eve got the heave-ho. The grapes were coming along nicely.

As perfect as Crete seems to us, many of the Greeks we meet would like to get away. A truck driver picks us up hitching and says, "Whattya think?" pointing out his windshield at the road twisting through the mountains and fields.

"Beautiful," we reply, "*kalo*—"

"No *kalo*," he says, "America *kalo*, Crete, *ochi kalo*." He shakes his head and launches into a tirade we can't understand about what he'd do if he could just get away like his cousin to Chicago or Boston.

"Yes, Boston, *kalo*," we say, "but Crete *kalo*, too." The driver scowls. There's always a worm in the apple. You have to eat around it, spit out some of that good fruit. It's hard to pity the guy just because he'd rather be living in Massachusetts, but we both know I wouldn't trade with him. It's all very nice to come down to the beach and live like a peasant, but I've got the choice. Being poor in the States with a beat-up '64 Chevy is not the same as being poor in Greece, or even being rich in Greece, with a government that denies you the right to travel with enough money to stay away longer than a few weeks.

The sad fact is that the Greek people aren't just poor, they're oppressed. The mood on the streets is subdued. There's a sullen reticence beneath the visors of fishermen eyeing the tourist throngs, a hang-dog resentment among the café loafers which may have something to do with their desperate history of domination by foreigners. In this century alone they've been overrun and/or ruled by Turks, Danes, Germans and now, in the cruelest twist of all, by those beloved stars of stage, screen and World War II—us.

We put the Junta in power in Greece, so we shouldn't be surprised if they are no longer our friends. As many Cretans speak German (from the war) as English, and the way current events and the Deutschmark are going, they'd just as soon keep it that way. There's a slow boil beneath the surface of things which is just as well mentioned now as later, although our minor hassles with villagers on the beach are no more than the kind of friction that arises whenever young travelers rub shoulders with the natives. The main gripe of those furtive men married to the heavy-set women in the long black skirts isn't political, it has to do with our naked bodies. They never actually see them, for they won't venture out beyond the rocks, but they know they're there.

The wind is angry. It kicks the sand and whips the waves. Africa looms across the darkness like a threat, breathing hot breath with all the ardor of impending rape. I lie on the Kalamachi beach, resolving to enjoy it, inviting my senses to abandon. The moon is full. The sea is bright with cold light as we gather for the last time, participants in a ritual we make up even as we disband. Geoffrey has finally slept with Anika, but his yearning is all the more intense, for she carries a sort of perfection about her that makes him superfluous. He entertains her with light verse, drawing a smile or an occasional caress, but it's clear that she won't miss him and he's already in mourning.

Otto, the skin-head Teuton, is up a tree. Perched in the fork of branches too slender to be anywhere near comfortable, he makes some kind of obscure personal statement, getting drunk and spilling wine inadvertently, but inevitably, on the bench sitters below. Alain, one of the two French hippies, wanders in a drunken stupor toward Kamelarion, a village four kilometers away. His girlfriend Sylvie, the mother of his child, is near tears, for he's told her he'll be heading on to India, leaving her to return to the south of France alone.

We set out a delicious spread and drink our fill, but the melancholy is thick. I play my little junk-store quitar, picked up in a flea market in Athens, but after each song the night is more silent than before. Something is amiss.

We sit and talk, picking among the vegetables for a piece of cheese, a piece of fruit. The hours pass slowly. Suddenly Alain comes back, covered with blood. Some villagers in Kamelarion stopped him and when he answered with drunken incoherence, beat him. He says he felt nothing. He laughs at the surreal sensation of fists pounding him, of his nose opening up and cascading over his lips. Alain is beyond caring, already lost in some mystical headset that will carry him east, but Sylvie is distraught. She sees an endless road of beatings and humiliations for her lover, even as he turns his back on her. Larry and Jan are moody and tense, undergoing an uncertain end to their affair. Cheryl and I are no better.

Several weeks back, Sylvie rescued a kitten from the burlap bag of a Greek woman who was heading to the sea, having decided there were enough cats already. The kitten has become a communal pet, pampered and adored as it laps up sweet condensed milk from a plate. We're just about ready to return to our rooms to wait out the moonlight and pray for sleep, when one of Otto's friends, dropping from an adjacent tree, lands on the little cat, which lets out a cry, then goes still.

Someone cries, "You broke its neck!" Geoffrey steps up to take charge, but he's unable to do anything and staggers away. The kitten is lying in a crumpled heap, twitching with the last signs of life. Suddenly Anika walks forward, kneels beside the cat and in a single gesture of shocking, resolute violence, picks up a large rock and dashes its brains out. She rises, her dress spattered with gore, looks around, then disappears into the night. Geoffrey is numb and filled with shame. I have yet to move.

Sylvie stoops down, gathers up the kitten and carries it in both hands, held aloft like an offering, to the water's edge. She's framed in moonlight, her silhouette piqued with sharp edges of broken light from the waves, as the cat, rescued from the sea, washes into the surf. It's too symbolic, much too precious, this hippie rite, but we play it out. Sylvie kneels by the water, counting her losses as we watch from the dunes behind her. Our lease is up.

The Istanbul Connection

TWO THINGS HAPPEN toward the end of our stay. First, we make up our minds to travel east. Cheryl's persistence has finally paid off. Our month on Crete has shown us how cheaply one can survive, and the quality of life we've begun to discover has us hungry for more. We write to Marie in France and to her old boyfriend Richard, Cheryl's brother, back in the States, to see if they'd care to join us on a little overland escapade. Both answer yes, but Marie needs more time to sell her *bijoux,* so we make plans to meet in August.

The second development is triggered by a telegram from our old friend John the jeweler, who asks us to call him collect. That's much easier said and done in Boston than on Crete, where it takes us four hours in a post office to make the connection and learn that John would like us to meet a friend of his who's leaving the country for the first time and will be arriving in Athens the day after we expect to land there from Heraklion. The timing is good.

We ride the ferry back to Piraeus, take a room in the same old sleazy student hotel, then go down to Syntagma Square to wait outside the American Express office for one David Austin, described by John as a master goldsmith. We stop about fifty people that morning who just might fit the vague description John gave us, before Cheryl spots our man in bleeding madras trousers and a short-sleeved shirt, with a Nikon slung around his neck, looking like the most woeful parody of an American tourist ever to step out of a *New Yorker* cartoon.

He'd been ripped off by the cabbie on the ride in from the airport, ripped off by the travel agent who booked him into a hotel manned by surly Greeks at three times the going rate, and is already so jet-lagged and culture-shocked he'd like to turn around and head home. We sit him down at a nearby café and hit it off immediately. David pulls out some slides of his work and floors us. We've been touring the great museums of the western world and his work is equal to the best we've seen.

After that we serve as his guides, leading him to the doors of the museums, where he takes over, deepening our appreciation with his expert commentary. We encourage him to check out of his hotel after he's hassled by the manager, who assumes the only reason I keep heading up to his room is for paid sex. On the other side of the drachma, we bump into that world-traveling hippie, Lee, who was so forthcoming on Mikonos, but now turns up his nose when he sees us with someone who fits his stereotype of a rich tourist.

After one week in Athens, David announces his desire to visit the museums of Istanbul. Cheryl and I had been planning to stop there on the first leg of our journey east, but we don't have enough money to go there twice, so David insists on providing the air fare. There's no way in hell he's going to tackle those Turkish streets alone.

We land in Istanbul after a one-hour flight and fight through the queasy, closetlike atmosphere of the airport. Faces intrude and hands grab at our bags. The signs are printed in Roman characters, but make no sense at all. People shout at us, ordering us this way and that, but not knowing who or what to believe, we believe no one, mistrust everything, ignoring the clamor of cabbies pulling at our arms to keep on walking. These people are too close, they seem desperate. Suddenly it dawns on us. We're in Asia.

We ride the airport bus to downtown Istanbul and begin the long uphill hike to the old city, the *Sultanahmet*. Cheryl and I are pinching pennies, so David has to hike along with us through the blistering heat, forced to share our penurious life style. We tell him it's good for him. He's red-faced and irritated by the time we reach the top, complaining bitterly that it's his birthday and that this is not what he came to Europe to do.

The question of hotels occasions a compromise. Nothing at our price meets his standard of cleanliness, so the three of us wind up sharing one fairly clean room with three cots. This arrangement presents certain problems of intimacy, but David has a habit of taking long showers and Cheryl and I learn to make do.

Our first morning we head straight to the museum at Topkapi. We're all reasonably excited, but nothing anywhere in the West can prepare one for the sheer opulence of the Sultan's hoard. Picture harem chambers of tile and wood inlaid with mother of pearl; waterfalls through languid bedrooms; the old cartoon image of a turbaned satrap atop a pile of stones, drooling, "Rubies . . . rubies . . . rubies . . ." as a stream of red rocks dribbles through his fingers, reflecting in candlelight from the corners of his hashish-glazed eyes. Picture emeralds the size and shape of the human brain, backlit to reveal unearthly translucent depths; tea services of rock crystal and gold; gem studded Koran cases and thrones; perfect pools of amethyst and sapphire; daggers, tiaras and chess sets of ivory and onyx.

After seeing Topkapi, one no longer wonders about the fatal appeal of precious gems. One finds himself along with all the other tourists wandering the halls of this old palace with its almost comical lack of security, trying to fight back the fantasy of breaking a case, grabbing up fistfuls of whatever lies within, leaping the ramparts and swimming to safety (burdened to the extent of one's greed), across the Bosporus.

Even if one can put that thought out of his mind, there's no way to resist the sick fantasy of dancing girls herded by Nubian eunuchs and concubines on silken pillows. The palace reeks of love, lust and unbridled power.

Outside the streets are teeming. Old men fitted with heavy leather saddles march bent over, bearing crates of produce stacked ten high through the narrow alleys. One sees them later after work, or out of work, too old to carry on, wandering about doubled over, their spines permanently fused into postures of submission.

We sightsee for several days, visiting the Hagia Sophia, the cathedral built by the Emperor Justinian in the sixth century A.D. and later converted to a mosque; the Blue Mosque, constructed by the Sultan Ahmet at the same time the Taj Mahal was going up in the beginning of the seventeenth century; and numerous other mosques and churches, some of them stripped to brick, revealing man's infatuation with the arch and dome. Istanbul is a monument to monuments of faith.

Our fourth day we wander down to the Grand Bazaar, where Cheryl and David have a field day poking through little bowls of junk beads and hidden treasures. David picks out a handful, including a carved seal which he says is authentic, and Cheryl handles the bargaining. At first the guy doesn't want to deal with her, since she's a woman, but Cheryl gets him going by badmouthing the beads and laughing at the Turk's first price.

David shifts from foot to foot. He looks to me for help, pulls her aside and tells her he'll pay whatever the guy wants, then finally has to walk out, it upsets him so badly to hear Cheryl and the store owner screaming at each other across the table. The Turk is in heaven. These things mean nothing to him (I can't say they do much for me, either), so he's got nothing to lose. The process goes on for a full half hour and ends with both of them shouting "Last Price! Last Price!" Then the Turk wilts and Cheryl grabs his hand before he can change his mind. When it's all over, David's got his beads, Cheryl's wearing a big grin, and the Turk, in a sweat, walks over, puts his arm around me and says, "Good woman," implying, "Now get her out of here before she sees something else!"

Outside the bazaar, we notice that the mood of the city has turned festive. Martial music blares from the same loudspeakers used to broadcast the prayers of muezzins from the mosques. We're halfway across town before we find out why: Turkey is at war with Greece. Dodging across a soccer field,

I'm accosted by a group of young men with mad looks in their eyes, who ask, "*Yunanistan?*" (Turkish for "Greece?").

"No," I say, stopping short of telling them the truth, because the Turks, long angry for what they perceive quite rightly as our indifference and neglect (if our official attitude toward blacks was once "benign," imagine how sanguine our disregard of the Turks) are suddenly furious, convinced that the CIA, who installed the Junta in the first place, also engineered the attempt by Greek banana colonels to stage a coup on Cyprus. It's unlikely that our government was behind a move so likely to fail and in doing so precipitate hostilities between two ostensible NATO allies, but anything is possible. Perhaps the Greek colonels simply came across an old Rand Corporation scenario and thought it was an order.

Whatever the case, these skinny civilians, 4-F cousins of the heavily armed Turks at the front, are enacting elaborate pantomimes of what they'll do to the *Yunan*s or any other suitable victims who happen along, so when they ask me again where I'm from, I lie, saying, "Switzerland—*Suisse* . . ." holding up my trusty red rust-free army officer's knife, which fails to make its point as they close in and I start shouting, "Wait! Stop! Listen to me, I'm from Australia!"

"Australia?" they ask, "*Australia?*" cocking their heads. A little voice tells me "Keep it up," so I say, "Yes, Australia!" until they all get that look of recognition in their eyes and start running around grinning like monkeys in a rainstorm, shouting, "Australia! Australia!" shaking my hand and congratulating each other.

Australia's a good choice, a stroke of genius, really. It's easy to see why they've got such a good press: nothing but seas all around them, kangaroos and platypuses, treat their women mean—why, the Aussies don't have an enemy in the world.

The sun goes down, but street lamps and store windows fail to light. Istanbul is blacked out. Shark-finned '57 Dodge cabs, tangible evidence of the last time U.S. dollars flowed this way (the new cars are all Mercedes), prowl the streets with blue tissue taped over their headlights. It would be a good night to stay in, but driven by hunger we descend the hotel stairs to navigate the normally intrusive streets with remarkable anonymity. The Turks are in this together, and since in the darkness we are less obviously not them, we share in the communal solidarity.

The blackout brings a paradoxical security to this beleaguered cleft between Europe and Asia, a place that's been violated so many times by so many people that its inhabitants no longer seem to distinguish between pleasure and pain. They glow in this state of war, the streets are radiant. We take a dreamlike stroll through dense night air perfumed with sweat and the smoke of mutton roasting on skewers, dripping into pans filled with coals, bursting into flame. Voices babble and bodies gently collide, but there's no violence or fear. We pass from hand to hand without so much as a mark or bruise.

The restaurants are hung with dark curtains. They're ready for war, either with Greece, which means blackouts, box scores and business as usual, or with the big boys, the Soviets, in which case the curtains become shrouds and the whole country, a mausoleum.

We eat dinner, walk home slowly and turn in to bed, but there's no going to sleep. The sky is filled with aircraft, our minds with thoughts of Greek and American bombers. Everything is dark under overcast skies until midnight, when the clouds are blasted with heat lightning. A light rain starts to fall. The sky ignites and electrical leaves outside our window glow blue-green against silver heavens. Unseen planes drone on like the voices of a city at prayer. Thunder rumbles—Allah . . . Allah. Bolts of Oriental energy fly in jagged lines to the spiked domes of the mosques.

We've got to get out, but we linger over breakfast anyway, for we won't taste the likes of this rose-petaled honey again. War is hell, but an army marches on its stomach—like snakes —I see entrails strewn on paths. We stumble down to the spice bazaar to stock up one more time on dried fruit, bottled water and halvah, the world's best. *Now* we're ready to face the mobs, to rush in panic down to the train station to jostle in among the refugees.

With the airport closed, the only way out of the country is via the Orient Express. I hold my ground long enough to pick up three tickets for the five-o'clock departure, due in Athens at dawn. We hang out all day, unwilling to risk a change in schedule, board the train at four and find ourselves with five other people (since we're three, that makes eight) in a compartment designed to seat six, and none too comfortably at that.

Our fellow travelers include a young Greek, a mod jewelry store owner and his wife from New York City, and two Lebanese brothers who claim to be pharmaceutical students. The Lebanese make us all miserable by constantly closing the window. It's about a hundred and five degrees in this train, but they're shivering. We lend them sweaters and jackets, but they still keep closing the window and they'll wake from a deep sleep, freezing, if we crack it more than an inch. I'm ready to attribute this pathetic lack of resistance to their warm homeland, when Cheryl notices that they've got little packets of white powder inside their beat-up suitcases. That explains it—withdrawal. There's a war going on and these guys are smuggling smack.

The train rolls through the poppy fields of northern Turkey at ten miles an hour. You can almost get high breathing the air. There are miles and miles of sunflowers with storks jumping through the stalks. Lavender mountains glow in the distance.

Soon it's dark and there's no more view to enjoy as the train inches forward. The flight from Athens to Istanbul took one hour, but the return will take thirty-six. There's an elbow in every gut, a foot in every face. The Greek blows smoke, someone else breaks wind; it won't work.

Late the first night Cheryl and I brave generations of spit and dogshit to throw our sleeping bags onto the corridor floor, but our respite is brief. We're rousted at 3 A.M. by Turkish border guards, who shake us down, but for some odd reason leave the two shivering Lebanese alone. David stays awake talking shop with the two New York merchants whose idea of fine design is a gold Twistoflex. Our only relief comes in the form of thin glasses of sweet tea passed through the window by vendors at successive stations. David palms off a pair of these elegant tumblers to take home as a souvenir, but someone leans back and crushes them. The toilet facilities are unspeakable.

Arriving at dawn of the third day, we find Athens every bit as grim as we. Cheryl and I had hoped to visit the island of Samos, but it lies about a mile off the Turkish coast, so we settle on the first ferry out of Piraeus, knowing we're lucky to get away at all. The boat takes us to Paros, where David rents a hilltop room for a pittance, since the war has wrecked the tourist trade, and we set up camp on the far side of the island, thanks to a custom that keeps the beaches free. The Greeks are truly civilized. They permit one to be poor.

Paros is as magical in its own way as Mikonos or Crete, but something is missing. Perhaps it's the war, or maybe just me, but somehow, although the landscape is sea and sky as far as one can see, the beach lacks serenity. We're holed up, waiting.

We hang out for a week, then Cheryl rides the ferry back to Athens to meet up with her younger brother, Richard, six-two and lean with curly blond hair—a handsome headstrong kid with a taste for adventure and an eye for the ladies. Despite the fact that we've had our run-ins in the past (I've resented his profligate life style, he's resented my resentment), I'm glad to see him. His arrival spices the dull routine. Determined to get along on this trip, we test each other with nightly bouts of backgammon and *ouzo*.

Ouzo, nicknamed the "soft hammer," is a sweet anise-flavored *eau-de-vie* (brandy; literally, water of life), which sells for a dollar a bottle, pours out clear, but turns milky with the addition of water or ice. What it does to the brain is also unclear. We set up shots and knock them down in succession, seven in a row, slamming our glasses after each round in some macho ritual dimly remembered from *Zorba the Greek.* After that we roll the dice until our eyes cross as the soft hammer descends.

The porch starts to whirl and there's no stopping it, so we push back the tables, drop our drachmas in the Greek juke box and dance. There's a whole hard core with us down at the waterfront café, it's a summer camp for dissolutes (Simon, Nathan, Mark and Nancy), a haven of insanity in the midst of war. We jump and stomp, shaking up all that cold *moussaka* from dinner until the hammer impacts, cleaving our skulls. One by one we stagger off, puke, stagger back, and switch partners. Cheryl takes off with one of those backstabbing sons of the beach and I wind up with a young French art student, solacing myself for my misplaced *affaire du coeur* for Marie.

The frustration of our entrapment on Paros is driving us to extremes. Richard is found morning after morning washed up on the beach like driftwood, his head swollen, his limbs twisted about him in a vain effort to keep warm. Only David retains his perspective, walking the rocks with his trusty Nikon, finding inspiration for future work in the brackish pools of sea life.

Meeting up with each other was a real break. His dedication has restored my faith after my own dispirited attempts at jewelry, while our street sense has opened up a whole new set of possibilities for him. He and I take a long walk across the island just before he leaves. A farmer invites us in for some homemade *ouzo,* then we dine on rabbit and red wine in a tiny restaurant and walk home by moonlight, basking in the calm. David has found his traveler's legs. He's ready to push on to Crete. We tell him all we know about the island, then stand back, waving, as he climbs on the bus the next morning and disappears. In another week, we, too, are on that bus, heading back to port.

The war, meanwhile, has taken a turn for the worse. Down on the dock, women in black are weeping, repeating a scene as old as the stone walls dividing the fields. The boys are shipping off, walking up gangplanks to uncertain fates, forced to fight under a military in which they've lost faith. Long the enemy at home, the army has proven itself utterly worthless by being too weak to face the foreign threat, and the Turks are mopping up.

On board, the crewmen are truculent, fed up with tourists telling them what to do. A fight nearly breaks out when a hippie with a guitar asks them to turn down their radios. We ride through a brilliant blood-red sunset cut diagonally by ferries crossing our bow. We're leaving the islands for good. For better or worse.

Off to our left is the prison fortress of Kios, where the junta's prisoners are held. Late in the cruise the word comes in that the junta has fallen. The crewmen turn up their radios full blast and start smashing the dishes. Angered by the action on Cyprus and unwilling to suffer the consequences, the U.S. government (read: Kissinger and Nixon) has withdrawn its support and the puppet government has collapsed. The Greek people are jubilant, they're dancing in the streets. Marie, meanwhile, is setting a new land speed hitchhiking record *en route* from Avignon, and suddenly, after all this waiting, it's all coming together and the first leg of our voyage is but three days off.

> Personally, I have had occasion enough already to observe that a democracy is incapable of governing others.
>
> What you do not realize is that your empire is a tyranny exercised over subjects who do not like it and are always plotting against you; you will not make them obey you by injuring your own interests in order to do them a favor; your leadership depends on superior strength and not any good will of theirs. . . .
>
> To feel pity, to be carried away by the pleasure of hearing a good argument, to listen to the claims of decency are three things that are entirely against the interest of an imperial power. Do not be guilty of them.
>
> —CLEON, speaking to the Athenians,
> The Mytilenian Debate, 427 B.C.,
> Thucydides, *The Peloponnesian War.*

It does seem ironic that after all those years of protest and opposition to U.S. foreign policy of precisely this sort, I'm the one left holding the bag when the crowds converge on Syntagma (Constitution) Square, Athens.

"I'm on your side!" I feel like shouting, but in two months on the islands I've acquired a marvelous tan, but precious little syntax. Maybe it's not so ironic. I'm no less a tourist than anyone else scurrying around American Express, trying to get his money cashed. Drachmas are a dime a dozen.

Down on the square, across the street from the King George Hotel, several thousand people are chanting and pushing, awaiting the return of Konstantine Karamanlis, the conservative nationalist ushered home (but no one knows by whom) after the rug was pulled out from under the U.S. stooge, Papandreou. Latecomers jostle by me on the southwest corner and glare. Americans are easy to pick out.

The atmosphere is tense. Things are supposed to have changed overnight, but no one quite believes it. Tear gas and chaos seem imminent. The Greeks are edgy, unable to forget what's happened in the past, expecting at any moment the accustomed onslaught of military vehicles opening fire and plowing into the crowds. I've felt this kind of fear before, standing on the outskirts of other large crowds at the Pentagon and South Vietnamese embassy, but it doesn't matter what I did at school or how many times they've got my face on file, right now I'm just another Yank and like those Athenians blasted by Cleon, I want to be liked.

The crowd's chants may be Greek to me, but the signs speak loud and clear in English and French saying, "Kissinger Assassin!" I keep asking myself how we could have made enemies of the Greeks. It doesn't make sense. I'd like to jump in there with them, raise my fist and stake some claim to solidarity, but they neither need me nor want me, so I move instead into the relative calm of an airline office to see about getting out of the country.

The room is crowded, but the sight of those distinctly nonmilitary airline uniforms reassures us. We are all Westerners here. The world may be disintegrating, but we shall maintain our decorum. Those messy Greeks are Westerners, too, but Mediterranean, they push their way everywhere. It's a common occurrence while waiting in line to be knocked aside by some old Greek grandmother, charging ahead with the determined indifference of a water buffalo. We do not push. We wait. We shuffle, one foot at a time.

Way up at the head of the line, I spot an old high-school buddy of mine, Mark Smith from suburban Philly. I haven't seen him in eight years, but do I rush forward, clap him on the back and find out how he's been? Does he, his ticket purchased, his eyes coming to rest on mine, bound over, suggesting a beer and a sentimental tear for the best years of our lives? No.

We're thousands of miles from home, in a war zone, our futures and destinations uncertain, yet we pass without a word, without so much as a nod. There's a certain shame and humiliation attendant on our presence here, an obscene association with the U.S. presence being vilified outside that both of us would just as soon ignore. Mark and I will share a good laugh over this some time, back in some suburban bar, but today we're strangers, each of us alone with his own plans and desire to escape. I don't blame him when he turns and walks out the door. I'm not even surprised.

Now it's my turn at the ticket window. In normal times we'd be starting in Istanbul, the eastern equivalent of St. Louis in the days of the Old West, where Volkswagen buses and Land Rovers parked in a circle outside the Pudding Shop (Istanbul's famed hippie hangout) are like covered wagons in an overland train stretching back in time to the great Sanskrit civilizations of Asia. The open road *is* a kind of last frontier, but now the first stop on the traditional trade route is closed, so we'll have to start our journey in Lebanon.

None too confident of our carrier, I book four places on Middle East Airlines for two days hence, when the airport is expected to reopen, then hop a bus with Cheryl, Richard, and the newly arrived Marie to ride a few miles north to a small section of city seafront called Voula Beach.

Richard made some friends here on his last brief pass through town, and now we intend to crash in the caged-in refreshment stand where they work, to save our money for the road ahead. The problem is that Greece was quiet before, but now that the war has intensified, we discover to our chagrin that little Voula is directly under the flight path of the Athens military airport.

Every few minutes another plane screams in, pounding the ground, less than two hundred feet overhead. The din is incredible. The air is saturated with gasoline, it's like sleeping on the island of an Interstate truck stop. Blades whirl and hydraulics wheeze as the wheels clang into place, landing lights strafe us and these are just the Greeks! If the Turks come, we'll be the first to go.

It's madness, insanity to be here now, but nobody's listening to me and I might as well get used to it. Two days later we line up at the commercial airport to kick off into the unknown. Cheryl throws a fit to keep the guard from X-raying her film and Richard's still back at the bar, trying to drink up the last of his Greek money, but somehow we all make it onto the aircraft marked by the unfamiliar cedar insignia of the Lebanese fleet. Soon we're in the air over Cyprus, the cause of all this turmoil, looking surprisingly calm and unruffled from 20,000 feet, the edges of the bloodstained island washed with a gentle froth of surf. This is the last moment of detachment.

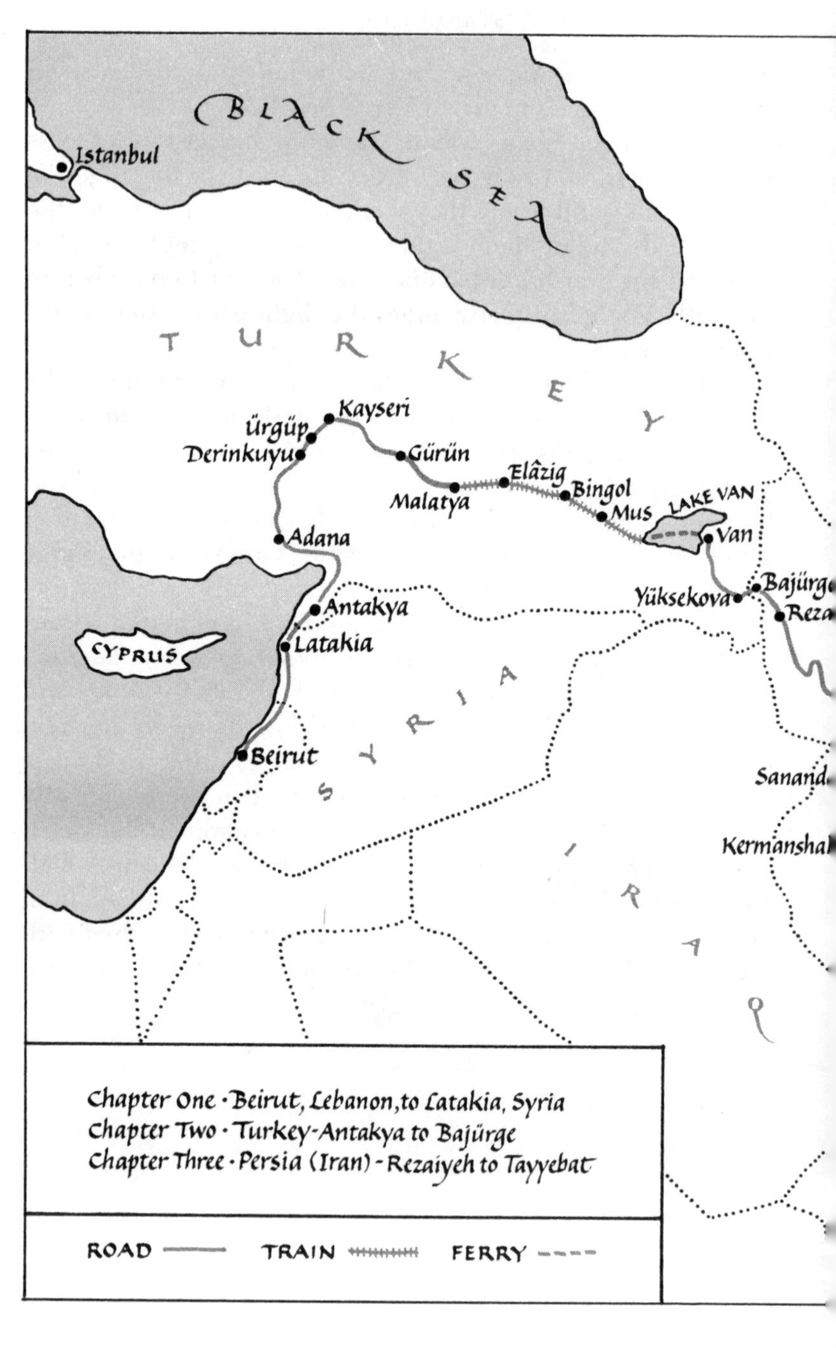
BLACK SEA
Istanbul
TURKEY
Kayseri
Ürgüp
Derinkuyu
Gürün
Malatya
Elâzig
Bingol
Mus
LAKE VAN
Van
Adana
Antakya
Latakia
CYPRUS
SYRIA
Beirut
Yüksekova
IRAQ
Chapter One · Beirut, Lebanon, to Latakia, Syria
Chapter Two · Turkey · Antakya to Bajürge
Chapter Three · Persia (Iran) · Rezaiyeh to Tayyebat
ROAD
TRAIN
FERRY

PART THREE

THE MIDDLE EAST AUGUST 1974

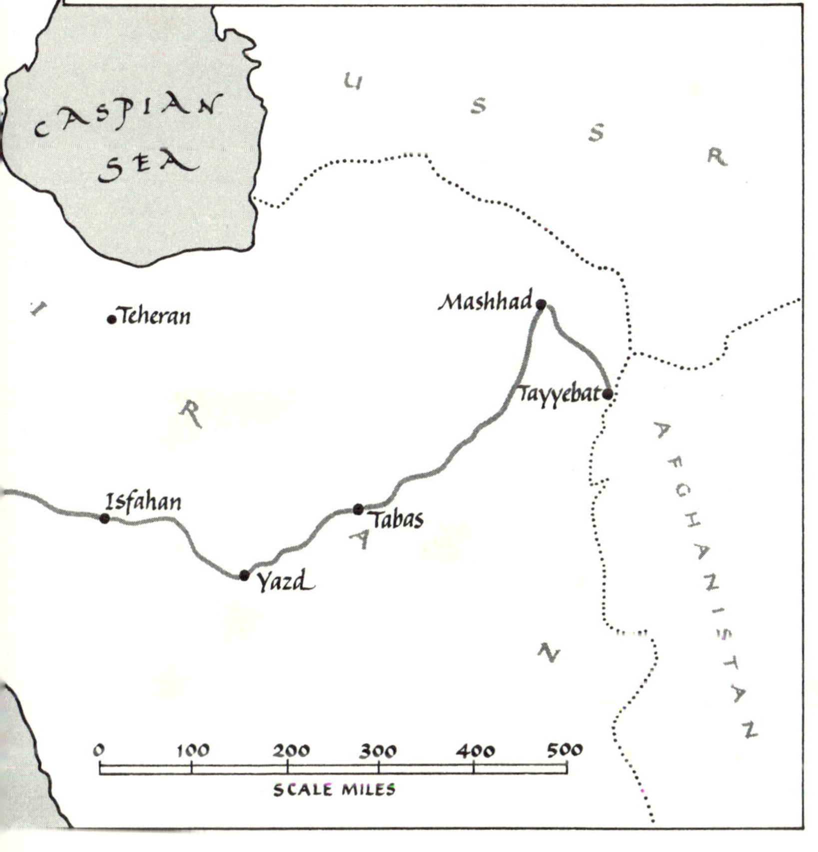

WE MUST HAVE taken off at twilight, for it's dark when we touch down and pass customs. I love this notion of passing customs—the guy walks out and says, "How many men on a Lebanese fire truck?" and you go, "Uh . . . uh . . ." and he says, "You flunk, back to the plane."

"Wait!" you shout. "Five—no, six!" guessing right, so he has to let you in, but not before he stares at your face, then dips his stamp and smears it across your passport photo, while signaling behind his back for somebody to keep an eye on you.

Some countries have really funny customs. They let you in for practically nothing, then halfway through you slip up and there's a sleazy guy standing there, holding a sign that says "Donations." *Baksheesh* they call it, a gift from a richer man to a poorer one; and once you hit Asia, it's a way of life.

The hard part about arriving in Beirut isn't passing customs, it's figuring out what we're doing here in the first place. The only one with any idea is Richard, whose eyes are half-glazed already from the mere thought of going out looking for some of that fine red Lebanese hash. We haven't evolved any ground rules for moving together, so when a cabbie slides up and takes two of us by the elbows, we're easy prey. Cheryl complains that the driver seems to be wasted on something, and her opinion is confirmed when he weaves his way out of the airport.

The cabbie asks what we want and Richard says, "Hashish,"

but Cheryl says "Hotel." "Hotel," says Cheryl again, finally getting her way, but the guy laughs when she tells him what she wants to spend. There are no fifty-cent hotels in Beirut. This is the financial capital of the Middle East, the place where the oil sheiks come to drop their cash and pick up their Rolls-Royces. The architecture is the best that new money can buy, pure Miami Beach, with high-rise hotels and condominium-style apartment buildings overlooking the sea. Our driver stops at one run-down place and comes back quoting a price of five bucks each. Convinced he's in on a kickback, we tell him to drive on.

Two or three more hotels at much the same rate convince us, but refusing to give in our first night on the road, Marie and Cheryl order the cabbie to let us down at a causeway high above a beach several miles down from the airport (we've circled town), saying we'll sleep out.

The driver protests, I protest, but somehow I wind up with the two women on the curb, while Richard drops his pack at my feet, hops into the front seat, unscrews his bottle of duty-free Scotch and hands it to the driver, motioning ahead like the Great Gatsby, saying, "Forward, Jeeves."

"Stop!" I shout.

"I'll be back," he hollers, and is gone.

This was not my idea in the first place. Our first night in a foreign country on a brand-new subcontinent with two attractive young women and carloads of Lebanese whizzing by and we're sleeping out and I can't even argue the point. There's nothing to do but wait. It's going to be an interesting trip. So far no decision has been made without someone wanting to do the exact opposite.

Cheryl and Marie sack out on their packs while I sit up, keeping watch. Two sleepless nights at Voula and now this makes three. I picture the kid careening from honky-tonk to gyp joint, trying to score. Hours pass. My fear for the women and concern for Richard turns to impotent rage at being stranded this way. I devise cruel and unusual tortures to inflict on the boy when he gets back (if he gets back) and am all but whimpering with frustration when somewhere around two in the morning the cab returns and the kid flops out, dead drunk. There's no sense even talking to him, he's incoherent.

Cheryl and I carry the packs while Marie walks her friend down to the beach, a hundred and fifty feet down a steep hill to a flat area hidden in shadows. I help tuck the kid into his sleeping bag, wondering how I'll get even now that he's aroused my maternal instincts, then hop into my own sack, exhausted.

Some time later, between three and four, I get a funny feeling, look up the hill behind me and see a set of dark shapes descending on the run. As my eyes focus, I begin to make out that the guy in front has a rifle and that there's a guy behind him and a rifle behind him and so on and so forth all the way up the hill and down the causeway to the troop carrier, where soldiers are pouring out single file, like army ants from a hole in the ground.

By this time the first guy is right above me, his automatic leveled at my chest, so I jump up, hands high, and start hopping around in my drawers, trying to explain in English, French and sign language that we're just a bunch of dumb hippies, not some crack Israeli paramilitary assault squad.

The commanding officer, about thirty years old with a trim mustache and a khaki shirt open at the chest, takes my passport, reads it, makes the universal sign for crazy (one finger circling the temple) and hands the document back. He says something to the guy behind him, who laughs and says something to the guy behind him, who does the same, and they go on so on and so forth all the way up the embankment. It would be hard to say who's more relieved as the rifle barrels lower, they or we, for we are merely surprised in our ignorance and stupidity, whereas they had been prepared for the worst.

I grin at the chief, who shakes his head and walks off, then climb into my sleeping bag as Cheryl and Marie lie back down and close their eyes. I hardly had time to get scared before, but the fact is, if any of us had made the wrong move in our sleep, they'd have cut us to ribbons. Over to my left, Richard is snoring. He doesn't normally snore, I wish to make that clear for his sake, but this night, with a bottle of Black and White under his belt, his chops are loose.

The next morning we dump some water on his head to revive him, describe what happened, ask for some smoke to cool our nerves and are told that his dope run was a bust, although he says he had a great time. I look over my shoulder to a pair of huge concrete tubes dripping human excrement into the bay below. Picturesque.

We pack up and straggle into the city past the American University to breakfast at a quiet seaside café, then find our way by bus to a hostel recommended as within our means. They must have thought we said hospital, because it turns out that we four are the only fully ambulatory people in the whole joint. We wind up sleeping dormitory style on bunk beds with the lepers and lesser communicables, males in one room, females in the next. The inmates pad about in prison-issue pajamas, color coordinated with the striped mattresses on which we throw our bags, trying desperately to ignore the tea-stained sheets. Our hosts are gracious and helpful, but the filth makes a mockery of their civility. My stomach is hardened through exposure to some of the worst dives in Europe, but this wretched bunghole in Lebanon makes me gag.

We get out early the next morning, trying to arrange a visit to Baghdad on our way to Iran, only to learn that there's a three-week wait for a reply from the Iraqi embassy, with a near-zero chance of obtaining passage. By contrast, we receive brisk and courteous service from the Iranian embassy, the very model of efficiency, are told our visas will be ready in twenty-four hours, then head back to the city to wander through the gold market (a disappointment).

Away from the luxury hotels, Beirut is a run-down, essentially awful place, a place calling for the development of some new kind of weapon, an anti-neutron bomb which destroys buildings, but leaves people unharmed. If ever a city deserved to fall, it is Beirut, but the people have it hard enough already, and this is well before the civil war that will reduce their lives to ruin.

People with money, of course, don't have to put up with the squalor; they live in the hills surrounding the city, cool and detached. The most powerful among them preserve their wealth and security through the use of private militias, whose competitions (with, among other groups, the PLO) reduce Lebanon to the status of a medieval fiefdom, with war lords and autonomous strong men. There will be no resolution of these affairs without a bloodletting, for even in 1974 the place is thick, swollen and ready to burst.

The next day, twenty-four hours to the minute later, we collect our passports, graced with the imperial seal of the Shah, then hurry to the bus station to buy tickets through Syria for the following morning. We pass the afternoon walking around town, talking to students who are happy to share the sordid story of their leaders' corruption and drug-smuggling, knowing we'll be leaving soon and repeating their tales to no one.

Unable to put off returning to our hostel any longer, Richard flags down a cab and we pile into the back seat, taking advantage of the extra leg room, leaving Cheryl and Marie with the cabbie up front. The driver talks non-stop all the way home about how nasty and dirty the Syrians are and how we shouldn't eat the food or drink the water, sneaking glances at us through the rear view mirror. As we near our home district and the streets get denser and narrower, he invites us to a little party at his place in those surrounding hills we'd heard so much about.

"Hills very nice, very cool," he says, "very good hashish," then sliding up beside our hostel, he turns with unfeigned disgust and asks, "Why you stay here? Come, you go . . ."

Richard and I hop out, saying, "Great, we'll be right back," but as we start in to retrieve our gear, Cheryl walks up, taps me on the shoulder and says, "Michael . . ."

"Come on," I insist, "let's go. What'd we come here for? You wanna meet people or not?"

"Meet people? *Meet people?* Are you crazy?"

"What do you mean?"

"Why don't you ask him what he wants? *Go ahead!*" She's

standing with her hands on her hips, very angry, and suddenly it dawns on me.

"Excuse me, I say, pulling him aside for a little man-to-man talk, "you weren't thinking that if we go home with you, you'll uh, wind up with these women, were you?"

"Yes!" he says, a big grin on his face. "We go to my place, make party, smoke hashish, then . . ." he jerks his head toward Cheryl and Marie, making me wonder who's more naïve, him or me?

"OK, buddy, what do I owe you?"

"No, no, *free* . . . you my friend, my guest."

"Forget it, pal." I hand him a buck.

"No, please," he says, shoving the money back, then realizing that he's blown it, he snatches the bill and takes off with one of those blood-curdling Lebanese oaths.

It's a good thing Cheryl and Marie are looking out for themselves. While Richard and I had been riding along, buying his line, the cabbie'd been shifting gears and copping feels with his elbow. In our vanity and greed we nearly sold them out for a free cab ride and a cheap high. Suddenly the old hostel doesn't look so bad after all. I take that back, it does, but it's clear that there are fates worse than dirt.

Dawn is an hour away. There's a cold, damp mist in the air, an early-morning calm that has the old men talking in whispers. Two of us wait with the bags while the other two go out searching for cigarettes and chocolate. The station gets crowded. Voices rise as the sun comes up and soon we're all pushing to get onto the bus. We ask several times to allay our nervousness and reassure ourselves that we are indeed on the right vehicle headed to the right place, then the driver arrives, surveys us with disdain and slams into first gear. The motor has been running for some time. The air is foul.

We pull out of Beirut onto the coastal highway running north. The country is flat, dotted with palm trees and shanties. Lebanon is reputed to be a country of great physical beauty, and I regret not having made it up to the mountains around

Baalbeck and El Laboue (which translates literally into French as "The The mud"), into the high country where the cedars flourish. Our route takes us past Tripoli to the Syrian border. When we get down from the bus to enter customs, I get nervous.

I'm a Jew. It doesn't say so on my passport, but it's written in my face, especially if you know how to read between the lines, and the Arabs speak this racial language as well as anyone. They yell, "Hey, American Jew!" to see what I'll do. They make me acutely aware of the fact that one is never a free agent in this world, that one must answer not only for what he does, but for what he's taken to be. I don't wish to be taken for anything, I only want to be taken to Turkey, so I adopt a low profile as we step up to the Syrian official, seated with his two assistants. They glance only at the golden eagle on my green U.S. passport and affix a set of stamps, three dollars, visa of transit.

Outside, Richard's got the Frisbee waiting. We start out at twenty yards and begin sailing it through the warm desert air, moving further and further apart as the guards gather in amazement. Cheryl clears customs and joins us and now they're *really* amazed. She whirls, she spins, she floats like a butterfly, stings like a flea.

We're drenched in sweat, glad to be using our bodies after the cramped bus ride, when suddenly Richard looks up and says, "Where's Marie?"

Richard and Marie are, or rather, were lovers. They met in Paris, then traveled together in Mexico, although their brief, passionate romance was all but over when she first passed through San Francisco at the end of that trip (which is where I met her). This new phase of their relationship is somewhat artificial, having to do mainly with our trek. Although they draw together at times, they tend to get impatient and argue over trivialities, a trait shared in common by all four of us. When Richard asks, "Where's Marie?" there's already an edge to his voice. They've had a rough morning.

We walk back to the customs room and find Marie, livid,

tête-à-tête with the Syrian official. The French word for arguing this way is *engueuler*, which means to give a little lip to somebody. Marie stalks the desk, giving him a mouthful. When we ask her what the problem is, she says, "These fuckers want five bucks!"

"Five?" we say, "we only paid three."

"I know. They say it's more for me because I'm French. It's not fair! Forget it!" As she stomps around, near tears, Richard storms out, adding to the confusion, shouting, "Leave her here! I can't stand it, she's nuts!"

Cheryl tries to reason with her, saying, "Come on, Marie, there's nothing you can do. Pay it," but Marie refuses, demanding to know why we, the U.S. imperialists, unsworn enemies of Syria in the Middle East, should pay less than she, sovereign daughter of the country that freed Abu Daoud. She even turns down Cheryl's offer to chip in, saying it's a matter of principle.

"Principle?" now *my* fuse is getting short, "Goddammit, there's a busload of people out there!" The Syrian official is folding his papers, getting set to leave, gesturing as if to say that he wouldn't issue Marie a transit now for any price. I plead with him, pulling Marie up to the table, watching as she lays her money down.

Principle? How the hell is Menachem Begin (or whoever follows) ever going to sit down with Yassir Arafat if people start invoking principles over a two-buck border surcharge? Marie thinks that we (the U.S.) are the bad guys. She forgets that the French have been pissing people off in this part of the world for a lot longer than Uncle Sam, who's just starting to get really mean in his dotage.

I'm not trying to make Marie look bad. We all have our moments on the road. Stress builds up, meals refuse to stay down, tensions accumulate, and if one isn't careful, he or she can easily wind up out of control. Marie hitchhiked down from France in two days without rest. She worked hard all summer trying to get her money together and now it's catching up with her. Borders are intrinsically insulting anyway, she's entitled to take offense. That's why we're traveling together. We help her now and next time it might be us. In her defense, although the sum may sound trivial, one should not underestimate the power of two bucks in Asia. In Marie's resourceful hands, they might last a week.

We're met back at the bus by angry stares from our fellow passengers, but once we start moving everyone forgets the inconvenience and goes back to his drowsy window watching. The ride through Syria is sobering. Tank installations are hidden under camouflage nets beside dozens of impoverished villages, which obviously could make better use of the money poured into the *jihad*.

A rest stop in the medium-size city of Latakia passes without incident. The Syrian people aren't nearly as nasty as the Lebanese cabbie who warned us about them. We stroll the streets, eating ice cream, attracting very little attention, then climb onto the bus for another forty minutes before the driver shifts into low gear to begin the slow ascent into the mountains. The barren terrain gives way to scrub pines. We're leaving Syria, approaching the Turkish border.

Turkey is where we want to be. Richard and Marie missed Istanbul, and we all regret skipping the Mediterranean coast, but we're finally back on the track. We'll check out the rest of the Middle East some other time. After the wars.

We get down from the bus and walk across to the Turkish customs house. When they start calling the passengers in one by one, we grab the Frisbee again and pass the time circumscribing large arcs of clear sky. The air is crisp and cold, it revives us. Turkey has what we're looking for, we sense it immediately.

Turkey

T. C. HATAY
Giris
Yayladag Hudut Kapisi
—Turkish passport stamp

Hatay is the city of Antakya, known historically as Antioch. *Giris* means either entrance or customs, while *Yayladag Hudut Kapisi* means just what it sounds like. We *yayladag* our *hudut*s across the *kapisi* and get on board the Turkish bus.

There are many classic bus rides in this world: there's the cartoon Mexican bus ride with its chickens and goats; the uptown ride through North Philly (from whose bourn no traveler returns); and the Greek mountain bus ride I once heard described, where the bus stops each time at a certain town before a particularly fearsome mountain pass, littered with wrecks, and the people get off in two groups—the men (including the driver) all run down to the tavern to get plowed, while the women and children stream into the church to light candles and pray; there are plush intercontinental cruises on hip Mercedes making the London to Delhi run, and dull hauls on Continental Trailways that turn one's soul gray; there are buses and then there are buses, but if you really want to talk bus, you'd better talk Turkey.

Turkish buses aren't the newest or fastest, and their seats aren't the best. There's bottled water on board, but who knows where the water was drawn? Who cares? We drink it, it's wet.

As the bus pulls off, red fringes above the windshield start to sway like tassels on a dancing girl, undulating, smooth, with a heavy-hipped grace. Then the music begins.

A friend of mine, who was stationed with the Air Force in Turkey, says the music is the worst thing about the buses, but I have to disagree. I can no more envision those barren mountains without the pulse of Anatolian rhythms than picture the Turkish flag without the crescent moon. The bus climbs from the border, clears the timber line, hits the top of the world, then hurtles down to hoofbeat percussion piped in on a sound track inspiring 70mm technicolor visions of Turkish, Syrian and Scythian horsemen galloping through the grass meadows and mountain tundra, scimitars glinting, twirling above their heads.

One approaches Turkey from the south as if one were not merely entering the country, but taking it. The music is hypnotic, the driver, possessed. He overpowers the corners, bouncing us up against the glass, approaching every switchback as if it were a test of his manhood. I get the feeling he woke this morning like an ancient warrior facing battle, thinking, "It's a beautiful day—if Allah wills it, a good day to die."

Coming in this way, one relives part of the history of part of the race. Here is where Alexander and Darius passed in the night. There is where they locked horns in the battle of Issus, 333 B.C. Cornering his adversary between the Cilician Gates (high mountains to the northwest) the river and the sea, the Macedonian neutralized Darius' numerical advantage and wound up slaughtering a hundred and ten thousand men (according to Plutarch) in an afternoon. It was also in a landscape like this (in Plutarch) that he took over the Persian's tent, regarded the trappings of gold and silk and remarked with that resonant mixture of admiration and scorn, "So this, it seems, is what it is to be a king."

Past Iskenderun on the coast, we continue on to Adana. Once out of the Syrian forests there are very few trees. One account has it that Alexander razed the land to hinder pursuit, but the timber may merely have been consumed in the blight of human years, as elsewhere in this once fertile crescent. Those forests which have been replanted are dedicated to Kemal Ataturk, founder of the modern republic, which means they can't be cut, although it is legal to pull off the branches. Most of the trees in Turkey are stripped as high as a Gypsy can reach from the back of a camel.

We arrive in Adana in darkness, physically and emotionally drained. Led into the hotel opposite the bus station, we drop our bags, eat at the nearest restaurant, then return to our room to sleep.

I say room, because from now until the time we split up, there's rarely a night that we don't sleep together. Cheap inns in Asia are set up dormitory style, each bed going for about fifty cents. If we weren't four, we'd have to take our chances, mixing in with whoever else happened to be passing through, but like this we can take over a whole room, throw a lock on it and call it home. It's not much, yet it's remarkable how much security and peace of mind are derived from slapping that padlock shut.

There are drawbacks, of course, to this forced communalism. One is never quite alone and must answer for his gaffes to a group, a disapproving chorus of critics with long memories and highly developed tastes. You can't fool or please everybody—not for long. The litany of past sins is recited each time one would forget. The slates are never quite wiped clean. One's karma stays with him, like a greasy film on a dinner plate rinsed in an icy stream.

The second drawback is love, or rather, sex. Richard and Marie could be getting it on much better, given the time and space; and Cheryl and I would certainly benefit from a little privacy, and I shouldn't have to remind you that Cheryl is Richard's *sister* (and that I've had a crush on Marie) . . . but when the mood turns amorous, the room goes still. There's a quiet scraping of wicker woven cots being pushed together, a nylon parachute rustle as the sleeping bags are interzipped, then dull moans and muffled noises of no particular shape and size building to bashful rhythms as the room fills with fecund odors, like a stable for Bactrian camels (that's two humps, not one).

When it's over, the edge may be off, but true satisfaction is rare. Sleeping bags cling to sweaty skin. Legs are thrown in all directions, and those moans are heard again as partners fall off onto separate beds. Travel third class may be exotic, but it's not an aphrodisiac.

From Adana we hop a shared taxi, called a *dolmus*, north. Cheryl points to a dot on her map called Derinkuyu, saying we'll stop there for the night. She's the only one who's done her homework, which tends to simplify things, although we wonder what she's thinking when we step out into a nondescript little town with one mosque, one hotel and two cafés filled with men. The walls are mud-tan and dung-brown. They're covered with cow pies used for fuel and insulation, bearing the handprints of the little girls who pattycake them into shape.

As soon as we step out of the cab we're surrounded by more kids than you'd ever expect to find in such a small place. At first we pretend that they're not there, but that's ridiculous. They're everywhere. This is our first taste of the *bwana* syndrome. The whole village is focused in on us. We have the feeling we're the first Europeans ever to have passed this way, or the first in a long while, neither of which is true.

These simple childlike people (they *are* children, dammit) are delighted by us. The girls edge up to touch Cheryl's dress and her long blond hair. The boys show off by tormenting huge white hounds wearing spiked collars around their necks (placed there by their masters to help fend off wolves), which in turn vent their anger on truck tires which they toss into the air like balloons. The dogs maul the giant wheels, but leave the kids alone, and one suspects that they've learned this distinction the hard way.

The little girls are gorgeous, bright and alert with onyx eyes, but the boys are disturbing. It may be their shaved heads which make them look so odd, or perhaps they're just aping their elders, who sit in the cafés while the women work non-stop, pounding their wheat, tossing off their chaff, grinding their grain, baking their bread and cooking their meals.

It's very unfashionable to generalize this way, to slander a whole race, but I'm not talking genetics when I say there's something wrong with the Turkish male. There's a thick, stricken look about his eyes, a born-again dullness that's obviously not the result of inbreeding, since the women are fine. My guess is that the vacant stare must be handed down from father to son via beatings which make unquestioning obedience a prime virtue. Lack of education and poor nutrition don't help, but whatever the reason, I can't help feeling that the Turkish male is somehow less than he could be. He's also lucky. His little girls are angels, and the women—ah, these brightly swathed women of Derinkuyu—Alexander had it right, "they are a torment for our eyes."

As the crowd grows, some of the men disturb their leisure to move in, giving an occasional kid the boot, making eyes at Cheryl and Marie. Fifty or sixty people are following us by the time we reach the main attraction of this town, the underground city hollowed out by second-century Christians. Turkey has been a most inhospitable place to groups out of power, and this eight-story subterranean refuge is a testament to their will to survive. Each basket of earth and precious square foot of space was carried out on someone's back. When those boys went underground, they weren't fooling around.

We locate the guardian, who lights a new electric light, which illuminates the first of the long shafts we descend on our way to the lower caverns. The entry is protected at intervals by large rock wheels, five feet in diameter, propped in slots and ready to roll across the narrow openings at the slightest kick, to seal out those above. Anyone not in when the doors shut could kiss it goodbye.

Once below, the Christians subsisted on accumulated stores, while breathing through air shafts running to the surface and drawing their water from a deep fresh well. In the dead of winter they might have been better off down below than up on the frozen plain. The city was connected by means of a nine-kilometer tunnel to another underground city at Kaymakli, where an estimated twenty thousand early Christians buried themselves to stay alive. It's cold down here. To hell with this notion of brimstone and fire at the earth's core.

Once we're out of the living tomb, with its memories of marauding hordes, the people of Derinkuyu don't look bad at all. The fact is, they're darned friendly. If the rest of Turkey is like this, we're in for a good trip. A group of little girls pull Cheryl and Marie over to where their mothers are baking bread in an outdoor oven. Before our friends know what's happening, the women are pushing them down, grabbing their hair, combing it out and braiding it into tight little knots. The children look on, beaming. Cheryl's got a pretty tough scalp, I can tell by the way she tears into mine sometimes, but the women are yanking so hard she's got tears in her eyes. She tries to smile, it's a great honor and all, but both she and Marie will have headaches for days until they finally undo the braids.

Later a dust storm kicks up and clears the streets. Sheep lean against the walls and all the little boys roll up and blow home. We rest a while at the hotel, then walk across to the restaurant, where the mayor joins us for a conversation in broken French. He has high hopes for the town now that the underground lights have been installed. That must be why we've gotten such a warm reception. Derinkuyu is looking forward to a resurgence. We tell him we're delighted to be here, he says he's delighted to have us, then we all sit back, sipping a delightful white wine and wishing ourselves well.

Cappadocia. The word conjures up images of a hit man for the Mafia. It's a compelling name for a place where the earth explodes into fantasy. Once the bottom of a sea bed, the soft sandstone has been eroded by centuries of wind into a sculptor's dream world of crazy spires, massive gum drops, cones, pyramids and grizzled profiles. In one spot alone we count more than twenty distinct faces of monsters and men. What is wrong with this picture?

The larger mounds were hollowed out and lived in by seventh-century Christians, Byzantine monks who fashioned 365 churches and cathedrals in this region of the Göreme Valley, carving Roman arches and keyhole-shaped doorways leading into chapels adorned with frescoes, genuine Byzantine frescoes unprotected, yet undeteriorated after all these years. Some of the mounds are still lived in and at least one of them sports a TV antenna. The land alone is incredible, like the badlands gone amuck, but the combination of natural forms with this extraordinary devotional art turns the region into a timeless monument, a spiritual link between the cave paintings of neolithic man and the great cathedrals of the West.

We descend into the valley by bus, looking out over the rooftops of a nearby village, where red peppers are laid out in great numbers to dry in the sun. Once down, we hike into the heart of Göreme, past scrawny grape vines, in and out of the river beds. We climb small hills to enter the chapels and dip our hands in earthen troughs where once the holy water lay, then sit back in the cool darkness of vaulted interiors, looking out. The world is bright tan with here and there a grudging spot of green. It's a world of nightmares and visions, a world for prophets and mortifiers of the flesh.

After one night in Ürgüp, a town which like its name is uglier than it is large, we get an early start hitchhiking east, for the first time on a direct line with our ultimate destination, Nepal. Cheryl sums it up quite succinctly, "When you're out on the road, all those ideas you had don't matter, and suddenly you have to face up to that fact and deal with it. Back home, nothing is as critical."

This is our first taste of the overland flow, standing with our thumbs up in the early morning air, ready to take whatever comes. We pass through the large town of Kayseri, then out into the rolling hills. We're approaching the country of the Kurds, arguably the most persecuted people in the world today. When the governments of places like Iraq speak of the rights of displaced people, they court contempt—they've been waging a genocidal war against the Kurds for years.

Traditional nomads whose range extends into the Soviet Union, Iraq and Iran, the Kurds are fierce fighters who recognize no borders or authority outside their own. When they stop an occasional Turkish bus to relieve its passengers of their possessions, no one resists, for to get on the wrong side of a Kurd is to face a vendetta.

This central region of Turkey reminds one of the American West on a scale that is somehow more vast, for these are the gates of Asia. Sheep graze around haystacks beside golden villages. It's harvest time, everything is in its hour. Every vista in every direction is sealed off by beautiful mountains.

We hang out the sides of cars and trucks, snapping photos, hoping to come up with something to remember as we speed through. We'd love to stop, would spend all our time stopping if we could, but out in the middle of Turkey one does not get down from a ride if he can help it. The next ride might be hours or days away.

The beauty and grandeur of Turkey are overpowering. That may be one reason why so many people throughout history have tried to overrun and possess her. We too are intoxicated with her savage strength, exhilarated by her indifference. She's taking us for a ride and we may never feel this free again.

After three days of hitching we get a lift in a small pickup truck with a canvas roof. The driver picks up a few more travelers along the way and we ride about a hundred and fifty miles to a tiny town called Gürün, in the absolute middle of nowhere. As we pull in, our driver uses a combination of hand signals and grimaces to invite us to bed down at his place, but we politely decline, having learned from the taxi driver in Beirut that there's no such thing as a free ride.

To avoid appearing ungrateful, we convince our man to let us buy him dinner. He sits down at an adjacent table in the small kebab shop and orders ten skewers of lamb, rice, soup, salad and a kind of local firewater called *raki,* served in old pop bottles. Richard joins him and the two of them get roasted, laughing and tossing off tumblers of booze. I admire Richard for his quick susceptibility to the idea of a good time, his easy rapport. When the old guy gets drowsy, we take his leave and retire to our room in the hotel directly upstairs.

As soon as the door shuts, we let down our guard, unstuff our sleeping bags, wash up and are brushing our teeth, when someone starts pounding on the wood. Nothing is worse than an attack like this when you think you're through for the day. Richard cracks the door to see what the fuss is about and finds our driver, furious now that he's had time to think about it, that we hadn't deigned to join him in that intimate soiree over at his place. The thought of the four of us in a hotel room must have piqued his demented imagination. His pride injured, his will fortified by all that *raki,* he says he wants money.

"No, no," says his good friend Richard, "we already paid you. We bought you dinner, *kebab, raki . . .*" but the guy wants more. He wants dessert. He wants Marie. When we refuse to fork her over, he goes berserk, screaming and shouting, trying to push his way in.

Now, if we were to take time to add things up, the petrol and wear and tear on his car at seventeen cents a mile the way the IRS computes it, chances are pretty good that we would owe the guy some change, but his pounding on the door scared me to death, and when he starts in toward Cheryl he makes a bad mistake.

The poor Turk. He's never heard of Capitaine Bijoux before. He doesn't know what a crazed East Coast hippie can do, he thought they were all alike. Out-Turking the Turk, my mouth full of toothpaste, I start to foam, shouting, "Let me at him (hold me back), let me at him!" charging the sucker, backing him up against the wall. He's terrified, I'm terrified, but I've got him now. "Let me at him!" I bellow, taking hold of Richard and bouncing him around until he gets the idea and grabs me back, yelling, "Michael, take it easy—" at which point I flip out completely and start strutting around like Muhammad Ali, saying, "*What's mah name?*" as the Turk looks up with pleading eyes and Richard says, "He'll be all right," calming me down, giving our man time to add up that mileage again and see if he hasn't made a mistake. Let's see . . . put down the two, carry the three—ah yes, just as he thought, a simple misunderstanding. He edges down the hall. He just remembered, he has to be someplace, see a man about a car . . .

I follow him down the corridor, calling, "Nobody comes in my room, *nobody* bangs on my door, *you got that?*" as a handful of men in the hallway nod their approval at my innate grasp of Turkish diplomacy. Richard shoves me back inside and slams the door and I deflate like a balloon, flying around the walls making a weird flatulent noise before winding up in a heap on the floor.

He picks me up and we slap hands. It worked, a perfect team, the soft guy and the hard guy, but the pit of my stomach is murky. I had no idea what I was doing. If the guy had called my bluff, the best I could have expected would be to wind up in a Turkish jail. There's no escape from this town, that's for sure. There's just one road in and one road out and they happen to be one and the same.

The next morning we hurry through breakfast, keeping an eye out for our friend, then hoist our bags and walk out to the street to hitchhike away. Once again we're surrounded by kids, but they're much nastier than they were back in Derinkuyu. There's an insidious aggressive edge to their behavior, as if they've done this before.

They poke and pull at us, trying to get into our packs. When we get out the Frisbee, they trip us and get in our way. We give them our spare Frisbee to play with, hoping they'll leave us alone, but they march it directly down to the river and ditch it. I suspect our driver is the accursed progenitor of some of these little bastards, who've been sent out to get even. Our karma is at a low ebb.

There's practically no traffic and those few trucks that do rumble by fail to stop. We wait three hours, then pick up our bags after much bickering and start marching east, not caring that the next village on the map is a hundred miles away, certain only that we don't want to spend another moment in Gürün. There's a peculiar lightheaded sensation that comes from doing something that one knows is stupid, a giddy liberation from care, and the moment one stops caring, things often start going right. Ten minutes out of town a bus appears. We wave it to a halt and scramble on, moving toward the rear.

Cheryl and Marie fill in next to some Turkish women as Richard and I plunk down on the back seat beside a guy with a three-stringed instrument indentified as a *sas,* akin to a dulcimer, the primary folk instrument of eastern Anatolia. The people of this region are excellent musicians and their tradition of village music still flourishes. The man with the *sas* begins to play and the other men around him start singing. The effect after our experience on the street is immediate. We cool out.

Some time later I reach into my pack for my Marine Band harmonica, which I first picked up on those long nights walking back from the library at Radcliffe. I can still remember that day when one of my sophomore roommates, a black premed student from New Orleans, finally turned to me after I'd backed up Tim Hardin singing "Misty Roses" on an old scratched LP and said, "Mike, that's the first time you ever played along with something that you didn't ruin it." I didn't know whether to thank him or quit while I was ahead.

I hold up the harp to show the guy what I have in mind, then blow a chord to let him know what key I'm in. The man's got a good ear and the bent notes on a blues harp are perfectly suited to the modalities of Eastern music, so we swing right in on a Turkish hillbilly rag. We tear it up.

He gets tired after a while, so I take a turn on the *sas,* which is easy to play if you can strum a guitar, the ladies in back keep clapping and the bus keeps rockin' an' rollin' along. When we reach our destination some two hours later and go to pay, the driver refuses our money. It turns out there is such a thing as a free ride, but they're rare and never when you expect them.

So far the emotional topography of our voyage has been up and down and sideways, like the path of a mite across a corrugated wall. Just when we're fed up with the Turks, we make music and friends. One moment seems to have little or no relation to the next. The obvious implication is that one should draw his conclusions in pencil and keep his eyes on the road ahead.

Our progress takes us to Malatya, a prosperous agricultural-industrial town in what used to be Armenia before the slaughter of that people, located at the edge of the Taurus Mountains, just west of the Euphrates. An upwardly mobile young Turk, attaching himself to us to practice his English, leads us proudly through the streets of his town, from the new city to the old in search of dice. Richard and I have had our hands tied since Paros, where backgammon occupied a niche reserved back home for literature and Monday Night Football. Dice are essential on the road, they help pass the hours of waiting between when do we leave and no place to go.

It takes most of an afternoon covering much of the town to locate a tiny pair of plastic cubes, then we sit, sipping tea, rolling doubles, mindlessly content. Back at the station, we tear paper into squares for makeshift backgammon on a board drawn directly on a concrete table.

Night falls. The train is due in shortly. We tear off chunks of bread and wait. Seven o'clock, eight, the train is late. Our mouths are coated with the metallic taste of tea. Richard waves the waiters around with comic insouciance, calling out, "*Chai* [tea], baby," every time his glass runs out. I roll a two and a one. A draft blows the markers off the table, so we give up the pretense of strategy and get down to basics. Double threes, he rolls again.

Eight o'clock, nine and still no train. Rick and I wander out along the spiked iron fence beside the tracks, to an outdoor park where they're showing a film. Two hundred men are lying on the grass, engrossed in the action. When we clear the bushes blocking our view, we get an eyeful of what passes for entertainment out here.

A huge guy with a shaved head and baggy pants grabs a blonde and throws her up against a wall. The audience howls.

He takes out a whip and she falls to her knees, then he walks up slowly, looming above her, waiting to take his pleasure. The men to our right grow silent. As he shuts his eyes, smiling, the blonde produces a knife from somewhere inside her sleeve and drives it into his guts, twisting it and sending him crashing to the ground in a pool of gore. Cut to:

SCENE 5. INTERIOR HAREM CHAMBER NIGHT

Loyal followers of the fallen leader stream into a courtyard, tossing guards and slaves into a reflecting pool, dragging off the women by their long blond hair. Blondes, everywhere blondes, every fair-haired wench between Ankara and Uskudar is in this low-budget extravaganza. The Turks on the grass are laughing and whistling as the camera pans in on ripped clothes and women screaming (quite convincingly). More blood, more gore, more laughter to our right and Richard and I have had enough. We hustle back to where Marie and Cheryl are huddled together, keeping warm in the cold desert night.

Nine o'clock, ten. My three friends are dozing in the café. I wander out to inquire about the train and draw a shrug, which is more than I deserve. Obviously it will come when it comes. Across the platform in another building, forty men are jammed into a waiting room. I edge through the door and find a place on the cement floor to listen to the music echoing off the green plaster walls. Three men up front are strumming stringed instruments in loose unison. One voice takes a verse and forty answer back. The assembled men rock on their haunches, staring out dreamily into landscapes that the music opens in their souls. The train is forgotten. They're thinking of tiny villages back home and little girls a shade too young to marry. The songs are a link to the past, to the lives of other men, who made them up for just such moments as this. A pulse passes from shoulder to shoulder as we float through time.

Outside, down the track, the double feature is ending and all that ugliness is staggering home to spend itself as best it can. Now the train pulls in, hot as a forge. The engineer is wired, wide awake and impatient as the station stirs and passengers stumble aboard. He wants that throttle open. Pistons paw the air like hooves as the train wheezes and snorts, pulled up short.

We climb into second class, sleep, wake and sleep again until day breaks and we peer through the metronomic visual click of telephone poles running past Elâzig, through Bingol and Mus to Tatvan, on the west bank of salty Lake Van, the largest inland body of water in Turkey (1,454 square miles). It's a half mile through open fields to the ferry that will carry us across to Van, the city, cradle of the ancient Armenian civilization and heart of the Vannic kingdom of Urartu, or Ararat, the name of the mountain on which Noah's ark came to rest. Lake Van just might be the last pool of the Flood. It's a mile high, crisp and cold, with sharp dark clouds etching lines across the sunset.

Topside, a retired Englishman takes out a large ledger and begins writing in a steady script. There's no telling what he's getting down in those archival pages. His is the kind of work I suspect is not for publication, but dictated out of personal needs accruing to one who's waited his whole life to escape the English fog and dreary offices out of Dickens, to find some meaning on the road. I've had to put my own journal away. It was forcing me to think too much, to find words from my old life to describe things I've never seen. I kept catching myself intoning, "Ah, the azure skies of . . ." whatever—when the skies weren't azure, it was just a good word, and it wasn't the skies that were of interest, anyway, it was the way the skies were making me feel, and I was having enough trouble just feeling without trying to write it down. There's a kind of literary corollary to Heisenberg's Uncertainty Principle: If you try to describe an experience as you're having it, you alter it. The only way to get it right is to go through it first, then think about it later, Wordsworth's experience recollected in tranquillity, unless you're like this old Englishman, who seems to know what he's doing.

Nothing much happens in Van, except as we're leaving,

when children too young to know better, yet too young to have dreamt it up themselves, pelt us with stones. I snatch a rock out of the air, suppressing the urge to whip it back, because there's no doubt that if I let it fly I'll nail one of them right between the eyes. That's not a boast, really, just a fact. Man's aim when he's out to destroy is uncanny, it's part of the reason he's where he is today, i.e., everywhere. He can lead his prey at full gallop, allowing for the wind, or throw a three hundred and ten foot strike from the warning track, but the one thing he can't do once he's let go is call it back, so I drop the rock, put my pack over my head and run after my friends, racing up the road. When a truck stops we hop on with a road crew, who laugh as the children follow us, made bold by our retreat.

We're heading out of town on a road indicated as not yet finished on a map that is five years old—the hitchhiking equivalent of Russian roulette. There's a train out of Van to the Azerbaijan city of Tabriz, in Iran, but when faced with two alternatives, we tend to choose the more difficult, the less likely. Our original detour at the start of this trip has gotten us into the spirit of improvising, and it's clear after that last leg from Malatya to Tatvan that very little happens on a train.

I read a novel once where a despairing man made it with a blind girl in a restroom, rocking back and forth with the rhythm of the tracks to a shattering climax, but aside from the sexual fantasies produced by that steady vibration between one's legs, trains are not fertile ground for experience. You're either cut off in your own little compartment, making small talk, or wandering up and down the aisles as the train rips off a hundred miles at a clip. Safe conveyance, although desirable, is not enough, so we find ourselves perched on top of this gravel truck, taking it on faith that we'll make it through.

A half hour southeast we get down at a crossroads by a gas station which looks like it's never been opened, then sweat out three hours with virtually no traffic before an orange pickup truck belonging to the government construction agency slides to a halt and we jump in. We ride an hour before reaching a small village serving as a checkpoint, which strikes us as absurd, since the road doesn't seem to be heading anywhere, but on second thought isn't, since this is the region of the Kurds, who are pursuing their war of liberation across three borders.

Overlooking the town are the weathered remains of an old fort, a vestige of the days when both the town and the road were more important. Our driver is inside a *chai* shop, having a drink, when a soldier comes up and orders us to appear before his commanding officer. Fishing out our passports, we descend a hill to a clearing by a stream, where a Turkish colonel is seated on a chair set like a throne on an Oriental rug. He ogles us, each in our turn as we step forward to present our documents, which he studies with the air of a man who can't read, but is trying to make it look like he can.

Finding nothing of interest in our passports, he browbeats us, trying to find out why people such as we would want to pass through such a god-forsaken part of the world. Are we Communists? No. Journalists? Heaven forbid. There's no reason at all for us to be here except that we are, and no reason for him to give us such a hard time except that he can. And does. And does a damned good job of it, too. We're practically kissing his feet when he finally hands our papers back and bids us leave.

Back on the road, our progress slows, but our good fortune in hooking up with the road engineer becomes even more apparent when we reach an area where they're blasting. He stops his truck, gets the all-clear, then takes his four-wheel-drive vehicle out over the edge, past traffic that's been backed up for hours and impasses that might not be cleared away for days.

This highway is being carved out with the greatest difficulty through one of the most remote mountain ranges in the world. Two years later a massive earthquake will strike, killing tens of thousands, leveling many villages and negating all the hard-earned progress, suggesting that there may be something about this region that doesn't *like* progress. That suggestion itself will be carried forward (or backward) by the religio-political impulse which will bring its own earthquake, shaking the foundations of the governments of this region by 1979, although we have yet to feel any tremors.

The high country of Turkey is rocky and wild, dipping over passes into river valleys coated with a soft green growth, grazed by cattle. We push on from one spectacular vista to the next until five-thirty, when we pull off the road into a work camp, a mess hall surrounded by barracks down a steep gravel path.

Our driver disappears into a wooden building, leaving us to stretch our legs, wondering where we are, until a kitchen worker appears with tea. Minutes later an aide-de-camp comes up and welcomes us in English, telling us he'd be honored to have us stay for dinner. Again we're amazed at our good fortune. First the ride and now an offer of that legendary Middle Eastern hospitality.

Richard and I are just getting comfortable, rolling for doubles as usual, when the aide comes back with his boss and the bubble bursts. The boss is a greasy, sleazy character with thick lips, bulging eyes, a glutton's gut and a vicious five-o'clock shadow, wearing huge rings and gold chains smothered in a jungle of thoracic hair. He swaggers as the aide flutters around, performing the introductions. The Big Boss doesn't even bother to hide his intentions as he holds out a limp hand to Richard, then whirls on Marie, taking her in from head to toe, breast to knee, zeroing in on the choicer parts of her anatomy. When he's had his fill he turns on Cheryl, snaps a few orders to his assistant, then disappears.

As all this is going down, Marie discovers that her wallet is missing. It must have been lifted from the truck while the colonel was shaking us down at the last town. That good fortune we were talking about is deserting us. The way the boss was looking at our women has me weak in the knees and obviously I'm not alone, for without a word we pick up our packs and start running up the gravel path, back to the road. The aide-de-camp comes tearing after us, crying,

"What are you doing?"

"Taking off."

"No, no, you can't" he says, tears in his eyes. I have a strong hunch that if he lets us get away, Big Boss will have his ass. Literally. "Where will you go?" he pleads. "It's almost dark . . . there are no more trucks . . . we've already put up the lamb."

The lamb gambit almost gets me, but one thought of those wolves down there straightens me right out. The odds are insane. They've got three hundred Turks on a hardship post, a boy Pander and a Big Boss tired of his steady diet of boys. The aide reaches up, grabs Richard's arm and *begs* him, "Please, stay . . . you must . . . *please* . . ." but the more desperate he gets, the more obviously imperative it is that we get out.

When a dump truck drives up, we throw ourselves in front of it. The driver tries to warn us, but we jump on anyway and land in a thin layer of cowshit. Richard, barefoot, gets a nice dose between the toes. As we ride off, the aide slumps back to face the music. I pity the guy, but it was his ass or mine. Marie's wallet is missing with a hundred bucks and Richard reports that our dice are gone, forgotten on the table. Things could hardly be worse. We have no idea where this road will take us, or where we'll sleep or if we'll eat, but it doesn't matter what happens next, I've never been so glad to get out of a place in my life.

Hanging on to the edge of the truck to keep our feet out of the slop, we ride two hours to a maintenance yard beside the highway, which has once again become passable as it nears the border. We're out of the mountains, on the plateau around the last town in Turkish Kurdistan, called Yüksekova. We hike down to the city lights a half mile away, find a bite to eat, then settle on a hotel. When Richard and I leave the room to wash up, the proprietor takes advantage of our absence to unlock the door and stick his head in on Cheryl and Marie, to "see if they need anything." The little ladies are getting tired of these intrusions. Each guy who sidles up to them thinks he's the first and adopts an air of wounded innocence when they tell him to bug off.

The next morning we walk out to the highway at dawn to hitchhike to the border, but this really is the last town in Turkey and no one seems to be going any further. Several hours pass before a young supervisor from the maintenance yard stops over and says he'll find us a ride if we'd like to come in for some tea. It sounds like another setup, but since absolutely nothing has passed us since early morning, we decide to accept.

Our new young friend, who also happens to speak English, sits us down on a veranda to find out what we're doing. He's happy to use his English, to air out certain complaints in a tongue his co-workers can't understand, but beyond that, as the conversation proceeds I notice a particular glow in his eyes each time he turns to Richard.

He's polite to Cheryl and even-handed with Marie and me, but it's increasingly clear that the boy wonder is tickling his fancy, driving him nuts traipsing around in cut-offs hacked off at the hip, his long legs tan against the short blond hairs and goddamn, if I had tendencies he'd be driving me nuts too.

The young Turk watches in awe as Richard hurls and tracks down the Frisbee, looking like a Greek god, then runs over to the garage to poke his head in among the mechanics. The kid has a great fascination for speed, he likes big Nortons and high risk, so he's right at home among the grease monkeys, who are trying to tune a dump truck. Richard offers a suggestion and when he can't make himself understood, grabs a wrench and makes the adjustment himself. The Turks stand back, amazed. A Westerner who can work with his hands? Unheard of. Oh, *American*, they nod, the land of surfer boys and beach buggies, Richard is the myth come to life and our friend is really drooling now. He nearly gets flattened when Rick hops in the cab and takes the dumpster for a spin, wheeling out, cutting hard and sliding donuts in the dirt.

Richard climbs down, gets clapped on the back, then returns to the veranda, trailed by the lovesick supervisor, who sends out for more tea. It occurs to me that before long he'll be asking us to stick around another day and it'll be shades of the night before. I'm not concerned for Richard's sake, he can take care of his own end, but as none of us has any interest in wasting another moment in the town of Yüksekova, we get up together and start walking out the gate. Finally our friend, forlorn, orders a car to drive us to the border. He shakes hands all around, saving Richard for last, holding on and staring into his eyes for all he's worth.

The car takes us to the Turkish outpost at Bajürge, just a shack with a sleepy-eyed sergeant, unshaven and slovenly, seated at a desk. There's a new border station across the road, but little to suggest it will soon be open.

Turkey has finally charmed us, with its breathtaking landscapes and half-baked adventures filled with sexual innuendo, and now as we stand outside this jerkwater cabin, quaint in contrast to the modern Iranian facility just past the turnstiles, I realize sadly that this is the last we'll see of it. I confess a sentimental tugging at the old heartstrings as our sergeant slaps his stamp to the dried-out ink pad, then applies it to my page, pressing just hard enough that I can barely make out the words of that traditional Turkish farewell:

Halkari Ili
Cikis
Esendere (Bajürge)
Hudut Kapisi

Persia

THE TURKISH GUARD DIDN'T even bother to check our bags on the way out, he knew that if we were stupid enough to be carrying any contraband, they'd find it on the other side. The horror stories (soon to be a major motion picture) that we've heard about Turkish and Iranian jails have driven all thoughts of illegal or controlled substances from our minds. There was enough to worry about in Turkey without getting high, and it's particularly nice being able to look those humorless Iranian customs men in the eye.

We assure them that we're clean, but they dive into our bags anyway, poking through the ladies' underwear, trying to relieve their dreadful boredom. Richard and I start skipping the Frisbee off the linoleum floor as they unstuff our sleeping bags, poking around for lumps, then call us over to stand, smirking, as we fold everything back up.

Outside a cab is waiting to take us to a nearby village that is little more than a *chai* shop with a name. When the late afternoon bus fails to arrive, it looks like a night on the old dirt floor, until the cab stops back, looking for fares to the city. At least ten people step forward, but we reach deep, something we rarely do, to top their fares by a dollar. To my surprise and relief, no one objects. We're playing by the rules, this is *baksheesh*, it works, and we're going for a ride.

Our destination is Rezaiyeh, on the west bank of Lake Urmia, a shallow, salty body of water about equal in size to Lake Van. The rolling hills to its west are deep green, lush with rain from the large inland seas. This is Iran's bread-basket, a prime source of this mostly desert country's grain, fruit, cotton and tobacco. Tractors chug along, stirring up little clouds of dust. Off in the distance a camel strides forward with an easy lolling gait.

Sunset. The horizon goes flamingo pink and green. As we roll on, our driver starts singing and the three men with him in the front seat join in, chanting the sun down. They really should stop the car, get out, spread their carpets and kneel (the bus drivers and all their passengers do), but it's late and we'll just make it by dark as it is, so they do the next best thing, turn this funky old cab of a car into a shrine, a tabernacle on wheels. The road adds vibrato and urgency to their voices as we downshift hard and strain up hills. They wring each worshipful note for emotion, shaking down the quarter tones like dogs with old shoes. They're not singing for our benefit, but we can't help feeling blessed.

Dropped off at a hotel in Rezaiyeh, we have a friendly but serious hassle over the rate, resolve it, shake hands with our innkeeper, then lie down, taking stock. Iran represents a whole new set of preconceptions to overcome. The question is how? The answer is, hardly; for hindsight will tend to disprove most of the evidence of our eyes.

I'm one guy who won't castigate the CIA for missing the boat in Iran. I didn't do any better; but, then, no one was depending on *my* intelligence. Our visit reminds me of a story I heard from a friend of my cousin's who traveled once in Algeria. While there he encountered a tribe of people whose teeth were all twisted and brown. Poor people, he thought, obviously their diet is deficient; how they must suffer with their teeth in such hideous condition.

When he got back to his sponsors (who knew the country better) and mentioned what he had seen, they told him that not only were those people not suffering, but that their teeth, to all outward appearances in the terminal stages of decay, were in fact fortified by an abundance of natural fluorides in the water, and were, in fact, far from being weak, capable of opening pop bottles and cans and crushing hard nuts like the beaks of macaws.

To my untrained eyes, Iran looks fine, but it's all cosmetic. The country might be likened to a handsome set of lousy teeth, bright and shiny on the outside, but rotten at the root. This is hindsight talking, I'm here for the first time, just passing through. I'm not about to get to the root of anything.

The first thing we notice upon hitting the street is that we're going *unnoticed.* It's a great relief after Turkey, where the men in the *kebab* shops used to line up three deep just to watch us chew. Westerners are everyday intruders in Iran, and as such, they are ignored by the people.

They seem to have better things to do than to worry about us. The men wear slacks and sneakers, and the women walk around in dresses and skirts, wearing bright scarves around their shoulders in token deference to the veil. Cheryl and Marie are delighted. The pressure on them has temporarily abated. The Iranians seem to be much (repeat: much) better off than their neighbors and Rezaiyeh seems modern and self-content.

The second thing one notices in Iran is the Shah. His photo hangs on the walls in barber shops, over the teapots in *chai* shops, behind hotel and cash registers everywhere. He's a nice-looking chap, although a trifle short, but his wife is a knockout. The twentieth century has had its queen. Farah Dibah. She's radiant and warm, smiling out over her people in white ermine on full-color portraits reverently framed and hung beside those of her spouse and son Reza, the *bar mitzvah* boy.

Farah Dibah. To whom shall I compare thee? Liz Taylor on a good day in her early thirties? Liz as she might have been had she really been a queen? No. The empress of Iran is no film star, no cardboard paste-up, but a dedicated hard-working woman, concerned (I know this, I read it in the papers) for the health and education of her people, especially the women and little girls, whom she hopes to lead out of the Dark Ages.

There are, of course, at least two ways of looking at the Shah, his wife and line. The first, at the moment silent, but apparently prevailing view in Iran is that they are all usurpers, milking the country of its wealth and enriching their supporters, while maintaining control through force of arms and torture. History will advocate this view most eloquently.

The opposing view, propagated widely by the Shah when we arrive, is that he is an embattled social democrat, doing no more to enforce his rule than anyone else who would govern this deeply divided nation of Persians, Kurds, Lurs, Arabs, Qashqais, Baluchis, Azerbaijanis, Bakhtiaris and Turkomans, forced to employ certain oppressive measures until he has educated his people and raised them up to a state in which they'll be able to handle self-rule.

Although the Shah has already instituted a number of land reforms unpopular with the clergy and numerous progressive social measures, he promises much more. Faced with demands for further rapid change, one Iranian professor in the Shah's camp remarked, "Yes, of course, but we must be patient—one revolution at a time."

That's the party line, but the party will soon be over. In 1974, however, it's still going strong and Revolution is just a code word for the slow implementation of the Shah's programs. Iran under the last of the ruling Pahlavis is thriving and lively, a land of mobility, petrol and plastic shoes. All the evidence seems to point toward the country's inheriting the mantle of the West, a garment with all the inherent charm, it would seem, of a hair shirt.

We spend two days in Rezaiyeh acclimating and learning to count in Farsi, the Persian language. Our path is taking us back along the route of Indo-European awareness, we're crawling from the end of the limb toward the trunk of that great tree pictured on the endpapers of old-fashioned dictionaries.

Having conquered the intricacies of one through ten we stop at the bank to exchange our money into rials, seventy to the dollar. Marie's Cook's traveler's checks are paid off at 2.2 times their actual value, because the clerk assumes they're for pounds Sterling, a fact that Marie fails to discover until she's halfway down the street, then ignores, taking the difference as cosmic compensation for her stolen cash in Turkey.

Dinner finds us in a basement-level cafeteria, dining on *cello kebab,* the national dish, white rice with a pat of butter on top and the ever-present mutton. Poor Cheryl is getting fed up with this diet. She's avoided eating sheep ever since she was ten years old and had a pet lamb named Amy. We make little bleating noises as she pushes the food around her plate.

Faced with a four-thirty bus departure the next morning, we go to bed early. One of the wonders of the human mind is the internal clock one can set when time really matters. In seven months on the road, with no wrist watches or alarm clocks, we never once miss a ride. Richard makes it close nearly every time, but just because he enjoys the rush of hopping on the running board.

The first one up bounces the other three, then we fumble into our clothes and walk down to the station, to wait on the concrete until the black night turns blue and the bus doors open. Light comes up as we clear the city, watching out our windows as a single tale of life, told in chapters strung out along the road, unfolds.

A farmer is sleeping on a wooden platform in his field. The next man rises, stretching, as we pass on. The next is building a fire. His little dog scratches, then barks. The earth spins and the light goes up another notch.

Farther south the foothills flatten. Smoke rises as the kettles go on for tea. The sun clears the horizon. A man has his hand over his eyes, watching as we race by. The next farmer squats, sipping his *chai.* We drive on. The next man throws his dregs onto the ground, then stands, rubbing his hands. Two miles later three men are hoeing the rows. And so it goes.

By midmorning we're out of the hills, into the desert of Kurdistan. It's hot and the bus is tiresome. Music plays over the loudspeaker, but it gives us no spiritual lift as it did in Turkey. Iranian music is highly stylized and overworked. The Ayatollah won't really be bothering anybody when he bans it.

My mind drifts. I see big buckets of caviar, black beluga, glistening like eyes. Dancers whirl to the rhythm of tambours and a tireless whining of strings. Red ochre, rainbow rocks, we push on past a number of small towns with tiny boxlike houses made of mud, stacked up along the hills. Pot-bellied men in loose white clothes replaster the roofs. Women go their way, drawing water, trailed by children tugging at their skirts. Each village is like the last as we drive on through the desert into the endless continuity of the present, the pastel ferocity of Persia.

Stopping for lunch in a village called Sanandaj, we make our way to the bakery, an adobe hut closed in on three sides. To our extreme left, a man is mixing flour. He passes his bowl to a second man, who kneads the dough, pounding it and slapping it hard against the platform on which they sit, before dividing the bread into loaves. A third man flattens them, rounding them into small pizzas, which a fourth man twirls and spreads over a round leather pillow, stuffed with straw.

He takes his cushion, reaches into the domed hearth fueled with chaff blazing up through a hole, and slaps the bread against the round walls, where it sticks. The baker withdraws his pillow, sets another pizza in place, then slaps it onto the hot bricks of the oven, withdrawing the first, fully baked.

A fifth man takes the hot crust and stacks it, passing it on to a sixth, who sells it. We hand him a few rials and walk away with four loaves, which rise in our stomachs as we stroll on, munching. The sight of that perfect division of labor (perfect except for the fourth guy, who seems to have the worst of it) has us mesmerized. We just do make it back to the bus, which is pulling out for the last leg toward Kermanshah.

One of our fellow riders is a Peace Corps volunteer, not too keen on returning to work after a short vacation. He talks at length, describing the isolation and frustrations of his post. After nearly two years, he has yet to gain the trust of most of the people around him, because everywhere in the world, Peace Corps people are assumed to be with the CIA.

He fills us in on the paradoxical position that women occupy in the Persian culture. Denied many rights by traditional law, the ladies are often the unheralded brains behind a family. Our teacher friend says that his little girl students are avid and diligent. They take the task and opportunity of learning seriously. That's part of the reason he's depressed. He's just been transferred to a class full of boys, who typically goof off, expecting everything to be handed to them. It is women, not oil, that may constitute the Persian Gulf's greatest untapped resource.

Fourteen hours after taking off at dawn, we arrive in Kermanshah, get a hotel, eat, then drag ourselves up to bed. The next day we climb on another new bus to speed down to Isfahan, the ancient capital of Persia. The long bus rides have been unkind to us all, but Marie is at a particularly low ebb, running a slight fever, although I'm less concerned about her health than with her state of mind. She and Richard are simply not working it out. They're hanging each other up, getting in each other's way and arguing over matters that have nothing to do with whether they're together or not.

Marie would like to walk out, she actually does so at one point, but Cheryl brings her back. Iran has been fine with the four of us together, but it can be impossible for a woman on her own, so Marie is stuck. We try to convince her to forget about Richard and hang in with us, and we tell him to cool it. Breaking up is never easy, but breaking up without breaking off can be torture. There's a lot of tension in the small room with the four beds. Everyone is weary.

One of our desires, being craftspeople, is to buy something handmade on the trip, so we stop in at least two dozen carpet shops to listen to their spiels, getting a feel for the kind of quality they would foist off on us. Isfahan boasts the largest bazaar in Iran, an indoor market as large as a small city, but it's a bit touristic, so we're on our guard.

The merchants throw down rug after rug, running their assistants ragged until the weight of guilt alone would make one buy, but although prices are about one third what they'd be in the States, they're out of our range. We forget about carpets and wander elsewhere through the bazaar, peering into dim shops where metal machine parts are cast in sand and men chisel the crosscut lines on steel files by hand.

Later we visit the Royal Square, site of the Masjid-i-Shah Mosque, constructed by Shah Abbas around 1700. It is covered with a ceramic glaze of mosaic blue tile and gold that make it one of the most beautiful buildings on earth. Across town is the Friday Mosque, the oldest in Isfahan, whose bare earthen walls and symmetrical niches echo with the slightest whisper. Skylights covered with sheepskin parchment let in a quiet light. It's a holy place. One doesn't need to be told that to know.

At night the streets are strung with lights, jumping on the occasion of the birthday of the heir apparent. It's impossible to detect a ripple of resentment. The people are out to party, it's carnival time. The air is yellow with hydrocarbons from all that indigenous oil. It's gay, but crummy, so we decide to push on.

Teheran, to the north, is jammed with the advent of the Asian Games (a regional pre-Olympics), so we reluctantly forgo our visit to the Crown Jewel Collection, consoling ourselves with the fact that we've seen Topkapi. We tell ourselves we'll come back, but have no idea how long it may be before that's possible.

With Teheran out of the question and Shiraz looking a bit too far south, we head down to Yazd on the strength of Richard's determination to cross the great desert of Iran. I've never been through any desert before and find the idea of crossing this one fairly absurd. There won't be any Stuckey's giving away praline candies out here. I raise my usual fuss, but all my stubborn arguments seem to boil down to one thing. I have yet to understand why I'm here.

"The point," says Richard, "is that *none* of us has ever tried anything like this . . . that is *precisely* the point!"—leaving me no choice but to shut up and fall in line.

Yazd, one more long bus ride southeast of Isfahan, stands against the desert wind on a line betwen Kerman and Qom, across the emptiness from Mashhad at an important juncture of one of the world's oldest caravan routes. It's known for its carpets, cotton, pistachios and opium, not necessarily in that order; its textiles and the underground water system that reminds us that once, in the glory days, Persians took the snow from the mountains and made the deserts bloom.

Persia was built upon the bones of the Babylonian empire, whose capital was first constructed by Hammurabi around 2100 B.C., then rebuilt by Nebuchadnezzar, cast by the Hebrews as one of the original Biblical villains. The history of this region is as ancient as civilization itself, so it's not surprising that even the word Iran sounds thin and reedy beside the mystical depths of names like Persia, Assyria and Mesopotamia. It's easy to see why the Shah slides off his people's backs.

Mohammed Reza Pahlavi, King of Kings, Light of the Aryans, rules like an alien impostor. He keeps his officers in sharply creased pants and little flat hats with short round brims. He skis, flies and reads widely, while the mood of his subjects is turning apocalyptic. The nation of Islam is in mourning. Its prophets wear black and rail at the gates. They will have their holy war. For all the relative youth of this religion, we may be living through a chapter in an as yet unwritten testament.

Qom is the religious center of the Shiite Moslems in Iran, but Yazd is the home base for the much more ancient religion of Zoroastrianism. Founded by a Persian teacher who lived from 669 B.C. to 583 B.C., and whose name is derived from the Greek form of Zarathustra, which in turn derives from the Persian word for Old Camel, this religion took many of the gods of the old nature religion of Persia, both righteous and malevolent, and placed them under the ultimate power of Ahura-Mazdah, whose cosmological hegemony was broken only by the arrival of Alexander, at a time when the Macedonian was knocking over the gods, idols and leaders of his world one by one and, not surprisingly, beginning to lend credence to certain rumors concerning divine deception in his own birth.

Imagine the cuckold Philip, how peeved he might have been, hearing the snickering as he handed over the reins to his unprecedented empire to a son whose mother, Olympias, allowed it to be understood that she had lain with a snake (and Zeus by any other form is still a snake). Afterward, it is said, Philip's passion cooled considerably, while the proud Alexander avoided the ignominy of such humiliation by not having any offspring at all.

It's not too far in either direction from the shadowy myths of yesteryear to a place like Yazd, where we find ourselves off the dusty street in a large inn built around a covered courtyard. The ceilings are high and the air is cool, kept moist by plants down on the central floor, but apart from the plants there are no frills, just beds and doors. This is a place for travelers, not tourists. The distinction is beginning to sink in. The innkeeper greets us with respect. We're honored guests, far from home, far from anywhere. The road's been hard, but we're still out for more, and our effort is starting to take on some dignity.

We're in the dead center of Iran, on our way to Mashhad, the last town in the northeast. Between these two places runs one dirt road about 450 miles long. On our left, to the north, the Dasht-I-Kavir, the great salt desert, site of ancient sea beds. To the right, the Dasht-I-Lut, the great sand desert. Four hundred and fifty miles might take all of eight hours in the States (we're cruising at fifty-five and keeping an eye out for cops, because the turn signal's busted), but this stretch of highway in Iran will take us nearly three days.

Thinking to make the trip by bus, we go down to the station, but are told that the daily run is booked solid for a week. A week in Yazd? "No problem," says Richard, staring me down again, "we'll hitch."

We don't have much choice. Rising at dawn the next day, we wait by the road for a lift up to the desert turn-off, where we get down at a roadside café to stare out into one of the finest empty spaces one could ever hope to see. There's just a few scrub plants and low hills, then far off in the distance, a rim of mountains.

The café owner says we're crazy, but twenty minutes later a jeep pulls up and a guy with the government archaeological survey tells us to hop on. When we tell him we're headed for Mashhad, he tries to argue us out of the project, suggesting instead a nice side trip to an old mosque he's trying to exhume. We decline, climb down forty minutes later, shake hands, then watch as he drives away, rising and falling, appearing and disappearing for half an hour across the desolate terrain.

This may be the stupidest thing I've ever done. We just rode off into the great desert of Iran, just like that, and all we have for water is a one quart plastic jug. We stand around looking worried until that daily bus appears in a cloud of dust, and it's so damned crowded that we're glad we're not on it, even if we croak. Meanwhile last night's meal and this morning's blazing sun are baking up a pretty mess in my bowels.

I climb a small hill just south of the road, cock a hip to relieve some of the pressure in my intestines and wind up suffering an indignity that takes me right back to the cradle. If you travel long enough, you're bound to get the runs. Cheryl had it so bad after Rezaiyeh I thought she would die. Marie and Richard have each had their days and now it's my turn.

I remember the Allen Ginsberg character in one of Jack Kerouac's books discussing his contention that the Asian method of wiping oneself with water from a rusty can is actually much more effective than paper swipes, and that the reason so many Americans walk around feeling guilty is that deep down they all know they've got dirty assholes, but out here the great debate over water or paper is academic. I can hardly justify taking our measly quart and flushing it through my legs, and tissue, under the circumstances, would be no more than a sop.

My only course is to ditch my briefs, which isn't so easy to do in the middle of the desert with three friends around without attracting a whole lot of unwanted attention. The only thing I can say for the entire humiliating experience is that it temporarily diverts me from the real problem, which is that if we don't find some way out of here, we're cooked.

Two hours later a truck finally drives up heading the other way, back to Yazd. We flag it down and get off at the roadside café, where I hurry out to the garden hose to do a little impromptu laundry. My stomach is still churning and my mouth is parched, but it's all I can do to down a Coke over some thirty minutes. I sit inside, propped up, trying to pour the fever through my forehead into the cool mud wall.

After noon, just as I'm beginning to get some strength back a big oil-carrying rig, actually a kerosene truck, pulls up and stops. The café proprietor says a few words in our behalf and we're invited to pay two times the cost of a bus ticket to ride on top. We try to haggle, but the driver knows we're stuck and stands firm. When we hand the dough over, the café owner grins, which means he got a cut, then we climb up and try to get comfortable, an effort we will soon abandon.

We're perched on a steel platform, six feet by four feet, built on top of the round drum just behind the cab. A horizontal ladder runs like the spine of a dinosaur down the length of the vehicle, with three or four little round vents poking up like mushrooms above the top. The ride is incredibly rough, but we're all agreed we wouldn't want to be back in Yazd, and that daily bus was a cattle car. We'd have gone eighteen hours without a breath of fresh air, arguing with women with babies who'd no doubt want the windows shut. Nobody shuts the windows on this baby.

The view is breathtaking. That flat featureless plain we saw from ground level reveals itself as a network of rivulets and gullies, fanning out in beds gone dry since the last spring rains. Great fields of earth run rust red and alkali white. We're in the midst of a tremendous 360-degree vista and we've got it all, no windows, no roof, just a clear and unimpeded view of this spectacular desolation.

The sky is light blue behind a veil of moisture driven up from the flatlands, moisture that will settle in the night, forming pearls of dew on the throats of desert weeds. Hot air rushes past at ten miles an hour, cooling and coating us with a layer of dust. The road rolls on, stretching out in an endless ribbon that dips behind a hillock and emerges slightly off center at the next rise, like the furl of a flag. We roll on and on, but the mountains at the other end show no sign of approaching.

Hours later we reach the first pass and descend into a second immense emptiness, sealed off in the vast interior. The drone of the road has receded into background noise, a gray babble of silence, which the wind stirs like a thin soup. There's nothing to say, nothing to point out, nothing to do but squint and ride, hanging onto the rails, propped on our packs, drinking in the arid beauty with our eyes.

To our left stand the remains of a Mausoleum, a beehive dome glowing orange and rose at sunset. Far off in the distance, an oasis stretches across the road, with a hundred palms behind a mud wall. We pass beneath the gates and stop in a *chai* shop, the only inhabited structure in this city which once housed thousands, but push on quickly, for there's one more hour of light.

The horizon explodes in spectral bands as the sun sets and

all that color rises to the high clouds above our heads, goes gray around the edges, then dies. That ten-mile-an-hour breeze from the motion of the truck now gets cold and our platform turns to ice. Marie and Cheryl have already turned down a chance to ride with the two men in the cab. They break out their sleeping bags and fluff them up into little nests.

The truck rolls on without stopping. When Richard and I can no longer ignore nature's call, we tightrope the ladder to the back of the rig, then lean out, trying to relieve ourselves, but the tight vibration of the steel drum, together with the muscular control necessary to maintain our balance, makes it impossible to relax the proper sphincters and proceed. We stand there, legs spread, arms akimbo, cursing, then get down on our knees to shuffle to the edge and try again, but nothing works.

We walk back to the platform to lie out under the stars as the wind picks up. The night is freezing cold and the constant motion is breaking us down. I started the day with a fever. Now I'm near exhaustion and can't rest. Each time I relax the truck jumps and snaps my head. We've all got headaches from the kerosene and we can't even light up to pass the time, because the whole thing might explode.

Finally, after sixteen hours, with our nerves on the verge of rebellion, we stop. Richard and I run to a ditch by the side of the road as Cheryl and Marie disappear into the *chai* shop. Our driver is circling his truck, scratching his head. It seems we have a flat, but fortunately we can get some tea while waiting the two hours it will take the assistant to patch it, get it back onto the rim, pump it up by hand and slap it onto the axle. That done, we climb back on, reminding ourselves not to grit our teeth, lest we grind our fillings to dust. At dawn we enter the town of Tabas, roughly halfway to Mashhad.

Tabas, like those towns we passed in eastern Turkey, will be leveled in a few years by a massive earthquake, killing many of the people we're seeing now as we walk through the first stirrings of this sleepy September morning. We get some breakfast, find a hotel and crash on and off until the next morning, when we again try to hitchhike east.

As we're standing by the curb, a group of women in full *chadris* comes down to see what we're about. The notion of a veil is highly misleading, considering what the devout Moslem woman must actually endure. The *chador*, or *chadri*, is a black or gray garment falling like a sack from the crown of the head right down to the ankles, with a thick webbed netting over the eyes, a material that barely allows the women to see out and absolutely precludes the possibility of anybody looking in.

There's no peek-a-boo going on, they watch the world through a mourning gauze, chattels of the men who hide them. The fact that no males outside of their own family may gaze upon them suggests a brand of male insecurity bordering on, if not well into, the pathological. Still, these women of Tabas have spirit.

Richard and I move down the street so as not to inhibit them, then watch as they crowd around Cheryl and Marie, laughing and stroking the arms of our friends, daringly bared from the elbows down under the blazing sun. The sight from a distance is ludicrous, two young women with a bunch of bubbling old bags. Actually, I have no way of knowing how old those women or garments are, but it's better to laugh at the situation than to take it to heart, although there's something so dehumanizing about this setup that I refuse to accept it as ordinary or chalk it up to simple cultural diversity.

After several hours with no traffic, we run down to the bus station to purchase four tickets for the midday run. We have another five hours of dirt road to endure before hitting the paved highway north to Mashhad, then another hour to a rest stop, where I eat quickly, then wander out back into the fields.

Off in the distance, a shepherd is playing a flute. His sheep graze steadily, shuffling forward, not even stopping to raise their heads. When they're done in this field, they'll move on to the next, and the next, and the next. The scene is out of time and timeless. Despite the highway and the busy roadhouse behind me, it's clear that it will never change. There's too much of it, the emptiness is too vast, human beings will never make a dent in it. There'll never be anything more out here than sheep, shepherds, snow-capped desert mountains and the quiet wind.

Mashhad. Millions flock to this city to visit the shrine (*meshed*) of the Imam Riza, the burial place of the Harun-al-Rashid (764?–809), whose legend reached all the way down into Arabia, where he figured in more than a few of the Thousand and One Nights.

Mashhad, with its Golden Mosque, is the most important pilgrimage site in Iran, second in importance only to Mecca to the Shiite followers of the Imam Ali, Mohammed's cousin and the husband of his daughter Fatima, whose reign ended in 661, when he died fighting the Kharijites and his son Hasan abdicated to Muawiya, the Prophet's former secretary. Muawiya is credited with unifying the Moslem empire, but he failed to either placate or eliminate Ali's other son, Husein, who maintained the faith, perpetuating the schism that endures today.

The greater rift, however, is between Islam and ourselves, noses pressed against the iron gates, forbidden entry under penalty of death. The mosque itself is beautiful, the Golden Dome, dazzling, but it's hard to ignore the fact that they might kill us just for walking in. Ethereal and violent, Islam refuses to make itself accessible to us.

Our first night we go walking in the Medina, the walled-off inner city jammed with visitors from the hinterlands, who stay with relatives or throw their blankets where they can. The people resent us. It's OK to be out on the street, but not to come in and see them like this. Maybe it's not so cool on the main streets either, they just can't do anything about it. I don't know if it's political or religious, but I do know when I'm not wanted. One man starts shouting and waving his arms, then we get caught in a cul-de-sac and have to return right past him. Perhaps he was trying to warn us. Am I overreacting? No. It's honkeys go home until an alley spills us onto the street of its own accord and we make it around the Golden Mosque, back to our hotel.

The next morning we're at the Afghan embassy, looking forward to moving on, when an Iranian kid in western dress walks up and asks how we like Mashhad.

"Fine, great," we say.

"Good. What will you do when you're done here?" he asks.

"Go to Afghanistan."

"No, *today*," he says, "you come with me, I show you all Mashhad."

"Hold on, bucko, we don't have any money."

"Money?" he laughs, "you are my guests. My name is Ali." This Ali character obviously didn't come down here just to befriend somebody, but he looks harmless enough, speaks good English, and although he's obviously into some kind of hustle, we've established right off that we're not buying it, so we've got nothing to lose.

When we come out of the Afghan office an hour later with our visas, he's waiting with a car. We all pile in and Ali takes us around town, pointing out this and that until we're really beginning to wonder what he's up to, when he turns around and asks, "You like carpets?"

"Carpets? Yeah, sure we like carpets, but . . ."

"Good. I take you to best carpet place in all of Mashhad."

"We already told you. No money."

"So? You look. Nobody makes you buy. Nobody can make you buy if you have no money . . . many peoples have no money. This is Mashhad. All peoples come here for carpets . . . I take you to best place."

Impeccable logic. Mashhad is located near some of the Turkoman tribes most famed for their weaving. We had hoped to go shopping and there's no reason to expect that what Ali shows us will be any worse than what we might dig up on our own, so he parks by the market and leads us through the back alleys past a number of carpet repair shops, up a rickety set of stairs to a small room piled high with rugs.

The boss is out, so Ali arranges to bring us back, then drives us across town to a tree-lined square, where we enter a semi-private club serving drinks, where attractive dark-haired women sit tapping their long fingernails to western music on a jukebox. After we get our burgers, Ali asks Richard if he'd liked to sell his blue jeans. The two kids (Ali's about eighteen) are hitting it off, and for once it's without sexual overtones.

As they talk, Ali begins to open up about some of the contradictions of his life. He knows what's going on in the rest of the world, but the closest he ever gets to it is talking to kids like Rick. He can listen to Mick Jagger singing "Let's spend the night together," but can't get a date for the movies without risking life and limb to the girl's father, brothers and uncles. "Change will come," he tells us hopefully, and we have no reason not to believe him.

After lunch we return to the market, thread the alleyways and again step upstairs to the store, where the boss, whose car Ali's been using, is waiting for us. We sit against the wall as he starts throwing down rugs, watching us for reactions, trying to type us, although we don't give him much to go on. We saw at least five hundred rugs in Isfahan without even being tempted. The boss holds a folded rug, gives it a great buildup, then throws it onto the floor. Nothing. Ali takes off and the boss tries again.

He slowly grows weary trying to satisfy us within our price range (300 to 400 dollars) and slumps against a wall, letting his assistant do all the handling, continuing with his big buildups, but with decreasing hope. This is no small accomplishment, bringing an Iranian carpet dealer to his knees. If Cheryl, for one, were any less discerning, he'd have thrown us out long ago, but each time she turns thumbs down, you can see that he agrees.

He tries to talk us into buying something to resell, but the little lady puts her foot down. "We're in this for love," she tells him, "not money." His eyes roll back in his head. If this weren't the off-season, he wouldn't have time for such nonsense, but by now it's a point of honor with him to keep going.

Four hours and hundreds of rugs after entering his shop, the guy's a chain-smoking wreck. Merchants buy in lots of a hundred. He can't believe what we're putting him through for one lousy rug. Finally Cheryl points to a carpet atop a tall stack to his left, but the boss says, "No, is not for you. Too much money."

"Come on," we say, "at least let us see *something* we like, even if we can't buy it." Goaded by this insult, he points one last time to his flunky, who glares at us with eyes that would kill (he still has to fold everything back up), then dumps the carpet onto the floor.

Cheryl, Richard and I jump up, shouting, "That's it! We'll take it!"

"What? Take what?" he says.

"The rug, we'll buy it."

At our feet is an antique Bokhara carpet, 4′ x 6′ in natural camel's wool with cream-colored medallions of lambs' wool accented with faded pomegranate red and indigo blue. It's the style that's spawned countless imitations, made over a hundred years ago in a village now in the Soviet Union. The care and craftswomanship with which it was woven have all but disappeared.

"It's a thousand dollars," says the boss, having already made it clear that his prices are fixed, but he offers to take a deposit, the rug to be forwarded when we earn the balance back in the States. We figure we can trust him; if he double-crosses us we'll write a letter to the Shah or come back ourselves (we're already looking for an excuse) and personally break his arms.

We want the thing, and suddenly the boss is not too keen on parting with it. It would make a nice sweetener for one of his big rug moguls. It's good psychology on his part to let us think we've put one over on him, but in this case I have a feeling our stubbornness has paid off. The traveler's checks are signed, the hands are shaken, he's shaken, we're shaken —it's a deal.

Ali joins us on our last morning in Mashhad. No doubt he got a handsome commission for hooking us in, but he's willing to pass up the next round of potential clients just to talk to Richard. He borrows the car again, takes us out to lunch, then drives us to the west side of town, to a small café across from the bus station for the farewells.

Next to the door, a falcon shackled in chains is perched on the handlebars of a bicycle. It has a sad, trapped look in its eyes, not unlike the look on the face of our young friend. Ali feels his life passing him by. His values may be a little warped, he likes his fancy clothes and still covets those dungarees out of all proportion, but apart from that, his dreams are like our own. He knows that life can be free. He speaks with hope of the next twenty years, when Iran will emerge from the bonds of the past.

Ali, of course, is mistaken. It will take longer than we can predict for Iran to handle its national trauma. Perhaps Ali will get out in time and wind up with compatriots in Paris or Beverly Hills. I hope so for his sake, because it's too late for him to turn back. We shake hands all around, then he and Richard embrace, vowing they will meet again. They've known each other just two days and already it's like this. They're young, their hearts are open. Richard has his back to me, but the Iranian kid is crying.

The bus from Mashhad to the border at Tayyebat takes three hours. A group of men in loose-fitting clothes is seated up front. When we reach the last stop they're herded off like convicts, pushed and shoved down the road. I have no way of being sure, but suspect that they're Afghans who've crossed the border illegally and are about to be booted back. We line up at customs and are stamped through without a search. On this side of Iran the drugs flow the other way. The turnstile swings shut and seals us off in no-man's-land, just thirty miles, but worlds away from Afghanistan.

Chapter One · Afghanistan – Islam Qala, Herat,
Qala Nau, the Sabz Canyon,
Bala Morghab, Maimana,
Mazar-i-Sharif,
Kabul & the Khyber Pass

Chapter Two · Pakistan – Peshawar to Lahore

ROAD ——— Unpaved roads between Bala Morghab & Mazar-i-Sharif

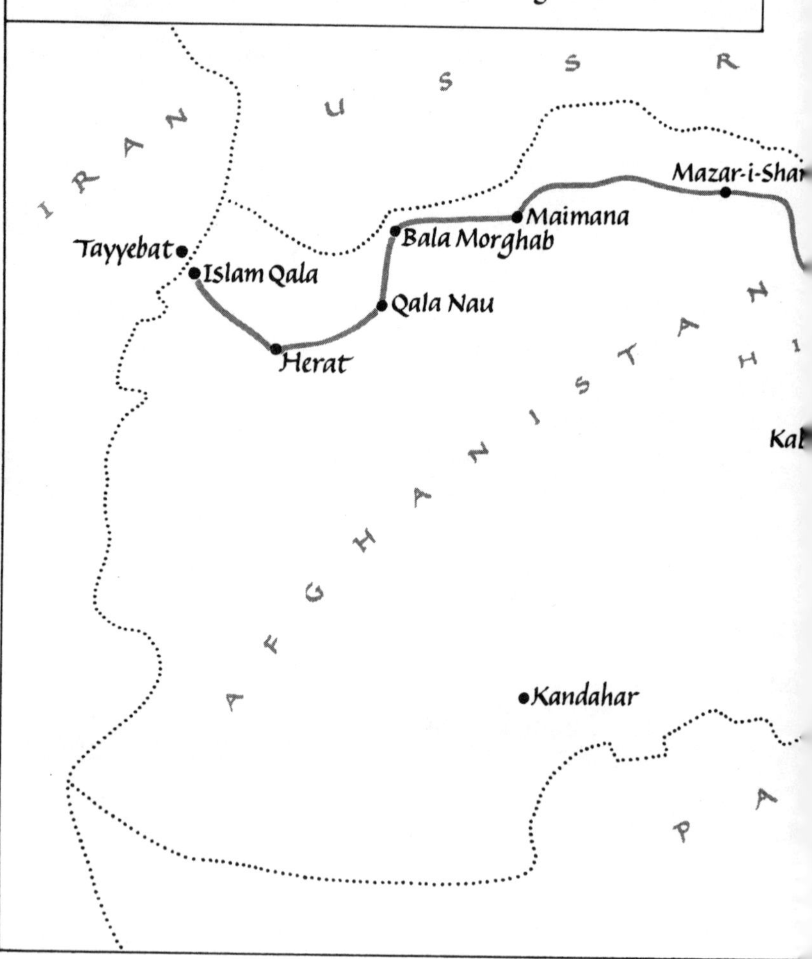

PART FOUR

THE WILD WILD EAST

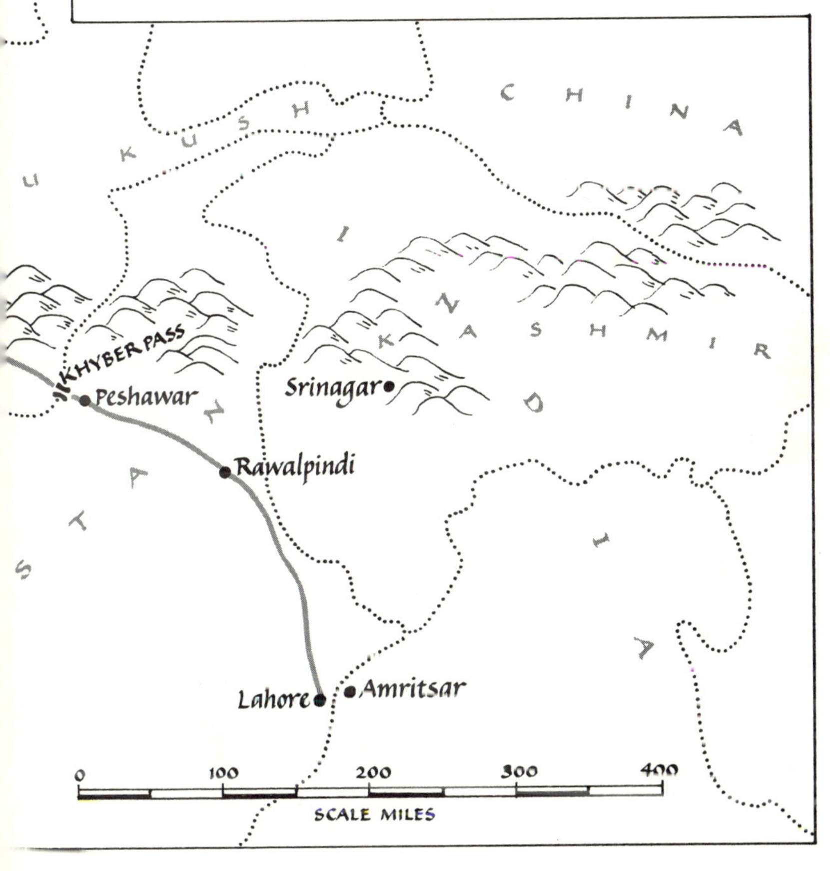

OUR DRIVER'S WAITING on the other side, wearing baggy white pants and a shirt down to his thighs. He's got bare feet, a dusty tan and a big goofy grin on a young man's regular old face, the face of a kid from down the block in Philly. His turban, wound around a little felt hat, has a three-foot tail that floats behind him as he leads us over to the beat-up Mercedes minibus meant to convey us to the real Afghan border at Islam Qala.

Ten of us climb in and settle back. An aging Indian con man on his way back home tests our knowledge of local prices. We're consistently high, but he assures us that we're not doing too badly. The little jitney rolls about twenty minutes down the road, then stops. We stare out the window at acres and acres of emptiness as our driver gets out, goes over to a small stream, dips a tin can and carries it back to pour the water over his radiator. He repeats the action two or three times, then climbs back in, starts up and lurches away.

Fifteen minutes later he stops again. The road, by virtue of the stream running along its shoulder, has trees every thirty or forty feet. Elsewhere there is nothing. Off to our left, up a small rise, young camels, muscled like middleweights, roam freely, breaking into gallops. They have the run of the range until they reach a certain age and are broken and tethered. Still, there are worse things than being a camel out here. Camels are prized possessions and these Afghan camels are fine-looking animals.

We power up a hill past a truck in low gear, roll down the other side and are heading up the next rise when that truck, having built up a good head of steam on the descent, overtakes us on the left and starts to pass. At that moment an equally large truck heading the other way appears over the crest less than fifty yards ahead and it's suddenly obvious that someone is about to be run off the road.

When the first truck veers right, our driver has no choice but to go with him. We get scraped on the front left panel and wind up on two wheels on the narrow shoulder, tipping toward the creek bed. All of us jump left and lean hard until the chassis slams down and the battle-scarred Mercedes wobbles to a stop. Our driver shuts off the motor and steps out, ashen. We follow. He dips his little can in the stream, pours it over the radiator until everything cools down, then persuades us to climb back in.

We drive until sunset, arrive at Islam Qala and are herded inside a two-story wooden house that serves as the border station. It takes half an hour for the guy to come out with the forms, telling us to list our valuables, so we can't dispose of them on the black market. That done, we step out onto the porch.

We're standing in the darkness, waiting for the rest of our group to make it through, when a young Afghan appears out of nowhere and motions for us to follow him, repeating the word, "Hotel . . . hotel . . ." We're debating whether to trust him, we usually wind up trusting somebody, when an official in a dark business suit rushes out, grabs the kid by the shirt and slaps him three times, right across the face. Whap, whap, *whap!*

The kid falls to the floor, crying, "Yes, *sahib,* yes, *sahib.*" He clings to the guy's shoes, not even daring to raise his eyes until the official, a big bruiser, possibly one of those Russian advisers, stands him up and flings him into the night.

Now the guy turns to us and says, "You go with him, you get rob, maybe you get *kill*—" he makes the sign of a throat getting slit—"we do nothing. *Nothing!* This boy no good!" He spits in the air where the kid was last seen and says, "You stay *there*—" pointing past us to a large clapboard building—"*Government Hotel!*" End of discussion. Sounds OK to me.

When Marie comes out we march over and discover to our surprise that despite the monopoly exercised over the tourist trade out here in Islam Qala, rates are cheap. Ten afghanis per person per night. Fifty-five afghanis per dollar.

We take our key and walk through the star-pricked darkness to the far annex, where we find our room. Except for the bare electric-light bulb and the minibus that brought us here, we are no longer in the same century as when we left Iran. I have my doubts as to whether we're on the same planet.

For once Richard and I agree on what to do. Back along the road, when we'd mention we were heading to Afghanistan, people would roll their eyes and say, "Ah, Afghanistan, going there to smoke, eh?" although the truth was that I hadn't even thought about it. I might be one of the few, but my primary purpose in heading east was not to get stoned. I've tried to make it clear that I had no real purpose in making this trip, but now that I'm here, I'm not about to pass up the local delicacies. That would be like going to France and not drinking wine.

Marijuana and hashish had been around a long time before American hippies began using them in the sixties. Sometimes we act as if we invented them, when all we did was take advantage of the good boo filtering back from the jungles of Southeast Asia (one more effect of that war) and bring it out into the open.

My own opinion is that drugs, although altering our consciousness somewhat, in the end only confirmed what we thought we had seen before. It's one world, and if you see it from enough angles, the illusions begin to cancel each other out. Drugs complicated our lives when things would have been hard enough had we marshaled all our strength, but in the end they were a significant factor in the cultural fusion of sex and rock-'n'-roll politics that finally stood up to the lingering authority of the McCarthy era and let it be known that things were not as certain people would have us believe.

The Afghans have a totally different attitude toward smoking than one finds in the West. It is not forbidden at all and there's no stigma attached. There's been something of a crackdown in the last year, but only because of the change in governments, and because the U.S. is paying them off, and because the local police are not averse to putting on the squeeze. Nobody stays in jail out here if they fork out fast enough. For some reason the Afghans have trouble seeing getting high as a crime against the state.

I haven't thought about drugs for months, but less than thirty seconds from the time Richard and I leave our hotel room, a young Afghan pulls us over behind a small shed and flashes a piece of brown hash about the size of a cigarette lighter, asking for a buck and a half.

We're probably getting ripped off, but are nervous enough to want to conclude the transaction quickly, and we figure that the young man deserves his *baksheesh* for being the first to turn us on, so we pay his price and head back to our hotel room, where Cheryl and Marie are starting to unpack.

"Back already?" asks Cheryl. Marie looks up with a knowing smile. We lock the door and hook the shutters. Richard takes out a pack of matches, heats the hash, crumbles it and mixes in a bit of tobacco (European style).

"Wait a minute," says Cheryl, "I want to brush my teeth." Marie joins her at the sink and Richard leans back, relaxing. He's got all the time in the world. When everything's in order he strikes the match (the splinter sails like a flare across the room), applies it to his bowl, inhales deeply and passes it on. I take it, toke and burst out coughing. Just as I'm catching my breath, the pipe comes around again. And again. And again. The smoke hangs like skywriting in the center of the room, read out by a lady in a husky, heavily perfumed voice, saying, "Hello, sailor. Welcome to Afghanistan."

We wake in no great hurry to face the sun, piercing the wooden shutters in thin vertical strips. We have no desire to move or be disturbed, but soon there's a knock on the door. Richard opens it a crack and peers out. It's our driver. He wants us to shake a leg and follow him. He gets a whiff of stale air from the night before and grins. Richard asks if he'd like some, but he signals "Not now," then steps into the hallway so the women can get dressed.

Richard lights another bowl and when the door opens a second time, clouds of smoke filter out. Our driver laughs and leads us to his Mercedes mini, where a dozen people are crammed in, furious, for they've been waiting almost an hour. We take our seats amidst a storm of icy stares, but we're so loose we have to laugh and that just makes matters worse.

No one told them they had to wait in the car. So what if they're late getting to Herat? What the hell are they going to do in Herat, anyway? These people may have made it as far as Afghanistan, but obviously they haven't learned a thing. Faced with a delay, instead of getting out and making themselves comfortable, they clenched their fists and held onto their seats, as if it mattered where they'll be riding. We didn't ask them to wait. If the bus took off we'd have caught the next. It's our driver who made them wait because he wanted the extra fares. There's just no way they'll get away with laying a guilt trip on us, we're hung over and we haven't had breakfast. It's pathetic. The ride to Herat takes two hours and not one of these assholes cracks a smile. They call this the White Man's Burden.

Finally the bus arrives and we climb up to the second-story restaurant of the hotel where we take a room, to catch up on breakfast and look out the window at Herat, the spitting image of a fort town in the days of the American frontier. There actually is a fort sitting in ruins just behind us, and the streets are patrolled by horse-drawn carts called *gadis*, bright with embroidered blankets and bells. The drivers are whip-cracking, turbaned Afghans, who gallop from one end of the strip to the other trying to scare up fares. The stores have wooden walks in front of them, like Dodge City, with hitching posts and troughs for watering the animals.

Away from the main drag, the city recedes in mud housing, indistinguishable from a distance from the desert ground itself. Herat blends in at the edges, it's feathered into the landscape. The houses last a number of years, but when they get to be more trouble than they're worth, the people pick up and move on to newer digs, leaving whole blocks and apartments in the midst of heavily populated sections to fall to ruin. The cycle of succession is brief, generations fade quickly. As the Afghans say,

> "We come from the earth, we live in the earth,
> and to the earth we will return. We are made
> of dust."

Herat has mile-long walls built on prehistoric foundations by Alexander the Great, who captured the city and refounded it, before it was destroyed by Turkomans, rebuilt by the kings of Ghor, then destroyed again by Mongols in the thirteenth century. Tamerlane (Timur the Lame)—a Mongol Moslem who slew 80,000 in Delhi and ordered that pyramids be built out of their skulls—took the town in 1383. His successors, the Timurids, ruled in splendor until 1506, turning Herat into a garden spot filled with mosques and centers of learning.

On the west side of town stands a remarkable adobe mosque beside an ancient graveyard. This domed structure exemplifies the true Afghan style, the hollowing of great mud bubbles whose contours arise from some primeval spiritual and architectural cauldron. Across from the building, through a field littered with flat stones marking graves, lie the remains of the oldest mosque in the country, a howling void into which the spirit of all these scattered dead have flown.

Beyond those half-suggested walls and down a hill, three towers dominate a flat expanse of valley. The towers are great pipes, hollow throats a hundred feet high, which sound a quiet moan each time the wind touches their lips. They are primitive, shocking, almost comical icons, minarets thrust like phalluses into the universe.

Afghanistan is closer to its past than any place I've ever been. It has not outgrown it, nor does it wish to. From here on we must pay strict attention, being careful to avoid using standards that don't apply. Not that things are not what they seem, they *are* what they seem. That will take some getting used to.

Back at our hotel, we encounter a trio of young women who are circumnavigating the world in the opposite direction, having begun in Australia and already been through India and Nepal on their way west. Two of the three are so lovely at seventeen years old that it's astounding to think of the part of the world they've just crossed. The third, all of twenty-six, serves as Big Momma and protector, but they would never have made it had it not been for a kind of instinctual reaction the sight of these innocents must have evoked in the hearts of the men they've encountered along the way.

Like male dogs which won't attack a pup, the Afghans, and before them the Pakistanis, Indians and Indonesians, must have been paralyzed before the overwhelming vulnerability of these sweet young things. Unlike Cheryl and Marie, who are full grown, and thus, fair game, these little ladies have been the beneficiaries of the convoluted morality and chivalry of the region. They claim to have been everywhere and done everything, right down to drinking the local water, but I take their advice with a grain of salt and two drops of iodine. If they made it through traveling that way, good for them. They're charmed. We'd be foolish to expect the same.

Late one afternoon Cheryl and I drop in on an Afghan silversmith, not a master by any means, just a guy trying to eke out a living by whatever crude techniques he has at his disposal. He's the Afghan equivalent of Capitaine Bijoux, a man born at the wrong time into the wrong trade, overannealing the filigree wire and wondering why he's not getting anywhere. Unlike Capitaine Bijoux, however, he has no escape.

The only promise in the whole dingy operation belongs to his son.

This young man, aged nine or ten (and others like him whom we encounter in the shirt shops and carpet stores), can converse on a rudimentary level in four or five languages with the tourists who make up the walk-in trade. He wheedles and cajoles like an old pro, while retaining that youthful sense that all this bargaining for survival is still just a game.

He can play on your sympathy, make you laugh, or insult you just to get a rise out of you and keep the ball rolling. Like an experienced angler, he toys with the line, jerking the bait, threatening to withdraw it just before you bite. He's got the body of a child, but eyes that have been around and seen a lot. He reminds me of pictures I've seen of my father, kicking around in the thirties back in the States. Somehow he must sense what I'm thinking, for he moves in for the kill. These kids are sharp. They size you up, they make you pay.

After three days in Herat it's time to move on. The four major cities in Afghanistan form a diamond, with Herat in the west, Kandahar to the south, Kabul, the capital in the east and Mazar-i-Sharif to the north. There's a paved road from Herat to Kandahar to Kabul to Mazar, but no road at all running northeast to Mazar-i-Sharif from where we are. The only way to traverse this wild back country is via four-wheel-drive Russian trucks, for which one must have a government permit; must, in effect, sign his life away and relieve the Afghan government of all responsibility.

Instead of putting us off, as it's supposed to, this news only whets our appetites. We run all over town, from office to office, threading the bureaucratic maze to get our papers in order. As soon as we get the final signature, we return to the truck yard to reserve our places for the following morning.

I wander off late in the afternoon for one last visit to the site of that ancient adobe mosque. As I'm entering the grounds, an Afghan comes up, takes my arm and says he'll be my guide. Usually I manage to put these guys off, but this fellow is determined not to let me tour the site without him. He's an even match for me physically and we're on his turf, so if it comes down to push and shove, I'll be up against it.

He wanders beside me, pointing out things I don't want pointed out, making explanations I can't understand, all but robbing me of this last moment I wanted alone. Suddenly he pulls me over to a small hole in the side of the large mosque, climbing in and motioning for me to follow. I hesitate. What kind of fool would jump into the darkness with a man he neither liked, nor was particularly sure he could handle? I poke my head in cautiously, half expecting to get clubbed, but as my eyes clear I begin to make out eight or nine Afghan kids who've turned this dark alcove into a hangout.

They're not awed with its holiness or beauty, they're squatting there, playing games, smoking a joint which they pass my way as soon as I cross the threshold. I take a long drag, feeling myself losing connection to the bright world outside. I sit on my heels, listening to their laughter bouncing around the walls. When I ask why they're smoking grass instead of hash, they say, "Oh, no, hashish for tourist, make you crazy . . . Afghan smoke this"—pointing to the weed and passing it on.

There's a deep conspiratorial feeling in the air. It must have something to do with having so much fun inside a mosque. The boys start singing and beating out a rhythm. Our heartbeats synchronize, we're back in the womb.

When it comes time to leave, the young man who had declared himself my guide takes my arm and hits me up for a contribution. He lays it on a bit thick, trying to get me to believe that these boys are hungry and might not eat tonight unless I help them, but I cut him off. I don't need any reasons. Sometimes you pay and sometimes you don't. Sometimes it's worth it and sometimes it isn't. Sometimes it's blackmail and other times just *baksheesh*, and if dropping a dollar is all the tribute it takes to say thanks for an afternoon of such unexpected atmosphere and mystery, I'm getting off light.

The next morning we're walking around, checking out the Russian trucks in the yard, kicking their tires and wondering which one will be ours, when the man comes up and points out the smallest and least impressive of all, telling us to climb on. Along with the four of us there's an American student working on his Dari (one of the two main dialects, the other being Pashto), sixteen Afghans, one driver and the boy in back.

This kid's got the most romantic job in all of Afghanistan. He runs the ride. He gets the people on, sees that they're set, checks the road, then bangs the side of the truck, calling out "*Borubachai!*" which sounds like the beginning of a Hebrew prayer, but is really his way of telling the driver to get going, a call with all the impact of the late Ward Bond cupping a hand to the side of his mouth, sitting up in his saddle and roaring "Roll 'em!" to the pioneers.

He stands on one foot outside the truck, on a metal step down by the bumper, and rides that way all day and night, holding on with one hand, ready to jump down at the slightest sign of trouble. If the truck is running out of room on a mountain pass, he's over the edge, telling the driver what to do. When a wheel gets caught and we need a push, one word from the kid and all sixteen Afghans are down there with him, heaving to. By the time we figure out what's going on, the truck is free, the Afghans are storming the bulwarks and the kid is back on that one foot, eyes out over the cab, impassive, imperious.

Our ride begins in flat country outside Herat. We bounce through lightly stubbled grazing lands and creek beds, the seasonal turf of nomadic tribes who come and go as they please across the borders, including that of the Soviet Union, a few miles north. We'll ride about twenty miles without seeing a thing, then 'way up high one black tent will dominate a bluff, overlooking a valley in which we're just a poor pitiable thing, crawling along, choking in our own dust.

All morning we push through the Paropamisus range, through the region of Band-i-Baba, until mid-afternoon, when we reach the town of Qala Nau. The American student (CIA? Even I'm getting suspicious) gets down with a few locals and we spread out, little suspecting that two minutes across town our driver will stop at another *chai* shop and pick up another dozen sweaty riders, who jump on with a shout.

The scene is chaotic. We're sailing the high seas of landlocked Afghanistan. Our frigate is a two-ton land cruiser, with its canvas roof rolled up over the ribs. On the floor of the truck are burlap sacks filled with dry goods and grain. On top of the sacks, Afghans in tatters and rags, the direct descendants of every cutthroat from Alexander the Great to Genghis Khan. They don't have rings through their ears or parrots on their shoulders, but that's all they lack to complete the picture. The tails of their turbans are wound around their faces to ward off the dust, proving that their fashion is not only stylish, but eminently practical. The best we can do is tie on our red bandannas, adding one more set of outlaws to this motley crew.

Naturally, the biggest, ugliest, sliimiest guy, the kind of guy who can be counted on to go too far for everybody, plunks himself right down at Cheryl's feet, looking up with a grin that says that even he doesn't know what's in store. Every few minutes someone leans over the edge to discharge a mouthful of green slime called *naswar*, a kind of green tobacco snuff that can only be held in for so long, then is drooled out in a horrible long line to the ground. If you don't duck down when the wind shifts you're liable to get a faceful.

The truck is bouncing so much we're constantly landing in one another's lap. The women are being felt up, leered at and leaned on. The big guy starts feeling *me* up, he doesn't give a damn.

There's just one spot of calm in the midst of all this madness. Right in the center at the rear of the truck, a Mongolian man sits cross-legged on a single bag of grain, taking up no more space than he needs, leaning on no one, supporting the rigors of the ride with a beatific grace. He is the Buddha out on the Dharma trail with a consort of thieves. He looks up with a quizzical tilt of his head, as if to say, "What's the problem? It's easy. Look at me."

The worse it gets, the more radiant he becomes. Suddenly my inflexibility is shown to be not only a physical limitation, but a spiritual one. I'm a pretty good athlete in the western sense, I can run, jump and go to the hoop with either hand, but one thing I can't seem to do is deal with myself in my own space. There's a territorial imperative about my existence. I slop over borders. I consider it manifest destiny that my right leg be allowed to rest over *there.* I am, if not the ugly, at least the uncomfortable American.

Past Qala Nau, we enter an immense area known as the Sabz (Green) Canyon for the trees clinging for life to its flinty slopes. The Afghans look up, beaming and repeating the word, "*Sabz . . . sabz . . .*" until we nod back and say, "Yes, *sabz,*" as if it's the greenest thing we've ever seen. I have to wonder what they'd think if they ever saw the forests of Pennsylvania in the late spring.

I play a little harmonica, with the Afghans on rhythm, and Richard shows off his Buck knife to great general approval. There's little that these people appreciate more than a good piece of hardware. Soon night falls. Whenever the going got rough during the day, we had to get down and walk, but now when we reach the tricky passes the kid in back insists that the four of us stay put. He doesn't trust those guys out in the dark. He's not about to vouch for our safety if they get us out there alone, so we ride atop the baggage like Maharajas, watching the Afghans pick their way over the rocks.

With everybody crammed back in on the other side, we ride on, bouncing and rocking, our kidneys weeping, our legs falling asleep and waking in agonies of needles and pins. There's no solace in the landscape now, it looks like the far side of the moon. Even the Afghans are subdued. There's nothing to do but hold on and endure until we pull, some eighteen hours after starting, into a small square beside a *chai* shop in the town of Bala Morghab, three kilometers from the Russian border.

We sit right down to dinner, four plates of rice awash in a thin broth, with two small pieces of potato each floating on top. We send back for meat, but there is none, so we hoard those spuds, and by the time we get to them we're so damned hungry that they taste like steak.

Just as we're finishing, a soldier with a rifle comes up to escort us to the government hotel, a whitewashed mud structure, where we're told it will cost us ten afghanis each to throw our sleeping bags onto the floor. Marie and Cheryl set up a furious protest which the guard endures patiently since he can't understand a word. He knows who and where we are much better than we. We don't have a leg to stand on or a bed to lie in, we're stuck.

Bala Morghab. If Herat was a frontier town, this is the kind of wilderness backwater that might have a name like Last Chance or Devil's Gulch. There are absolutely no women; women don't come to a place like this, they have no business here. We don't either, the eyes would seem to say as they follow us down the street, but the feeling is more guarded than hostile. They're just looking us over as we do the same to them.

Bala Morghab is a town in the middle of nowhere, a classic town in a succession of nowheres where we've lived our lives over the past two months, each one different, yet bringing on that same sensation of being lost and alone. There are two main streets with mud stalls, a few walls around a few fields and nothing else. We're in the center of Asia with vast plains and deserts on every side. We could panic and there'd still be no way out.

The Morghab River is a silty green stream just wide enough to have an island in the middle with a few cows grazing its banks (the word *morghab* itself means "bird of water," or "duck"). It flows north, threading its way along some path of least resistance into the Soviet Union. As I look out across those rounded foothills, I realize that actually *is* the Soviet Union, where my grandfather walked, where his grandfather fled, no doubt, in some poorly chronicled diaspora following another historical moment gone sour. Sentimental or not, I hear footsteps. I've passed this way before.

It's been a long hike since Philly and I've wasted a lot of time along the way looking for something, myself, anything which might distinguish me from all the other little noises of the postwar baby boom. It's a common problem, not a very admirable one, a dilemma that owes its origins to having been born into the middle class.

To those coming up through hard times, the middle class is a dream, a goal, but much of our effort in the late sixties was devoted to finding our way out of its comforts, which had surrounded us like fluid of which we were unaware, like water to a fish. The story of the Buddha is instructive, although I'm not suggesting that I or any like me should be judged by his example.

After Siddhartha was born, a priest prophesied to his father that the young prince would remain in his homeland as long as he didn't see four things, a sick man, an old man, a corpse and a renunciate. His father tried to arrange things so he would never leave

> and gave orders whenever his son moved from the palace grounds guards were to precede him and to make sure that there were no aged, or sick, no dead and no renunciates in the streets. He set about providing his son with every possible pleasure in life, sheltering him from all pain and unhappiness.
>
> Siddhartha grew up in this way, living life fully, tasting its every pleasure. Yet an insatiable curiosity drove him beyond these pleasures and they quickly paled and left him listless . . . the prince began to wander farther and farther afield in search of something new, something to fill the void that he could sense in his understanding of life.*

* From Thubten Jigme Norbu and Colin Turnbull, *Tibet, Its History, Religion and People*. New York: Simon and Schuster, 1969.

All it took was one eventful trip through Kapilavastu (mothers, take note) for the young man to see all four of the proscribed things, and "Siddhartha immediately knew what had been missing from his life, the inescapable truth of decay and suffering."

We, the young princes and princesses of the American middle class, also sensed our lack. We too had been protected, and in an effort to unprotect ourselves and get down to those truths which had eluded us, we hit the streets, let our hair grow, and took on risks we never thought existed. The result in our case was not a vision of release from the cycle of suffering, but a cultural upheaval that left us scattered, all over the place. We might have been the new rage, but in the end were no more than foot soldiers in the passing parade, left to wander in search of our personal dreams, to chase after the images of adolescent poets, seeking the approval of people who were themselves no more than reflections of the same set of conditions that had produced each and every one of us.

Some of course, have done better than others. Some have found new meaning in new lives, but it's taken me until today, until Afghanistan, in the middle of this proverbial nowhere, to finally get it straight. These Afghans are so unlike any people I've ever met, that it's obvious that I too am unlike them, unlike anyone within a two-hundred- or even two-thousand-mile radius. I might be middle-classed or American, but I don't have to answer to it. There are just two classes of people relevant out here, Afghan and other. I'm other.

There's no more cultural garbage or baggage to haul around or explain away. I've got a pack on my back, I'm walking in the marketplace in the blazing sun and that's it. From now on I won't have such a hard time justifying my desire to write. I won't waste so much time asking, "Who am I to say?" I'm the guy in the tan shirt who wants a Coke. The babble of voices is receding and I'm beginning to pick out my own above the din. I've walked just long enough in the marketplaces and nowheres of this world to finally come to rest in my own two shoes.

Sunset. The faithful gather at the river. Religion is coming in for a lot of abuse in this tale, but there's nothing better that anyone could be doing than praying at the end of a day like this. The hills glow to a soft murmur that reminds us they will glow again, that life unfolds according to some plan that we can much more easily worship than comprehend.

Darkness puts a chill on the expansive heart, and hunger drives us past the *chai* shop with its greasy plate of rice, to a restaurant Richard noticed during the day. It's a seedy-looking joint, so ominous in the dim light that Cheryl and Marie both balk before stepping in. We walk up to the porch and stoop through the door, then remain bent over, for the ceilings are well under six feet from the dirt floor. We head past two groups of men seated around low tables on the ground, to a place against the back wall where we can keep an eye on things and I can pretend I've got a chair.

Dinner is a veritable banquet, rice, potatoes *and* meat, worth three forks in the local *Michelin*, except that Afghans eat with their hands. Three fingers, then. We scoop it up and stuff it in, tearing the bread and mopping up the gravy. You really get into your food out here, when you're done you have to lick yourself clean.

We're sitting back, waiting for tea, when a young Afghan scoots over (everyone looks like he's skulking in here because of that low roof) and squats next to Richard, asking if we want some hash. Rick sniffs the hard-packed dry stuff, then hands it back, asking the Afghan if he's got anything better. The dealer pulls out a second grade, which Richard also refuses. He's still looking for some of that real dark fresh resin, and he can afford to be choosy because we've still got some left from our first night at Islam Qala.

Fed up with Richard's gringo connoisseurship, the Afghan asks, "What you want? I have everything—hashish . . . pills . . . *opium* . . ."

"OK," says the kid, "let's see it."

He's really just buying time, doesn't actually expect the guy to come back, but ten minutes later the Afghan's kneeling at our table again, holding out a piece of paper bag so old that the fibers are starting to rub loose, with a gumball-sized gob of gooey black paste in the center. Richard takes it and looks it over. There's no way he can badmouth this stuff, it's pure.

"How much?" he asks.

"One-fifty," says the Afghan. That's about three bucks.

"I'll give you seventy-five."

The dealer grabs the paper back, saying, "How much you give me, eh?"

"Seventy-five," says Richard again, then the Afghan says, "A hundred," and Rick says, "Sold." They shake hands, but as they're holding on, the guy adds, "And twenty-five *baksheesh* for me," and he won't let go until Rick agrees. Suddenly, all over the restaurant, the waiter and patrons start turning around and applauding. They've been following the whole thing. They're all smiles as we get up and head out the door back to our hotel, wondering what to do with it now that we've got it.

I don't know much about opium except that I'll never find it any cheaper or fresher and that trying something once is supposed to be perfectly acceptable behavior for a philosopher, and my cousin is a philosopher, so I figure maybe I'll tell him what it was like.

We divvy up the paste, smear it on four squares of newsprint, fold them up, then swallow them down with disgust. Nausea is too tame a word for what happens next. We spend the next thirty minutes gagging and retching. Finally, to escape the confines of our room, we grab our sleeping bags and climb a narrow flight of stairs to the hotel roof, where we settle down, trying to relax and suppress the urge to heave each time that taste comes back.

Opium, when smoked, is said to produce a dreamy narcosis, a deep down. When swallowed raw it produces a hallucinogenic drug trip in which the mind is perfectly alert, sharp, crystal and calm. The body disappears. It ceases to be a factor as we lie together, heads on stomachs on heads on stomachs, intertwined like an Escher illusion under the vast Afghan sky.

Shut your eyes and it's daylight. Open them and the universe is exploding with stars. Waves of not only sensation, but emotion, pass through us. The four of us are one, closer than we've ever been, closer than we'll ever be. We hold onto each other, keeping warm, glowing with a hypnotic bliss, at one with the night.

Some time later—very late, in fact—someone remarks that he or she is getting cold. We're all probably cold, although I, for one, can't feel it, but I accept the fact that it's time to move. We grab our bags and start crawling toward the hatch from which we emerged, but that single flight of stairs now looks like a hundred feet, straight down. Richard drops out of sight, taking an infinitely long time to descend before stopping at the bottom to lend a hand to Cheryl and Marie. When they're done I crawl out along the rail, inching my way like a worm until my chin hits the floor and I follow their dim shapes back to the room.

As soon as we lie down the fun is over. I sleep fitfully, waking frequently to swear I will never do this to myself again. It's sweltering, and my body, so peacefully oblivious the night before, is drenched in sweat. I uncover and get the cold shakes. I prod Cheryl to make sure she's still alive, but the verdict is still out when she lifts her head, then lets it fall to the floor with a thud. Marie is no better. I drag myself to a sitting position against the wall, watching as Richard attempts to do the same.

Convinced we'll be no better off lying down, I suggest going out for tea. It sounds simple enough, but getting a leg through the hole in my pants takes all my strength. I catch my breath, try the next leg then go for my shirt. Richard is crawling toward his shoes. Somewhere inside I'm laughing, but it hurts just to think about it. We struggle to our feet. I grab Marie's sunglasses and slip them over my face, asking, "How do I look?" Richard turns away and starts out the door.

The sun beats down cruelly, robbing us of whatever last bit

of energy we possess. This is the sun that drove Camus' stranger to murder. Three blocks downhill to the *chai* shop take half an hour, one step at a time. We lean against the walls to rally, then push on. Himalayan explorers speak of this kind of agony at 28,000 feet with no oxygen.

As we slump against the mud bench at the *chai* shop a handful of Afghans crowd up to look into our eyes. The word is out, but Richard and I play it cool. So cool, so hip, so positively whipped are we that we can barely open our mouths to tell them,

"Yeah, man," we say, our teacups rattling in our hands, "it was great . . . far out . . . *too much*."

It takes us another day to pull ourselves together, then we leave Bala Morghab on the third morning for another day-long drive through the back country to Maimana, a larger town with a military installation featuring a number of Red-starred jeeps and trucks. Maimana is just developed enough to be of no particular interest, so we pick up with our same driver the next morning for the last leg of our journey to Mazar-i-Sharif.

This final bit of road in the northwest quadrant of Afghanistan runs through a flat expanse of open desert. There's really no road at all, but a series of trails among which our driver picks and chooses, or, if he feels like it, he can light out on his own, forging his own route with the same latitude he'd have on the open sea.

The terrain is sandy, with low rounded hills rising like the bottom of the ocean it once was. Ready to cut loose after three days of grueling work behind the wheel, our driver begins veering into the sandy patches, spinning hard and sliding out, showing off like a high-school kid on a hot date. The problem is that our vehicle is no low-slung coupé, but a top-heavy lorry fully loaded with twenty-five people perched along the gunwales.

I'm at the rear left corner, holding onto the awning struts, hiking out, while at the front dead center of the truck, just behind the cab, sits a fierce Ahablike Afghan with deep-black brows and a raging white beard, the most impressive specimen we've encountered anywhere. He's got one hand up the rigging and his spine against the spar, like he's strapped in to ride out the flood. His eyes are fixed straight ahead, and he's muttering incantations under his breath, and I swear it's the force of prayer that's keeping us upright, for the driver has lost all concern and is hanging out his window, laughing like a maniac.

When the desert finally runs out and we pick up the short paved road into Mazar, our friend Ahab has to pry his knuckles from the pole and flex his hand to restore the circulation. If my imagination's not playing tricks on me, he looks my way and nods in recognition of my stalwart efforts as first mate. We had established an axis between us. That nod and subsequent entry in the ship's log means more to me than the praise of kings (which has been in markedly short supply lately). For one Rudyardesque Kiplinglike instant we remain there, eye to eye, man to man, then I slip below to see that the kegs are still tied down.

All afternoon I've been sitting next to a young Afghan nomad, strikingly handsome with long eyelashes and deep dark eyes, and his wife, so beautiful it's all I can do to keep from staring. Seeing her face is a shock after the sight of all those women covered up in *chadris* in the towns, but the nomadic men and women live and work equally. They have well-defined roles to play, but they're not too dogmatic about their religion, and no one would think of ordering a woman to cover up where only the eyes of her tribe and the sky are upon her.

At one point the nomad takes my hands and holds them palms up for inspection. They're lily white, soft after several months of not working, not a callus on them. Now he shows me his, great brown stumps that look like they've been used to plow the earth directly. I look over and shrug. He shrugs back. Life is unfair, that's one thing we can both agree on. I'm ashamed of my hands next to his, but deep down I think he pities me.

The contrast in our lives is a constant mystery in a place like Afghanistan. By our standards they're suffering terribly. They all go barefoot and their feet are chronically gnarled, swollen, dried out and cracked as the caked mud on which they walk. Often they're bleeding. They may not be as painful as they look—the sensation must be long gone—but they can't feel great.

Still, the Afghans are fiercely proud of the way they live and wouldn't change lives or shoes with me for anything. When I look at this nomad looking at me, slightly condescending, I know he feels I've missed a lot. The thousand and one nights of a million and one stars. The direct contact with every element of personal existence. What do I have to offer him? Shoes? He'd throw them out. Tools and technology? He can take it or leave it. The question is—the central question, in fact, of this conflict between East and West and old and new—what would he have to give up in return?

We're driven crazy with guilt and greed when we think about the undeveloped and unexploited. We think they would live as we do, given the chance, but many of them wouldn't. I'm wandering into the realm of the noble savage here, caught between idealizing and rationalizing the difference in our states, but if the goal in life is to realize one's potential, to be fully human, I wouldn't want to judge between myself and this young nomad (with his beautiful bride), swollen hands, sore feet and all.

The truck stops at sunset and everyone gets out to pray. The sky is a brilliant red orange. Across the road, forty Afghans explode from a large highway cruiser to run down to the desert to kneel. The silhouettes of a camel caravan come walking toward us. There's a babble from all sides. They are praying everywhere right now, in every village and town.

Once done, the forty Afghans get up and run back shouting to fight for position on their highway truck, the kind of high-walled wooden rig you might see hauling used tires back in the States. They hang onto the sides, packed in so tight that the ones in the middle appear to be held up by the crush.

As they roll into the cities, these Afghan trucks come alive. The men wave their hands and start chanting and cheering like a high-school football team coming back from a win. In the old days they'd have shot off their guns, but the new government has disarmed them. We've been pretty adventuresome all along, but we wouldn't get on one of those things on a bet.

Back in our own machine, we roll into Mazar-i-Sharif, the largest city in northern Afghanistan, famed for its blue mosque, surrounded by pure-white doves, a testament to the fanatical vigilance of the locals. There's not one black or speckled pigeon among the hundreds that flutter about the holy square, suggesting that anything else that lands there has its neck twisted off or winds up in someone's stew. Afghans have a great fascination for feathered creatures. Cockfighting and betting is a national passion, store owners keep songbirds in cages above their doors, and the markets are filled with vendors balancing little bird feet on their dirty dark hands.

Our timing in pulling into Mazar is slightly less than optimal, for the holy month of Ramazan (the local pronunciation of Ramadan) has just begun, and the devout Afghans are fasting during the days. They can eat each night, but tend to get a bit testy in the late afternoon, and a surly Afghan is far from the easiest person in the world to deal with. We go shopping, but feel awkward accepting their traditional offers of tea. Their thoughts are elsewhere. They have no heart for bargaining. Empty stomachs are a constant reminder of a vengeful Lord.

Waiting outside the bus station one afternoon, I get into a "conversation" with an old Afghan who doesn't let the lack of a common language stop him one bit. He wants to let me know what he thinks of things, starting with my shoes, which he points to, saying, "Shoes no good. American shoes no good. Afghan shoes good. Look."

I've just said that most Afghans go barefoot, but this guy's got flat bedroom slippers with the heels crushed underneath. Obviously his idea of a good pair of shoes is one that you can get in and out of easily. I'm growing rather fond of my Clark Treks and might actually argue the point, but when he starts in on my pants, he's quite convincing.

"Pants no good. American pants no good," he says, pulling at my dungarees. "Look . . ." He makes me stand up to show me how tough my jeans are to move in, how tight they are at the crotch (and when an Afghan reaches for your balls, you pay attention), then he stands up to model his own. They're loose and cool, free flowing in soft white cotton. "Afghan pants good. American pants—*stupid.*" He makes a face. I could have sold these Levi's for a profit in Iran, but out here I couldn't give them away. The Afghans couldn't care less about outlining their asses in blue denim, and when it comes to style, no one can touch them.

This is all very interesting and I'm beginning to catch the drift of his cultural critique, but my friend has more important things on his mind. He takes out a bill worth fifty afghanis and points to the picture of the man in the middle. "Shah," he says, then talking eloquently with his hands, he indicates, "before this, we have Shah—very good. Shah good." I point to the money and nod.

Now he takes out a newer bill, points at the seal on the back and says something like "*Jamourie*"—which I take to be a term referring to the new government, the one which deposed the old shah in a coup in 1973. "This very bad," he says, "Afghan no like." He makes a face, points to the second bill, then grabs at my pants again, letting me know that the two are of equal value in his mind, which is to say, nil.

Slowly I piece together a history from the mystifying talk which follows. The Shah was a laissez-faire Moslem, under whom his people were free to carry their guns, smoke dope in their shops—in short, to do as they pleased. Then last year while the Shah was in Italy his former premier Mohammed Daud Khan led a coup and suddenly it's not all right to do what has always been done. Suddenly there are Russian advisers and military hardware, and the Afghans find themselves under the domination of a foreign power and foreign ideas.

History has shown what the Afghans think of outsiders giving them orders. When, in the early nineteenth century, the British first marched in they met little resistance. Then they got fed up with the harsh winter and tried to march out on January 6, 1842. Afghan guides led them up to the Khyber Pass, where armed bands were lying in wait. 4,500 British troops and 12,000 camp followers were annihilated that day. Just a handful survived to tell the tale.

If this old guy's unhappy now, in 1974, with phase one of the Soviet influence, you can just imagine what he'll be feeling when Mohammed Daud is ousted by Nur Mohammed Taraki in April of 1978; then Taraki is overthrown and killed by his deputy Hafizullah Amin in September of '79; then Amin pushes too hard to institute reforms, the natives grow restless, Amin is assassinated and a puppet named Babrak Karmal is installed with the aid of 100,000 Soviet troops backed by tanks and planes, and there's no more Afghan money in circulation to point to to make things clear to a passing foreigner, just Russian rubles. It doesn't take much imagination for me to see the old guy weeping in the snow, or running up with sticks and stones against those Soviet tanks and being gunned down and ground undertread.

It's going to be quite a fight, because the Afghans, often crushed, are never wholly beaten, and the Russians never seem to get dislodged once they've got a foot in the door. I'm afraid that in this case, however, the greater the fight is, the greater the ultimate tragedy. Things are calm right now, in 1974, but the people are not content; they don't want change and they're not seduced by progress. They want Afghan rule and rulers and flat shoes with no heels and baggy pants. The so-called contributions of the twentieth century are proving to be nothing but a false and vicious rumor.

Mazar-i-Sharif to Kabul is a straight run southeast on paved roads, a piece of cake were it not for the touch of the runs that has us dashing for the door each time the bus stops. By the time we reach Kabul, the capital of modern Afghanistan, we're depleted. The back roads and pitiful poor fare have taken their toll.

After checking out the downtown hotels, we move on to the hippie quarters and find a small place with a courtyard occupied by a bearded gnome of an Italian expatriate named Robin. Although a world traveler of the first order, who once spent two years in the jungles of Africa posing as a doctor and administering necessary medicine to thousands, Robin has just had his money stolen like a rank beginner, and is forced to camp here in a tent, to cut hair and draft horoscopes to raise the cash to carry on.

Robin holds court daily, holding aloft his chillum, a kind of vertical pipe filed with hash, and calling out, "*Bambooli!*" the local equivalent of come and get it, until all the little hippies come out of their rooms to gather at his feet. He's a free spirit, a Sufi dancer, and before that a philosopher in the Italian universities, but now all his philosophy is in the stars. He keeps busy compiling an opus of mystical knowledge which is already three volumes thick.

The other main character in our week-long convalescence in Kabul is our hotel owner, the guy who is letting Robin stay in exchange for the services he performs. The owner is a huge dark hulk of a man with a wild shock of black hair, a pudgy fleshy face and the soft hands of a born sensualist. Although he seems to be a man of formidable intelligence, the only English he speaks is a litany he recites each time he passes, trying to entice his guests into betting him on a game of chess.

"Come, you play," he says, never varying a word, "you win, one kilo hashish, very very *good*—one Scotch, case beer, one movie, taxi—click click," he clucks his tongue and shakes his hips, indicating that by "movie, taxi" he means one hot date with the local trade.

We're warned off early by Robin, who claims he was a prodigy back in Italy, an entrant in numerous blindfold tournaments, but who says he can't touch our host, who seems to be something of a chess genius. "One kilo hashish, very very *good,"* he whispers as I pass him in the hall. The boss is a man with a mission.

After several days of this baiting, I decide to take on the big man and check him out—without betting, of course, because I'm a crummy chess player. I sit facing him in the yard, make a few thoughtful moves, surprise a Knight and actually have him wondering, when I slip up. The big man was getting nervous, but seeing through my charade his mobile face surrounds a sneer as he picks up his Bishop and slams it down with a guttural "Ha!"

I move again and he repeats the action, going "Haa! Haa! Haa!" surrounding me in phlegm until my Queen's been had and my King is running through the jungle like the Emperor Jones. The boss wraps me in his fine web of strategy, wondering whether to finish me now or save me for a light snack later in the week. When he's done, I'm not only beaten, but humiliated. "One kilo hashish, very very *good,"* he tells me, but now when he says it, he laughs.

Kabul is a fine place for recuperating and putting some flesh back on our bones. Fresh apple and carrot juice go for two or three cents a glass. There are a variety of restaurants serving European food, including Italian and German, and a great number of things to do.

Had we been here a month earlier we might have witnessed the national sport, Buzkashi, in which opposing tribes or villages of mounted men try to drag a sheep or goat stuffed with sand and rocks around a prescribed course before depositing it in a circle and claiming victory. The Afghans are superb riders in a country where a horse is the single most valued possession. One test of a good Buzkash player is his ability to remain in the saddle while bending to the ground to pick up a needle with his lips. The sport was introduced to the country by Genghis Khan in the thirteenth century, although in those days the Mongols used to drag around a live human instead of a stuffed goat.

In 1219, while the Afghan ruler Ala-ad-Din Mohammed was

marching on Baghdad, Genghis Khan first rode in from the east. Din returned with 400,000 horsemen, which he deemed insufficient to confront the invading hordes, but his son Jalal later rallied to crush the Mongols near Kabul.

Genghis, incensed, sent his own son to pay back the Afghans, but when the son got killed the great Khan took matters into his own hands, captured the citadel at Bamian (where the Russians are camped out right now), gave orders that no living thing be spared and turned the whole country from Kandahar to Balkh (that *is* the whole country) into wilderness.

There's a legend that the Khan heard a rumor after the massacre that one small cat had survived, and that he sent out twenty men with orders to find it and bring it back to be slaughtered before him, or all twenty men would be killed in its place. Two small towns which stand today in the region of destruction are Char-i-Zoack (city of the red earth, named for its red clay, but also for the blood which flowed) and Char-i-Golgola (city of howls).

Nothing much has changed. Each new turn in the road reminds us how the Afghans, with the most pitiful inheritance imaginable, have had to struggle in every era to maintain it. This is the original land of the free, although life out here has been more rigorous than any of us can imagine. There's a cannon in downtown Kabul that's set off each day at noon. About fifty years ago they used to strap wrongdoers across its muzzle and blast them all to Kingdom Come.

Ironically enough, I never worry about my personal safety. The fact is, it's much more dangerous to walk the streets of many American cities than to travel anywhere in Asia. These people can be fierce, but they still need a reason. There doesn't seem to be any of the senseless, anonymous interpersonal violence we face back home. Whatever fears I felt back at the beginning of the trip have proved groundless. Occasionally we get scared when we don't know where we are or what's going on, but we never feel menaced. We're free to come and go pretty much as we please.

On a typical day Cheryl and Marie get an early start to head down to the market. Cheryl's got her camera hidden in her bag, she's always on the lookout. They reach the old section and slow their pace, poking their heads into the shops and stalls, taking their time and missing nothing. It's better when the two women are alone together, because Richard and I are always rushing them. We have no patience for detail.

Cheryl's already given up on buying any lapis lazuli, a gem stone found only in Afghanistan, because the good stuff, the Royal Blue, is locked up in government vaults. Anyone caught smuggling it out is likely to have his hand cut off and the black-market price reflects that risk. The stores are glutted with the lesser stuff, full of calcite and flecks of pyrite (fool's gold), but it's easy to resist.

There's no charge anywhere for looking, however, so they poke through stolen treasures in the thieves' market and stand watching artisans weaving handkerchiefs out of shimmery synthetics on hand looms. They stop for a while by an old school to peer through a wooden window into a classroom where patriarchs in white beards tutor small boys in the Koran. The Afghans are an illiterate, but not an uncultured people. They are great philosophers, and many of them can quote at length from the holy books and traditional poetry. Although the predominant religion here is Islam, the historical traditions which predate its imposition give the Afghans a typically independent bent.

Cheryl and Marie load up on dried fruits to munch surreptitiously (it's still Ramazan) as they move on. The market is Cheryl's stomping ground. Bargaining is essential out here, and while normally retiring, she can easily spend ten minutes arguing over the equivalent of two or three cents while buying a soft drink. The thought that a vendor will jack up his prices at the mere sight of her is enough to drive her wild. It's not just a matter of respect. She's the one who started off months ago with a small bankroll and a vision. Our seven months on the road will wind up costing seven hundred dollars each, excluding air fare home, but including food, transportation, lodging and the deposit on our carpet. Obviously there is not much room for extravagance. The native vendors may think we're rich and that it doesn't matter, but they learn.

By now Cheryl knows all the tricks. If she's sure she wants something, she'll get up early so she can be the first customer of the day, for an early sale is supposed to bring good luck. Otherwise she'll wait for the last minute for the same reason. This tactic is especially effective during Ramazan, because the vendors are starving by the end of the day and their business sense is all tied up with their karma. There's nothing unfair about her tactics, she's just tough. Nobody gives anything away, and the handshakes and smiles when the deals are closed are always real.

At one point I'm hanging in with Cheryl when she stops in a shop to select an embroidered bib to serve as the front panel in a custom shirt. The old store owner and his son stand there looking at her, working up the nerve to take her measurements, but they're so flustered by her breasts underneath her leotard that their hands are shaking as they apply the tape.

Cheryl sees that it's twisted and calls them back to try again. The kid reaches up around her waist. The old guy's in a cold sweat. She takes his hand and puts it where it belongs, but he can't even see to read. She finally gives up, knowing that if it comes out wrong—as it will—she can take it in at home. All she really wants is the embroidery. She walks out laughing, trying to figure it out. There's nothing but women's clothing in the whole store, but if that old guy had to face her breasts one more time, he'd have had a stroke.

Cheryl and I are walking one day in a large park in downtown Kabul, when a blacktop basketball court appears to our left. At first I think it's a mirage, I have to pinch myself to make sure I'm not hallucinating. Three or four kids are goofing off on the sidelines, while another two go one-on-one without intensity.

Before I know it I'm out on the court, asking to see the ball. They toss it over. I bounce it a few times, set up, then fire a shot that falls three feet short of everything. One of the kids retrieves it and throws it back, so I line up and the same damned thing happens again. Air ball. It's not even close.

I'm reminded of those times at practice when the principal used to walk out in his shiny black shoes, motion for the ball and make an ass of himself like I've just done, hunching up his jacket and tossing a brick at the bottom of the rim. The wheel has turned. Now I'm the old fart in the street shoes.

Wait a minute. I'm in shock from four months on the road, but it's not that bad, so when they toss the ball back, instead of trying again, I bounce it over to the better of the two kids whose game I've interrupted, then set up in front of him, signaling for him to make his move. He fakes left, goes left and I slap it away.

I retrieve the ball myself this time, hand it back to him, smother a jumper, then stop a drive and pick him clean. Like the coach always said, your shot may desert you, but there's no such thing as a bad night on defense. The kid sticks the ball on his hip and looks over at his buddies, saying, "*Khoob, khoob,*" meaning, Hey, this guy's OK. He says a few more words in Afghan, tosses me the ball, then they all take off and scatter toward the housing development across the way.

I have no idea what's going on, but as long as I have their ball it's obvious they'll be returning, so I get to work, finding the range, getting the feeling back in my fingers and wrist. Fifteen minutes later every basketball player in Afghanistan is down at the court. The word went out fast and now the big boys are showing up to check out the American in the funny shoes.

A game forms up, but as we're about to start, a tall, whining weasel of a kid, kind of an Afghan Eddie Haskell, storms up, announcing that he's ready to play. Since we've already got ten men, they tell him to wait, but he immediately starts calling people out, threatening a fight.

Since it's obviously on account of me, I give my place to the new guy and take off. It's the right thing to do, but I kick myself all the way back to our hotel and all night long because I wanted that game so bad I could taste it.

I sit around the next day, chewing my nails until three, when Cheryl and I walk back to the court and—lo and behold, that wasn't every ballplayer in Kabul yesterday. I can hardly believe my eyes. There's talent everywhere. My young friend from the day before comes running up to shake my hand and introduce me to the team he's hand-picked just in case I came back.

Starting at right forward, six-one and nineteen years old, incredibly handsome with deep dark eyes, a trim mustache and the legs of a gazelle, Omar the Afghan Sharif. He heads to the hoop, takes a pass and leaps way up over the rim to drop it in.

At point guard, a short blond guy in his middle twenties, a dead ringer for Jimmy Lynam, the old St. Joseph's College star (now the coach), who waged those epic double-overtime battles against Villanova's Wali (né Wally) Jones in the heyday of the Big Five back in the early sixties.

Then there's my friend, about sixteen, a heads-up little guard; myself, an undersized swingman, and our center, six feet eight inches of big-time bona fide ballplayer, a blue-chip Afghan with a big dark beard, who waves from the corner, where he's dropping twenty-two footers through the bottom of the net. This guy could play ball anywhere. If we were back in the States, the college recruiters would be out here right now, strewing rose petals in his path.

We warm up in a smooth drill, match up and start running against the next five best players in town. I've played basketball all over, in Boston, Philly, France and San Francisco, where you have to allow six inches for the wind, but this, without a doubt, is the best game of my life.

The flow is incredible. Our fast break looks like one of those old Red Auerbach training films. The big guy rips it off the boards and shovels off the outlet. I clear it to the center, cut off the tail and wind up a trailer on a three-point play. We're wheeling, dealing and shooting the eyes out of the hoop and soon there's a crowd of hundreds three deep around the court.

Somebody has been coaching these guys. They didn't learn

this riding camels in the desert. Maybe it's the Peace Corps, more likely the Russians, but whoever it was, they did a fine job. Basketball's got a language all its own and these guys are fluent. Back in the States, ballplayers, black *and* white, communicate in a kind of street hip, hand-slapping jive, but when I turn around to do the same, saying, "Hey, man, nice play, now look . . . set me a pick an' I'll . . ." I realize with a shock that I'm not back in Philly, these are *Afghans* standing in front of me and they don't have the slightest idea what I'm talking about.

I can't help feeling a momentary letdown as they shrug their shoulders and head back up the court, and I get a lonely little twinge each time they make a call, because we invented this game and by international convention traveling is still "Traveling!" and a hack is still a "Foul!"

When the rout is over we shake hands and throw our arms around each other, jabbering and not even caring that we can't understand. The crowd cheers and Cheryl runs up, ignoring all the sweat to plant a nice little kiss on my cheek. I'm telling you, you can have your high-school heroes and your NCAA's. All I need to be happy in this world are these four guys from Kabul, a pair of sneakers, and a sharpshooter coming in off the bench.

Late in the week, Richard and I take out the Frisbee and move into the narrow alley outside our hotel to play a game of killer hockey, in which one of us fires the Frisbee, ricocheting it off the walls, while the other tries to keep it from getting past. After a couple bruising rounds, Richard winds up and lets go, but the Frisbee catches onto his finger and sails over the high wall to his right.

"Come on," he says, "give me a boost."

I figure it would be just as easy to walk around, but instead of arguing I cup my hands and he steps up for a look over the top. As he's peering over the edge, wondering what to do, I make the mistake of saying, "Come on down," and the next thing I know Richard is saying, "Give me a push," hoisting himself to the top of the wall where ceramic tiles are set in mortar that's long since lost its strength. Halfway up the tiles break loose and both the kid and the wall come tumbling down on my head. The tiles shatter on impact and Richard winds up like a duck with a broken wing, lying on the ground with his shoulder twisted beneath him. Dislocation.

Not wanting to risk resetting it myself, I yell for Cheryl and Marie, then run to the street to find a cab. We pile the screaming kid into the back seat and speed across town to the hospital.

Once inside, Richard immediately starts yelling for morphine, while off to his left, on another glazed metal table, lies a young Afghan kid, nine or ten years old, with a shattered leg and pieces of fibula sticking up through his shin. Apparently the kid got hit by a cab which ran up on the sidewalk, but he doesn't make a peep. The doctor, who's already been summoned, arrives after a while, eyes the two of them, then takes Richard first with a look of mild distaste. He gives him that shot, wheels him into the back room and waits for the anesthesiologist before performing the necessary manipulation.

The Afghan kid is still waiting silently. His operation will be a long complicated affair, which may be the reason that Richard went first, but there's an implied contempt for us Westerners in the surgeon's action that he doesn't try to hide. Make no mistake, we're soft. At each new misery we weep and moan, thinking that if we do so loudly or long enough, some miracle of modern science will be brought to our rescue.

Taxis, morphine, skilled surgeons in foreign lands, these are our due. We want them and we want them fast. Afghans, on the other hand, take what they can get, and if it takes forever, that's just too bad. This little boy's got a compound fracture of the leg, but he'll put up with his agony until he passes out. He'd live with it the rest of his life if that were the only way he could get by, and he wouldn't expect any sympathy.

The doctor explains what we can do if the shoulder pops out again, then shakes hands with Richard, whom we lead out in a blissful trance, his arm in a sling. The timing could be better, for we plan to move on, but there's no good time to get injured on the road, and at least in Kabul we had a hospital to go to. Richard will be able to take care of himself with one hand, there's not too much he has to do besides stuff his sleeping bag and hoist his pack, so we'll just wait two days for the shock to wear off, then climb on the morning bus to Pakistan.

The Khyber Pass

EAST OF KABUL, irrigated fields give way to empty valleys where the black tents of nomads collect in basins. The calligraphic form of the word *kabul* suggests a basin, and the word itself is a compound locution meaning The Dew on the Rose. This is the last we'll see of these people, and it's a little sad; we would like to have done more. Time and money would have taken us into the bush, into the Hindu Kush, the high mountains around Badakhshan, but now all we can do is hope we'll return, take our short month in Afghanistan as a scouting trip and plan to come back in style, with our own Land Rover, to go where we please and stop as long as we like, to get a little closer to the Afghan nomads and hill people, who are still no more than romantic strangers to us.

With a tourist's indifference we've called all the tribes by one name, the Coochis, as in, "Oh, look, another Coochi tent," even though they've got more tribes than languages and the languages alone include Pashto, Dari, Nuristani, Baluchi, Uzbek and Turkoman. Afghanistan is the great melting pot of the East, the breeding bed of Dravidians (Indians), Semites (Arabs and Jews), Greeks, Scythians, Turks and Mongols; and in latter times the English and now the Russians. The men are of every conceivable racial and facial type. Shave an Afghan and strip him of his turban and you've got a cabbie from Brooklyn. Stick a cabbie on a camel and he'll be right at home in Ghazni. There's a strong and surprising link between the heart of the inner city and the heart of this Asian wasteland.

Just as the outlaws, castoffs and huddled masses of Europe wound up in the States, Afghanistan is a last resort for a different set of refugees.

The barren hills grow rocky as the land rises to desolation —we're approaching the Khyber Pass. We climb a ridge across the way from a baked-out village behind a salt lake fronting a range of hills topping one another into the vast outer reaches of the Himalayas. Everything is gray and still without a hint of life. The air cools and our hearts start pounding. For all the cruelty of the scene before us, this is one of the most romantic places on earth, romantic in the sense of the passion of history, the violence with which it's played out, the spectacle of its grand march. Ghostly echoes of bagpipes and drum. Indian officers saluting smartly, reporting in their singsong tongue.

We climb slowly through mountains growing more impossibly steep and forbidding, to the Afghan border, where Richard's cheap commercial rug is impounded pending *baksheesh* to the order of five bucks. Five bucks is all he paid for the thing, but they tell him it's an antique treasure. Somehow it's fitting. Held up at the Khyber Pass. Worse things have been known to happen.

Now we're in Pakistan, a no-man's-land if there ever was one. Huge fortresses from the nineteenth century sit high across the valleys from one another. Cold clouds squat above the peaks, sending a bitter wind that rattles the windows. The whole ride is one extended moment, so breathtaking and beautiful that Cheryl puts her camera away. This is no time to fiddle with shutter speeds and light readings. Focus on one thing and you miss a hundred more.

Our Pakistani driver is insane. He thunders around blind curves, making me wonder if he has any brakes or sense at all. There's nothing to do when the center of gravity shifts but hang on for dear life. We're scared to death, but that's hardly an inappropriate emotion out here. As the blues man named (fittingly enough) Taj Mahal once said, "If you ain't *skeered,* you ain't right!"

Pakistan

THE RANGE BREAKS and it's all downhill along a road straightening out as if someone were pulling a string, into the flatlands of Pakistan. It's raining as we come off the mountain, streaming in sheets. Lightning flashes, then the rain stops, but the wind increases. Everything glows a misty orange as dust billows up from the plains. The horizon disappears.

Soon the rain begins again, slanting down, soaking the fields. Water buffaloes wallow in the mud by the side of the road. Afghanistan was the desert of the interior, but Pakistan smacks of jungles to the south and east. We're not just shifting centuries, as at our last transition from Iran, but entire modes of life.

As the bus pulls into Peshawar the shower ends and the sky goes a deep and brilliant rose. The atmosphere is bruised. Down on the street, we're met by the usual horde. Finding one's way through each strange new town is not as tough as it may seem. The fact is, we don't have to do a thing, the people come in search of us. They know, for example, that the bus from Kabul arrives at six, so you can count on them to be out there, screaming and shouting as you climb down in a stupor,

"Hotel!" "Me, follow me!" "English, good English, hotel, very clean—come . . ." They take you by the arm, assuming a tone of intimacy, showing off the full range of their vocabulary and nine times out of ten it works. Nothing is more welcome than a modicum of communication and we know from experience that all the hotels are alike, so the brightest, most fluent boy usually becomes our man. Our only other guide, apart from our instincts, is a little yellow book called *Head East*, by a West Somerville, Massachusetts, group called Head Guide Publications (a subsidiary of Hippo Productions, Inc.), which may tell you something about its slant.

In Peshawar, this first city in Pakistan, our accommodations are at the beautiful Rainbow Hotel. Psychedelic murals by stoned-out hippies on trips past adorn the walls. Signs saying "No Drugs" litter the halls. We spend three days here trying to get on a single-engine aircraft up to Chitral, above Swat, to visit the hill people, who may be doomed in their battle against the Paki high command. Here's one more irony to add to those that will be heaped upon us by the eighties. To check the Russians, who will have taken Afghanistan, our government will likely rush arms to a government that has been equally ruthless in suppressing those tribes still fighting for their independence.

Weather in the northern valley is too rough to land, so our flight is canceled each day just before takeoff. We start out determined to get up to Chitral, to make up for our failure to visit the northeast of Afghanistan, but eventually have to give up, because there's no guaranteeing that storm up there won't last another week.

Our last night in Peshawar, I go walking through the marketplace, hemmed in by crowds milling about the street vendors and movie houses. Lanterns throw a warm glow on the faces within their circle of light. The darkness is alive with voices and smells. Hawkers push green betel leaves which they cover with a red paste, then sprinkle with a white powder for customers to pop into their mouths and chew until their lips, teeth and gums are grotesquely discolored. Little dough balls fry in a crackle of hot oil.

As I'm walking out the dark end of the main street, heading back to the hotel, a three-wheeled cab, like a golf cart or mail truck pulls up and the driver asks if I want hashish. He holds out a sample. Not really thinking, I take a quick look and resort to one of Richard's old tricks, saying, "Do you have anything better?" The guy grabs the hash back and says, "Come, I take you to store."

For some reason I climb in, get driven off into the night, and within two minutes have no idea where I am. We roll over bridges and across town until he turns a corner and pulls up into a small crowd by the curb. Standing in a circle are a dozen Pakistanis, headed by two, not one, dead ringers for Sidney Greenstreet, the fat villain and arch rival of Humphrey Bogart in *Casablanca.* One of them wears a red fez, while the other is totally bald. I have two choices, to turn around and start running for my life, or to enter, not at all convinced I'll ever get out.

The bodyguards part and escort me into a small room, where Sidneys number 1 and number 2 plump themselves into chairs. I'm directed toward a rope bed of the sort we have back at the hotel, which is where I wish I was. I wait. The Fez begins, "What you want? You want hashish?"

"Well," I say, my voice quavering, trying to maintain some semblance of self-respect, "it depends on what you've got."

Sidney the Skull snaps his fingers and a man comes out with a bar of dope. I look it over quickly, sniff it, then hand it back and say, "I'll tell you what. What I'd really like to do is go get my friend. He's the expert. He's the one to talk to." Yes. I've found my out. Monsieur Rick, I must get Monsieur Rick. I've found my role in this melodrama, I'm the Peter Lorre character, the first one to duck behind the bar in case of trouble.

The Fez mutters a few words in Pakistani to The Skull, nods to my driver, then turns back to me, saying, "Go, bring friend. We wait."

I congratulate myself all the way back to the hotel, fully expecting that Richard won't be in and I'll simply not reappear, but sure enough he is home and when I tell him what's happening he can't wait to get going. We walk down to the golf cart with the fringe on top and ride back. This is now my third trip along the same route, but I'm still lost. They're waiting for us as promised and once again we walk the gauntlet into the dingy room of their Pakistani drugstore.

"Well," says Sidney number 1, "now we talk."

"Hold on," I say and everyone turns my way, "before we get started, I wanna say one thing: I'm scared; I've heard about people who sell you hash, then call the police and . . ."

"Oh-ho," the Fez laughs. "My friend," he says, "trust me, no police. Police trouble for you, trouble for me. OK?"

I nod and sit back, then Richard takes over, eyeing their first grade of hash and rejecting it. Next they bring out a cake of fresh-pressed pollen, which he sniffs, saying, "Not bad, but I'd like to get some Afghani."

"This is Afghan," says the Fez, with that characteristic eastern tilt of the head that says he both agrees and doesn't agree with you.

"No, Afghani is brown," says Richard, "this is green—see?"

"No, my friend," says the Fez right back, taking a deep breath and placing both his palms on his knees, trying to explain, although I can tell he has little hope we'll understand, "Afghanistan, Pakistan"—he waves in the air as if to indicate everything beyond these walls to the north and west—"is not two countries, no no no no, is one country, one people. All one, all same, peoples come here, peoples go there—same-same—you see?"

Yes. I do see. Something about the way he was tapping his breast, saying "one country, one people" made it perfectly clear. The governments out here are drawing lines trying to stem a flow that's gone its own way since the beginning of human time. His friends are up in the hills, fighting for their lives. If he wants to call it Afghan, he'll get no more argument from me, the question is, what's the price?

We're talking about a slab of hash the size of a large Hershey bar, a quantity that might bring two to three hundred dollars back in the States. Sidney number 1 looks at Sidney number 2, nods, then quotes a price of ten bucks for the whole thing. Monsieur Rick, undaunted, looks him in the eye, looks down at the hash, sniffs it and says, "I'll give you five."

Frustrated in our attempt to make it up north, we push on to

India. Pakistan is no more than a stop along the way. We ride through the West Punjab province, past old British garrisons guarding bridges across the Indus River, heading southeast toward Rawalpindi. Each time we stop, the Pakistanis along the road surround us, jeering and hassling the women. The Afghans were more than taken with Cheryl and especially Marie, who, with her dark hair, was perceived as one of their own, but they had too much pride and personal dignity to get too far out of line.

No such restraints, however, hinder the Pakistanis, who jabber and grab at the women, touching their breasts until we have to fight our way back onto the bus. I look out and see nothing human in their eyes, a reflection of the fact that to them we're not human. The women are whores, or worse, fresh meat to be swarmed over and devoured. Pakistan, away from the west where the mountain mentality still prevails, can be the worst of all worlds for a western traveler exposed to the streets. It combines the dense overcrowding of India and central Asia, a subtropical climate, and the hothead mentality of a nation of Islam on speed.

Inside the bus the harassment continues. Cheryl slams a guy in the ribs, but he still won't let up until I switch places with her. Richard, no longer inclined to play the White Knight to Marie's damsel in distress, is nevertheless standing up and screaming in the back, shoving people away from her. As freakish as these incidents are, they happen more than once. If anyone wants to make allowances or offer explanations as to why it's OK for the Pakistanis to act this way, go right ahead. You might even be right, but we're the ones putting up with these mobs, the same kind that will burn down the U.S. Embassy in 1979 after that ridiculous rumor that U.S. agents were behind the takeover of the Grand Mosque in Mecca, and our unanimous conclusion is that it's disgusting. Pakistan, if it is indeed to be our ally through the eighties, at the risk of even further alienation of the Indians, must be viewed with the greatest suspicion. Regardless of who the leaders are, the people are, to put it mildly, unreliable.

Sometime late we pull into the aptly named city of Lahore. Rather than lose all credibility by maligning every place we visit on a tour so brief as to disqualify me from any claim to objectivity, I offer the following as a purely personal anecdote, reminding the reader that behind every trick turned in a back bedroom on a set of dirty sheets, stands or lies a John. The Story of John Harvard in Lahore:

Arriving after midnight, we stumble half asleep into the first hotel we see, a dismal bus-station flophouse. The floors haven't been swept in months, it's even worse than the kind of joint we usually stay in, but it's dark outside, late, and from all we've seen dangerous, so we remain.

The next morning we get up early, eat breakfast and start walking around town, through thriving streets where huge-horned steers haul flat-bed carts loaded with freight. Small boys with large eyes and long eyelashes flash stunning smiles. The pace is fast, but since it is a large city we manage to get by without attracting too much attention.

Against a whitewashed brick wall splashed with movie posters and political slogans, a gray-mustached Pakistani man in khaki breeches stands in a trough, splashing water over the backs of brown and gray buffalo, who switch their tails and press closer to get under the cool liquid. Out in the country, they'd be neck deep in the streams to keep their skin moist and prevent it from cracking, but these are city herds of dairy cattle, kept in courtyards which occupy entire blocks.

We follow their spoor through the gates into stables where they're pent up, munching on hay. Most of the milk and butter one eats in these parts comes from buffalo. We dine one night on buffalo filet mignon at a local restaurant, a complete dinner, tender and tasty for $1.10.

About two o'clock in the afternoon, as we're heading back to the hotel, wondering if we'll be able to stand it for another night, a Pakistani youth rides up on a bicycle, asking if I want to change any money. Cheryl takes one look at him and says, "No," but I've been waiting to be approached, so I say, "Go ahead, Cheryl, I'll meet you in an hour back at that café over there."

"Michael, I really don't think it's a good idea."

"Don't tell me what to do. I'll see you later. Here's my traveler's checks, I'll just take fifty bucks." I shove the rest of my money her way and hop on the handlebars, waving as the kid pedals me off for parts unknown, ignoring the sound of Cheryl's voice fading in the distance, saying, "Michael, no-o-o . . ."

"Women, eh?" says the young man whose chin is practically on my shoulder as he pumps up and down.

"Yeah, women." Cheryl's been a fine partner, but it does get old, and nobody's gonna keep me on a short chain. It's great to be off on my own, seeing a part of the city I'd never otherwise see, and this Pakistani kid is turning out to be a terrific guy. He stops for tea, introduces me to the people in the *chai* shop and won't even let me pay. He steps out for a few minutes, making me wonder if I've been abandoned, then stops back, saying, "Come, we go."

Now we're down in the residential section, twisting through the alleys. After fifteen minutes I offer to switch positions, figuring I can use the exercise, and now I'm pedaling him as he calls out directions, smiling and waving to the passersby.

We emerge onto a main street, turn left and pull up beside a park, where a group of men are gathered around a skinny barber, who's administering a shave with a straight razor. Hopping off the bike and leaning it against a tree, I shake hands all around. My friend says a few words in Pakistani, receives some instructions and takes off, leaving me with the group of men. They all seem like nice guys, too, but a little strange. One of them gestures like he's got a rod between his legs, points to the barber and says, "Ten rupees."

"What?"

"Ten," he holds up his hands, "ten rupees," then he grabs that rod again and gets it going, pointing to the barber and rolling his eyes in bliss. Aha, ten rupees. Reasonable enough. The barber flashes a smile and nods. He's all skin and bone. His metal blade scrapes down the throat of his client, whose eyes are also rolled back in bliss. Obviously a man of many talents.

Now my buddy comes back and tells me it's all set. We leave the bike and go walking across the park to a building we passed on the way in. When we get over to the grassy front yard, I give him the money and he tells me to wait.

"Hold on," I tell him. "No way, José, I'll come with."

"No. You can't."

"Whaddya mean, I can't? Gimme my money back."

"No, you stay. This center for black market in all of Lahore. You stay. I go in. You come with me and finish . . . no deal, big trouble. You wait."

I look up at the windows of the modern building before us, trying to guess which office it might be. I picture ordinary-looking men in business suits surrounded by barefoot torpedoes, just waiting for someone to snap his fingers so they can rub somebody out. No wonder they don't want me in there, I wouldn't either.

"OK," I say, "I'll wait, but first give me something to hold onto."

"What?" he says.

"You have my money, now I want something of yours."

"Oh," he says, pulling out a wad of bills, "you hold this, I be right back."

"Good luck."

He disappears into the courtyard, turning toward the stairway to his left, as I sit down on the grass and shuffle through the money he's given me, a roll consisting of rials from Iran, afghanis from Afghanistan and a few Turkish lire, currencies of rather dubious liquidity, which despite their bulk amount to no more than seventeen dollars.

Five minutes pass. I've got seventeen dollars of his, he's got fifty dollars of mine. Ten more minutes go by. That makes a difference of thirty-seven. I get up and start pacing. People are looking at me, wondering what's the matter. I dash into the courtyard where my man was last seen, into the stairway and up to the second floor, but the doors all look the same.

What would I say, anyway? "Uh, excuse me, I'm looking for the black market center for all of Lahore . . ."

Right. I've been had. I run back to the barber shop, but the bike's gone and no one knows a thing. The barber, the ten-rupee man, strops his razor on a leather strap. Right. I come back with a cop, just to hassle them, but by this time even I know it's futile, so I flag a cab, hoping he'll accept some of my funny money for payment. We weave back and forth across town, looking for that café where I said we'd meet, but when we finally do find it, no one's there, so I pay the cabby in afghanis and walk back slowly to the crummy hotel by the bus station where my friends are waiting. Instead of one hour, the whole thing has taken three. Cheryl is terribly upset. She's been out on her own looking for me, and the streets scared her.

"What happened?" says Richard as soon as he sees my face.

"I got robbed. He pulled a knife." This is about as low as you can go, but I just can't help myself, I know I'll go stark raving mad if I have to listen to Cheryl saying, "I told you so."

I lie down on the bed, waiting some fifteen minutes to work up the nerve to admit the truth. Finally, "I lied," I say. "He didn't pull a knife, he conned me. This is all I've got left." I empty my pockets onto the bed, then turn to Cheryl and tell her, "Go ahead. Say it."

But she won't. She just walks around with this wry smile on her face all the rest of our stay in Lahore. I know I'm not the first person to get taken this way and I won't be the last. Lots of people get burnt on the black market out here, but like they say, you can't cheat an honest man. Even Richard Nixon supposedly lost a hundred in a flimflam in Delhi. What the heck, I'm in good company, the kind of company I deserve for being such a—go ahead . . . say it.

PART FIVE

INDIA

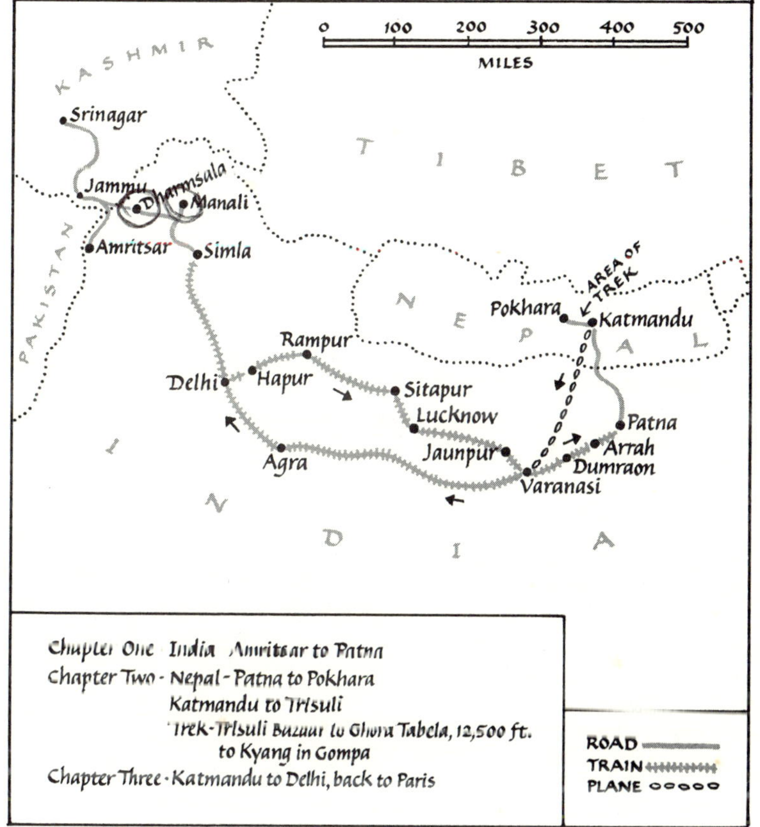

THE BORDER BETWEEN Pakistan and India stretches out about a hundred yards, with armed sentries all the way. Goods from one side are unloaded from trucks and carried on the heads of coolies wearing nothing but swaddling breeches to the other side, where the men dump their burdens and stroll back for more. There are four rows in motion, one fully loaded going to India, another toward Pakistan, with two rows of unloaded porters in the middle streaming either way.

You would think they would bring the borders together to save all the human wear and tear, but India and Pakistan don't like each other very much; they've been quarreling over small details like Kashmir ever since they partitioned in 1947. We join the coolies to carry our bags to the Indian side at Amritsar, prepared to pass customs under the gaze of the fabled woman psychic.

Fortunately, she's not in. The male customs officer in her place seizes on a pair of hippies ahead of us and strips them down. One good way to pass through a border out here is to look as if you haven't been here before. The people ahead of us, the ones whose toothpaste tubes are being emptied out, are wearing baggy pants, embroidered vests, bracelets, necklaces and gold earrings and one of them's a guy. We look like college kids beside them and are waved through without a glance.

One difference between Pakistan and India is immediately apparent in the navels of fine-toned ladies in bright silk saris, walking the streets with bundles on their heads. The baring of so much as one square inch of abdominal flesh in Pakistan might have started a riot. Here it gives the appearance, if not the substance, of liberation, but that'll do for starters. Cheryl and Marie immediately rip off the long-sleeved shirts they've been wearing since Turkey and let the soft breeze flow under their cotton T-shirts. We lie down beside a small tree, waiting for the bus, relieved that the cloud, or the veil, if you will, of the past few months has lifted.

Life in a Moslem country can be stark. It puts one constantly on the defensive. I realize that there are many reasons for me to have a built-in predisposition against the culture, but there's no denying the high level of sexual frustration, or the intense pressure it places on the Western traveler.

The bus arrives and deposits us in Amritsar, which pulsates with the particular rhythm of Indian streets. The four of us ride in two bicycle rickshaws to a hotel, then find our way on foot to the Golden Temple, sacred shrine of the Sikhs. The Sikhs, among the most interesting people in India, are easily the most visible, with their tight turbans, striking features and full beards. A northern race of warriors, they seem to run everything, from the buses, to the planes, to the Army, although at the time of partition their sympathies lay with the British.

The Sikhs' Golden Temple is a large open square inside a set of walls, with a highly polished marble walkway leading all the way around a reflecting pool with a chapel in the center. One circles the pool, feeling the smooth slabs under his bare feet (shoes are forbidden), drinking in a calm which comes as a relief after the teeming city streets.

We walk down a ramp to the center of the moat, where the chapel floats in the music of sitars and harmoniums breathing their reedy harmonies. Unlike certain Moslem holy places, where a nonbeliever can be killed just for entering, visitors are welcome here, and there's food and lodging offered to those who need it. Before this account gets too rosy, however, I'd better point out that a hapless dog who wandered in and slipped into the pool was first beaten, then dragged up a set of stairs by its tail to be thrown out. The Sikhs, in addition to being competent, can be arrogant and cruel.

Our plans for the road ahead are starting to diverge. Richard would like to kick back. His arm, injured in that fall back in Kabul, is slowing him up, but more than that, he's simply tired of hurrying, he'd like to spend more time in the places that interest him. Cheryl and I would, too, but our money's running low and we know that if we make it back to Boston by December we can work the Christmas season with my old friend John and bankroll ourselves enough to set up an apartment. Otherwise we'll go home a month later, totally broke, and stay that way longer than might be comfortable in the dead of winter. We have about a month and a half left to visit northern India and Nepal, so if we're not absolutely in love with a place, we'll have to move on. Marie decides to stay on with Richard, to give it one more chance, so we split up briefly, making plans to meet up a short while later in Srinagar, the capital of Kashmir.

It's a full day by train to Jammu and another agonizing day by bus before the last pass descending into the flat Kashmirian plains. The fields have already been harvested, and big bunches of red peppers hang upside down outside the houses. Huge trees, solitary giants, tower over the valley, which is bordered in all directions by mountains, especially to the north and east, where we get our first glimpse of authentic snow-capped Himalayan peaks. The floor of the Vale is flat, a green plateau.

Srinagar is built on a lake, along which runs a series of canals, with houseboats resting side by side. Hustled back in Jammu, we agreed to give one guy's place a look-see, so he telegraphed ahead to his cousin, who's waiting for us as we step off the bus, anxious to get our money before we discover any of our options.

I'm a little apprehensive, but the place looks fine, easily as nice as anywhere we've been. Our lodgings are in a flat-bottomed houseboat ("Class A," he assures us repeatedly) with a primly furnished living room of the sort one might find in a bed and breakfast in Scotland. There's also a dining room and a narrow hallway leading to two small bedrooms. Although something less than luxurious, it's private and picturesque, and at first we hardly notice the chill rising through the floorboards.

When we wake the next morning, we hurry out onto the street to restore the circulation to our frozen limbs. Dogs, taking advantage of the early morning sun, lie on the sidewalks, dozing. Little kids naked from the waist down pee off the stone walls into the murky water. Slop from thousands of buckets is dumped daily from the windows of houseboats into the catch-all waterway, mercifully overgrown with a lush velour of green surface plants like floating clover. Cheryl and I give in to the temptation to rent a small punt called a *shikara* and are propelled through the bright muck with a distinctive flicking motion of the rudder/oar by a Kashmirian gondolier, into the quiet backwaters where brilliant kingfishers with iridescent turquoise wings are startled into flight.

The afternoon of our second day we're joined by Richard and Marie, who didn't find Amritsar so exciting after all. They were scooped up by the same advance men who got us after we told them we had two friends on the way, and as soon as we're all assembled, sitting around after dinner, our hosts try to interest us in a little dope smuggling.

They tell us it's foolproof. They'll hollow out suitcases, stuff statues, disguise it in a hundred ways. We tell them we're not interested, but insisting that we try the stuff, the head man, a skinny Kashmirian who I knew was a little too slick to be playing this hotel game straight, hauls out a fifty-pound water pipe, which he fills with what he calls Number One, Kashmiri Primo. This stuff wins the blow-your-brains-out prize hands down. Onc toke has me splayed out on the floor, and Richard too, and he prides himself on his *savoir faire*, but our man in the little Kashmirian beanie takes the mouthpiece and draws on it for what seems like a minute and a half before expelling huge clouds of smoke into the room. It must be the air up here, the guy's got iron lungs.

Our third morning the four of us head to a nearby mountain for a horseback ride up to the peak. This may be the most touristic thing we've done the whole trip, but it doesn't exactly work out, because the horses are tired little ponies who can barely take our weight. At one point one of the four characters who latch onto us as "guides" switches Richard's mount and the poor thing pitches the kid forward, landing him on his bad arm and breaking a 200mm lens. Richard gets up ready to kill somebody, but the four clowns throw up their hands and I didn't see a thing. I was looking over the edge to the lower valley, unfolding its alluvial patterns below. All the melt-off from the mountains drains through here, bringing rich soil and plenty of water to the farmlands before everything winds up in that big lake.

On the fourth day we ride by bus to a stunning valley as green as a golf course, beneath a colossal set of permanent glaciers. Luxury hotels occupy the bluffs. Kashmir is gorgeous and there's a lot more to see, but prices are fairly high, so Cheryl and I decide to push on. We're saving our real mountain trip for Nepal. Richard, however, wants to stay, to get up into that snow and stomp around, so once again we wish him well, kissing Marie on both cheeks, asking her what she'll do if it doesn't work out between them.

"Don't worry," she says, "I'll take care of myself," adding, "Don't fight," to me as we start back to the bus. Marie might not have a future with Richard, but she doesn't want to be a third wheel with us, so we split, 'way off in the middle of the mountains, leaving our two friends in Paradise while we go in search of Shangri-La.

We're finally alone. It was helpful to share the early going among the four of us, I'm certain I wasn't the only one who benefited from the give and take, but any more and we might start getting in each other's way. Not only is Richard in no great hurry, Marie herself has absolutely no desire to return to

France. She wants to go even farther east and really live among the people. Both of them have been traveling several months less than Cheryl and I, who began last spring, and lately we've been feeling pressured, as if there were something wrong with our feeling that we'll have to get back. The only way any of us will enjoy the rest of our trip in peace is to go it alone, or in units of two, so we've broken off. *Vaya con Dios.*

The bus takes us down from Kashmir and up and around the switchbacks of Northern India's Himchal Pradesh (Himalayan District) on the road to Dharmsala. Green fields of tea coat the hillsides. Monkeys dash across the blacktop, leaping into trees to chatter and scold. This first sight of our free-swinging arboreal cousins in their natural state has us pressing up against the glass, crying "Monkeys! Monkeys!" to the great amusement of the Indians, who turn around in their seats.

The bus labors on. What appears to be a short hop on the map takes two days. When we stop along the way at various small villages we get our first good look at the saddhus, wandering holy men, who wait outside the bus-stop restaurants for a bit of whatever's on the bottom of the pot.

The younger saddhus look remarkably like what used to be called "freaks" back in the States. That term has retaken its connotation of aberration, but back in the late sixties a freak was anyone willing to let his hair grow long, on his head or under her arms. Freaks wandered about from city to city, rock concert to rock concert, commune to commune and demonstration to demonstration, glowing with instant karma in a movement that replaced religion with its own strange eclectic blend of politics and spirituality.

I suspect that many of those (read: *we*) so-called freaks might have made the same choice and become wanderers here, where renunciation is actually much more logical. Most of these saddhus were born into poverty, anyway. They could remain in their villages, eking out a miserable existence, or take the plunge and take to the road to try their luck and follow their destinies.

The saddhus aren't all holy men. Some of them spend much of their time hanging outside the government grass shops and train stations, hitting up the hippies for dope. Although there are great spiritual masters among them, the rest aren't necessarily frauds, but simply men who've cast their lot with freedom. They walk the full length of India, from the high mountains to the squalid streets of the south. They may not know where their next meal is coming from, but they pass on having seen the world. Saddhus are a welcome sight to the weary traveler. They look you in the eye with a gentle smile that says that they are just strangers, too.

Were ours a truly spiritual quest, we might be nearing the end of the trail, for the village of Dharmsala, where we're headed, is the home of the exiled Dalai Lama. He was forced out of Tibet for good in 1959, followed by more than 100,000 of his people, who resettled in northern India, Nepal, Sikkim and Bhutan to escape the domination of the Chinese, who first took over the country in 1950.

The Tibet they left behind was a powerfully beautiful, mystical place, described in this account by the French explorer, herself a Buddhist monk, Alexandra David-Neel:

> Shrouded in the moving fogs, a fantastic army of trees, draped in livid green moss, seems to keep watch along the narrow tracks, warning or threatening the traveler with enigmatic gestures. From the low valleys to the mountain summits covered with eternal snow, the whole country is bathed in occult influences . . .
>
> Up and up we went, skirting gigantic glaciers, catching occasional glimpses of crossing valleys filled by huge clouds. And then, without any transition, as we issued from the mists the Tibetan tableland appeared before us, immense, void and resplendent under the luminous sky of Central Asia.
>
> Since then I have traveled across the country lying behind the distant mountain ranges which, at the moment, bound my horizon. I have seen Lhasa, Shigatze, the northern grassy solitudes with their salt lakes as large

> as seas, Kham, the country of brigand-knights and magicians; the unexplored forests of Po and the enchanting valleys of Tsaring where the pomegranates ripen, but nothing has ever dimmed, in my mind, the memory of my first sight of Tibet.*

The true Tibet, that consecrated marriage of earth, sky and human spirit, is no more. If you ask our new friends the Chinese about it, they pretend it never happened, but although Chairman Mao declared its liberation, the rhetoric of socialism was quite a different matter when translated into action by Chinese generals in the field.

They kidnapped Tibetan boys to raise them in isolation from their families, forced marriages between the races, and through their oppressive policies created a resistance movement put down by the most brutal measures imaginable in 1959 when they shelled Lhasa with its population of 10,000 monks, killed upwards of 85,000 people, imprisoned another 25,000 and, according to eyewitnesses:

> crucified, vivisected, burned and buried alive thousands of monks and nuns—forcing them to copulate and then perform miracles to save themselves. Men and women were publicly tortured to death, children forced to execute their parents and whole villages sterilized.
>
> Investigating these atrocities in 1960, the International Commission of Jurists found the Communists guilty of "the gravest crime of which any person or nation can be accused—the intent to destroy, in whole or in part, a national, ethnic, racial or religious group as such." †

Even so, the fourteenth Dalai Lama, maintaining the detachment that has characterized Tibetan thought ever since they were converted from fearsome warriors, the scourge of the

* *Magic and Mystery in Tibet* (1932).
† From the report of John F. Avedon, "In Exile from the Land of Snows," *Rolling Stone Magazine*, Sept. 20, 1979.

Chinese, to devout Buddhists in the seventh century, issued a statement shortly after his escape which read:

> In spite of the atrocious crimes that the Chinese have committed in our country, I have absolutely no hatred in my heart for the Chinese people. We should not seek revenge on those who have committed crimes against us. The hope of all men, in the last analysis, is simply for peace of mind. My hope rests in the courage of the Tibetans and the love of truth and justice that is still in the heart of the human race.*

Such generosity of spirit, spread around the globe, would go a long way toward making the world a better place, but even with it the Tibetans seem sad and a little lost in Northern India. They seem earthbound, cut off from the particular force that their Tibetan homeland brought to their prayers. Even stripped of their domain, however, the lamas retain their personal dignity as they walk the streets in the strange and outrageous headgear of their sects, their hats strung with red cloth, looking like box kites, implying the message that "I am different from you. My concerns are somewhere between star and cloud. They need not interest you, yet they touch you like the night itself, which you also fail to understand."

Dharmsala offers a rich mix of holy rite with daily life. Little kids whoop and holler on the street under the all-seeing inward eyes of monks taking the afternoon sun. Merchants crossing the square set rows of bronze prayer wheels in motion, each turn sending a message in raised letters, like Braille, to a God whose eyes seem externally closed to the woes of the world. High lamas pass the time talking with women selling used clothes in the market, while young *trapas* (students) in maroon robes follow one another in regimented order down to the meditation hall. The young ones are being trained despite the calamity amounting to a holocaust, initiated into a faith which may have them saying, "Next year in Lhasa" a millennium from now.

* From the report of John F. Avedon, cited above.

Cheryl and I find lodging in a dormitory just down the hill from the Tibetan enclave, and one of our roommates turns out to be Mark, part of the beach-front crew from Paros. It's not such an unlikely coincidence—one is constantly crossing paths with the same travelers across Asia. We are not the only ones out here, which is part of the reason this trip is possible in the first place. Mark recommends a Tibetan restaurant serving flat noodles of the kind Marco Polo first enjoyed in the thirteenth-century court of the Kublai Khan. We wolf down a healthy portion of pasta and vegies and wake the next morning with a dose of Khan's revenge. We should have known better. Experience has shown that the more we enjoy a meal, the more likely it is to bring on the runs. I'd run back and throw a rock through their window, but I'm too weak. Each time one succumbs to the sickness, one prays it's not amoebic. That *oe* digraph crawls like a *bête noire* through our fears, for nothing besides hepatitis can end a trip faster than the dread dysenteric microbe. I see fanatical protozoans banging their shoes on a table, crying, "We will bury you!"

Fortunately, there is a cure for the low-grade, nonamoebic variety. Mark runs (walks) over to the drugstore and returns with an armful of small packets containing flaxseed hulls, a dry flaky stuff that turns gelatinous with the addition of water. The idea is to mix it up, swallow it down and plug yourself. A nice sticky quantity of white rice is said to do the same. I promise I won't talk about this any more, but I do want to pass it on—flaxseed hulls—Nature's Way—I've tried it and it works.

After three days in Dharmsala we take a two-day trip past Mandi, Kulu and Nagar, up a long narrow Himalayan valley to Manali, one of India's prime tourist spots, directly north of Delhi. A summer retreat for middle-class Indians, hippies and Tibetan hill people, who live in semipermanent tent encampments on the outskirts, the town boasts an abundance of general stores and a hustling market, filled with traditional objects from Tibet—wooden bowls and silver prayer boxes—and modern necessities, like ribbon, yard goods and rubber galoshes.

Whereas Dharmsala had an ecclesiastical feel, the Tibetans around Manali are just plain folk. The village women go around barefoot, or in flat black slippers, wearing red leggings all but hidden under long dark velvet gowns topped by black vests lined with vermilion. They're easily distinguishable from the hill people, who once ranged the high country, grazing their herds at well over ten thousand feet.

These ladies are brightly dressed primitives. They wear their hair in thick coils of black braid, sport gold earrings and necklaces of coral and turquoise, carry blood-red blankets around their shoulders and wear leggings above mukluks that make them dead ringers for the Eskimos and so-called Indians of the American Northwest. One sight of these Tibetans and one has no more questions about the provenance of the American tribes, nor of the existence of the land bridge which is said to have run from Siberia to the New World.

All these types and more mingle in the market, showing off their personal treasures, laughing, talking and trading. Young men squat in the dirt, playing a game like dice, throwing a wooden bowl with several markers down onto a leather pad, punctuating each toss with shouts like "Hik!" and "Phat!" the sounds the lamas make when trying to coax the spirit of a dead man out of the top of his skull, the only safe way for the soul to enter the afterlife.

Tibetans have what might seem as a fixation on death, were it not for the fact of death's obvious fixation on them. Life is such a brief span that it's seen as a bridge between worlds, and rather than shrink from death, as we tend to, they embrace its symbols and incorporate them into their rituals. Femur trumpets and human-skull cups serve in a religion which, while Buddhist, has been greatly influenced by the animist religions that preceded it.

Orthodox and enlightened monks disdain much of the superstition rampant in the country, but the ordinary people are just as likely to run to a sorcerer or a Bonpo magician if they feel that the spirit of their dear departed one is being endangered by demons in the limbo of Bardo, where they wander before rebirth. In certain rites bordering on necrophilia, a magician will lie down prone, mouth-to-mouth with a corpse, muttering incantations as he enters a trance in which he'll struggle for hours for both his and the dead man's immortal souls.

Wandering through the marketplace, Cheryl and I come across an old Tibetan women spinning a little hand prayer wheel as she sits in her stall. She's got some magnificent Chinese turquoise, but her prices are high. The time of bargain-basement trading in the Orient is over, these people have been picked clean. Five years ago they could still be had, but now they're down to their last precious goods, not only holding on to the memory of a culture, but trying to set themselves up for old age. That puts them in a rather firm bargaining position. Cheryl's been hoping to buy some stones to work with this entire trip. She was greatly disappointed that she couldn't afford the lapis lazuli in Afghanistan, and now it looks like the same thing will be happening here. The old lady wants fifty bucks for one stone Cheryl's picked out and twenty-five each for the other two. Cheryl walks away outraged, saying it's cheaper in New York.

About two miles north of town, across a foot bridge over a small, but powerful Himalayan river, we find the local hot springs. They're not the silty pools I'd expected, but sunken tiled rooms which fill with water heated by a geothermal source. Cheryl and I pay the guardian fifty cents each for our first hot bath since France. The dust of several subcontinents melts into the brine as we scrub our scalps and talk in whispers that rebound around the walls. We laugh, leaning back into the uterine intimacy of soft sloshing.

When we pass through the market on our second day, the old woman greets us with a bright smile. Cheryl pauses just long enough to ask if her prices have changed, then moves on when the woman says no. When we get out of earshot, I ask,

"Don't you even want to see them again?" but Cheryl answers,

"Don't bother."

On the west side of the village, footpaths lead through wild marijuana groves to remote mountain pastures. Halfway up we come to a thousand-year-old Buddhist pagoda, growing like a mushroom from the forest floor, then we turn down the hill and see Richard, sitting under a pine tree, staring off into space. Cheryl runs over and gives him a tremendous hug. It's only been a week, but it is a rather large continent.

These two mean a lot to each other. They make a mockery of the typical American nuclear family. Although they come from the same small suburb on the outskirts of Philly where I went to high school, which is where Cheryl met my sister, their upbringing was quite different. Their father is the son of a Jewish cop, while their mother is a farm girl, a coal miner's daughter from upstate Pennsylvania. Both parents are avid naturalists. Cheryl's father got an acknowledgment in Roger Tory Peterson's *A Field Guide to the Birds* for an observation he made when he was fifteen years old. They raised their children (there's an older brother, David) outdoors, and Cheryl was expected to do the household chores just as her mother had. The boys parlayed their father's interest in photography into a general interest in equipment and mechanics of all sorts, and their parents were successful enough to keep them well supplied.

Whereas college for me had been a foregone conclusion, Cheryl took off to work after high school and Richard wound up stepping out before graduation, a member of the late-sixties' teen-age dropout generation. It seems that 1967 was a rough year for schools, from junior high on up. He and Cheryl share a lack of concern for many things which count for me as obsessions. They also happen to be a great team. Lots of people stopped hassling Cheryl when Ricky walked up, looked down and said, "This is my sister," and there were quite a few stunts he might have regretted pulling if she hadn't been around to stop him.

Cheryl's all over him as I stroll up and ask, "Where's Marie?"

"I don't know," says the kid, "maybe you'll see her in Nepal."

"Oh, yeah?"

"I left her in Kashmir."

"I hope she's all right," says Cheryl—and, well, don't we all. Marie's finally done it. She's said goodbye to her American friends and phase and set out to prove herself. So long California, hello mystic Orient. She won't be the baby of the family when she gets back, her brother in the Army and sister in the underground will have to move over, Marie'll have been around, she'll have her own stories to tell. The nieces and nephews will start looking up to her, taking after her. It worries me quite a bit to think of her out there all alone; I wouldn't want to see Cheryl left that way and I wouldn't particularly want to be there myself, but there's nothing more to say. She's on her way.

Cheryl tells Richard that Mark from Paros is here and we all head down the hill, past those wild and crazy marijuana groves, to party. The next morning, our last in Manali, we wake to the sound of children singing in the schoolyard next door. The town is jumping with a large number of Tibetans in for some sort of tribal powwow. We walk to the market one last time to pick out a few doodads and knickknacks, a wooden bowl, a bright scarf, biding time before we have to face the old lady with the turquoise beads.

She, of course, has had her eye on us the whole time, whirling that thingamajig of hers, muttering an incessant stream of prayers, asking some reincarnated spirit of her ancestors to give her strength to handle the hardheaded blonde from across the sea.

Cheryl sits down and asks to see the stones. The woman takes them out and lays them on a velvet pad. Cheryl asks the price and the woman says a hundred dollars for three. Cheryl waits a moment, then makes her final offer. She's thought about it all night. This is not like bargaining with the Turks in the Grand Bazaar in Istanbul. Those guys couldn't have cared less about the junk we picked out, they enjoyed the fight as much as the money. This old Tibetan lady, however, is not in it for kicks. She cares about these stones and from all appearances Cheryl's picked out her best.

"Fifty," says Cheryl, "I'll give you fifty dollars, it's all I can afford. Last price."

The woman shakes her head, no. "A hundred," she says, looking Cheryl in the eyes. Cheryl shakes the woman's hand and gets up to go.

When we're past the edge of the booth, I say, "Come on, try again, you can't just give up, you didn't budge an inch, you'll never see these things again."

"No," she says, "it's not fair. If she only wants to sell to some rich tourist, let her. I know what I can pay. If she won't let me have them, I don't want them."

It seems a shame, because I'm convinced that no one in the world, except perhaps the old lady herself, could appreciate those stones more than Cheryl, but that's the way it goes. We're almost out to the street, when suddenly from across the square where the dice players are still uttering those guttural cries, the old woman's son comes dashing out, dodging through the bodies, yelling, "Wait! Stop!"

"See, Michael, I told you so!" says Cheryl, and I can't tell you what a relief it is; I've been waiting to hear that since Lahore.

"Come," says the Tibetan youth. "You very good, lady. She says yes. Fifty dollar."

"For all three?" says Cheryl.

"Yes, all three. You come."

He leads us back to the old lady, who, now that it's over, seems delighted to sell her things, even at a loss, to such a formidable adversary. Price is one thing, value another. Cheryl's price was low, but the worth she placed on the whole exchange, the way she looked into that woman's eyes, finally amounted to enough.

Fifty bucks passes hands, and the stones wind up in

Cheryl's lap. She's a little bit choked up. The old lady grins and spins her wheel. Now it's time to break out the Kipling, to blow the dust off and recite it so the old boy is spinning in his grave:

> Oh, East is East and West is West, and never the twain shall meet,
> Till Earth and Sky stand presently at God's great Judgment Seat,
> But there is neither East nor West, Border nor Breed nor Birth
> When two strong *women* stand face to face, though they come from the ends of the earth.

With the transaction completed, the old girl gets an impish look in her eye, reaches behind a curtain and pulls out a ceremonial headdress, a red felt cylinder eight inches high and completely covered with turquoise every bit as beautiful as what we've just bought. Our stones were for sale, but this is her treasure, the pride of a tribal chief, the dowry of a princess. The old woman wouldn't think of breaking it up or selling it piecemeal, her price is sixteen hundred bucks. Period. It's her legacy, her will, her grandchildren's education.

The way things are going today, sixteen hundred bucks is a pittance. Five years later it'll be worth eight grand. It's a shame we're so strapped, that we can't use what we know about stones to wheel and deal, but then our trip just wouldn't be the same. We didn't come here to get rich. We have to scrape and save to come back with a few mementos, and in the end it's probably better that way.

Richard stays on in Manali while we push down to Simla for the train to Delhi. The bus ride is typically long and hard. We stumble off in the middle of the night by a boarded-up station surrounded by people. All along the concrete ramp vendors stir up their iron kettles. We sniff around through the smoke, finally ask for a helping and get a runny portion of *dahl,* yellow curried lentils on a throw-away clay dish. A small piece of bread is balanced on the edge and bits of red pepper glisten in the stew, just as they will later, undigested, after passing through our guts. There's always a twig or a piece of rock to spit out. We eat, but never too much, for the dangers of overindulgence far outweigh the pleasure of satiation.

According to the accounts I've been reading, Indian wise men counsel against eating on the road. The reasons are many. First, it's hard to digest while traveling. One rarely achieves that state of calm conducive to proper absorption. Second, the food that's available is far from the best. But the most compelling reason for not eating on the road is that no matter where one looks in India, there's always someone no more than a few feet away who could use that meal more than you.

Poor people tend to gravitate toward the stations, hoping that something will fall or be thrown their way, and one can rarely swallow without being watched. Those Indian wise men have the right idea, but they also have a choice. If we didn't eat on the road, we'd scarcely be eating at all.

Food's been enough of a problem as it is. For the last two months we've seen nary a fresh vegetable. We're afraid of the salads because the lettuce is often unwashed, and even if it is washed, the water in which it's rinsed might be more dangerous than the lettuce itself. Everything that enters our mouths, unless we can peel it ourselves, must be cooked, and most often it's overcooked until any vitamins lingering are only there by accident. We're taking pills, which fortify our livers and turn our urine a reassuring shade of pale, but ever since Afghanistan it's been near privation. The occasional decent meal, like that filet of buffalo in Pakistan, is such a shock to our systems that it winds up doing more harm than good.

In five months of travel, bouncing over roads far more effective than any fanny vibrator in a health spa, I've gone from a playing weight of 178 pounds to a scant 145 with clothes on. That's what the ticket says when we drop ten paisas in the machine in the Delhi station upon arrival, 66 kilos. My arms are pipe stems, all the muscle is gone. I'm just about as skinny as the people on the street, but spread out over a six-foot frame thanks to all the scientific baby formula I enjoyed as an infant. I'm also giddy and lightheaded, all but blown away when the cab drivers charge us and start pulling at our packs.

Cheryl and I settle on a rickshaw, a bicycle-powered two seater. There's an early-morning haze over the streets of Old Delhi as our man goes pumping along, a surreal calm broken only by the bell going, "Ring ring . . . carload of sahibs here . . . ring ring, beat it, out of my way, two fat honkies and a hotel kickback . . . ring ring ring . . ."

We slow up at a bridge and coast down the other side into New Delhi, through denser more mechanized traffic onto a street lined with cheap hotels. For $1.50 a night, the most Cheryl and I have paid since reaching Asia, we get the use of a basement room with a big double bed and a gracious overhead fan. We drop our gear, nap for an hour or two, then step out onto the street into the crush of midmorning.

I'm in a kind of hallucinatory shell, bombarded with sights and sounds that only half penetrate. This nutrition thing has gotten the better of me. We stop for a mango milk shake from a street-corner vendor and down it on the spot, feeling a momentary rush as the sugar hits our bloodstreams.

Having decided on a visit to the Delhi zoo, we go looking for a cab with a meter to avoid hassling over the fare with cabbies notorious for jacking up the rates for foreigners. Finally we locate a guy with a motorized mail cart, point to his meter, are told that it works, then hop in, announcing our destination.

The driver highballs it around several squares, skirts a fort, then straightens out onto a busy boulevard. I don't ask that he take the shortest possible route, just that he not insult my intelligence by taking us past the same spot two or three times. When we finally pull into the parking lot by the zoo, the meter says four rupees twenty. At eight rupees to the dollar, that's about fifty-five cents. I reach into my pocket, add a two rupee tip and am getting out when the guy says he wants eight rupees ten.

"Whaddya mean, eight-ten?" I say. "The meter says four-twenty."

"No, eight-ten, eight-ten," he says, "meter broke. This old meter—new meter, eight-ten!" He holds out his hand.

This is exactly what we wanted to avoid. My nerves are shot. They're all chewed up and floating down my bloodstream on little corpuscular rafts and I'm not about to dicker, or dick around.

"Listen, fella," I say, hiking up my pants, falling from where my hips used to be, "that meter says four-twenty and that's all you get. Four-twenty and two rupees tip, I'll see ya' later. Come on, Cheryl, let's go."

When the cabbie shoves the money back, I close my hand and it hits the ground, so he picks it up and starts running after me, shouting,

"Eight-ten! Eight-ten! Old meter . . . new meter . . . eight-ten!"

I'm so far gone right now that when he grabs my arm I just pick him up and throw him away, turning to Cheryl and saying, "Well, that's that," slapping the dust from my hands, but the driver bounces up, comes running back with a full head of steam and shoves me some fifteen feet up against a tree.

What the hell is going on? I'm not only lightheaded, but so physically light that this human twig just blew me away like a 210-pound pulling guard. I can't believe it. He comes right back and now I shove him and *he* goes reeling and all the while there's this little voice in the back of my head going, "Oh, God, don't let me hurt him." We go on like this, back and forth, rocking and socking each other fifty yards across the parking lot, all the way up to the front gate.

It's ridiculous, insane, Cheryl's screaming, "Michael, stop it!" and I say, "Whaddya mean, stop it?" and wham, he slams me again. This little sucker just won't learn, so I bounce him onto the hood of a government limo and am about to close my fist, when the Zoo police finally come running out to separate us. The cabbie starts yelling in Hindi, and Cheryl and I take advantage of the lull to pay the entrance fee and slip through the turnstiles.

Cheryl's a fierce bargainer, but getting into a donnybrook over a difference of one rupee ninety is a bit much, even for her. If I don't get some real food into my gut and bring myself back up to a human condition, I'll wind up in a cage like one of these emus.

The zoo's a little run down, it would be hard to justify animal luxury when people are starving out on the street, but the creatures are still incredible. They've got gorgeous antelopes and strange jungle cats with huge goblin ears to catch the night's secrets. Around the corner, a band of Indians is throwing stones at a tragic white tiger.

I'd like to tell them to stop, but after what just went down I'm in no position to start giving orders. I'm afraid there's another lesson in here somewhere. If I can be reduced to a state of such utter irrationality by a little privation and prolonged hunger, I have no reason to expect anything but the same from people who've lived most of their lives that way. If we in the so-called civilized world would have people deal with us on our own level, we'd better start at the beginning and see that they're fed. Otherwise we're probably doomed to an endless succession of useless brawls, and we'll wind up taking our solace, such as it is, from beating up on lightweights.

As a northern town, Delhi has less human suffering than one finds in cities like Bombay and Calcutta. Cold winters drive out the very poorest, but the poverty is still appalling. Children of five or six sleep in the train stations, then wake, shivering, to hold out their hands as prosperous Indians brush by. The calculation is simple. Millions of people are hungry, it's nothing new. Why give to one when there's another right behind? Where do you draw the line? Sorry, kid.

I'm glad we've taken the hard way, overland, for now we can draw on a sense of who we are and where we're from that's not available to anyone who flies in cold, steps off a plane and suddenly has to deal with these conditions. Anyone advocating the cessation of welfare back in the States ought to come to India for a while, to see what it's like when the poor confront you and follow you through the streets. Such people might find their blood money cheap compared to the cost of living in a society where misery surrounds you, where there's no way to wall yourself off.

India herself could do much better. One district may be starving while another shows a surplus. There's little sense of the people pulling together as a whole. The only real concern of the middle classes is that they not sink back into the mass. Everyone's got his own problems. Keeping a society from falling to such depths is not a matter of compassion, but self-interest of the first order.

Attending to our own needs, we feed up at a Sikh hangout in New Delhi called the Milk Bar, where we enjoy such delicacies as milk shakes, broiled burgers, French fries and Russian salad. The customers aren't American hippies, as one might imagine, but businessmen from the airlines and government agencies across the way. The air is conditioned and the service brisk. We didn't come to India to eat this kind of food, but then I didn't expect to look like this when I got here. Burgers know their way around my frame. For the first time in months I've got little burger biceps and a tiny pinch around my middle.

The two things we must do in Delhi are secure visas for Nepal, available at a beautifully manicured embassy a cab ride down the road, and obtain reservations for the flight home. Several sources along the way have recommended the services of an agency called Tripsout Travels, one of a host of 
outfits catering to the freaks-going-home-on-a-shoestring trade. We reserve places on Air France for half fare, about 245 dollars each to Paris. Our tickets are stamped for November 20. That will leave us ten days to get from France back to Boston in time to get to work. Those December winds on the Charles are a long way from us here in the heat of the Delhi

streets, but we feel them all the same, blowing cold down the backs of our necks.

We take one last afternoon to wander around Old Delhi, a circus of humans, cars, rickshaws, bicycles and Brahma bulls. The sunset is pink, its color heightened by the *putt-putt* of tailpipes. 'Way up high on large billboards, Sikh sexologists in turbans, full beards and pointy mustaches, with bandoliers strung across their chests, clutch rifles and hand guns, promising sure-fire cures for impotence and incontinence. In ten short visits, they seem to say, even you, the scrawniest henpecked little Hindu in Delhi will be confidently cocking that trigger and blowing 'em away.

It's a comic carnival, only this is one show that never folds its tents. With my American love for solitude and space, I find it hard to see how anyone remains sane here. Obviously sanity is one thing in one place and another somewhere else. No wonder meditation is so important in India. For some, all the space they'll ever achieve must be found within their own minds.

There's an exaggerated quality about much of official life in India, but the railroad carries its devotion to form to new heights. It's almost as if the bureaucracy were grafted onto the native religion, so that while on the surface its adherents are merely pushing paper, deep down they're paying homage to strange gods and placating primordial fears.

To use my student card to purchase a ticket to Patna, about six hundred miles east of Delhi by train, I must first report to the under-assistant adjudicator of exceptions. He, naturally, is not in, so I'm directed from one out-of-the-way office to another all the way around the back of the train yard, into a record room filled with yellowed slips of paper from the early years of the British Raj.

I'm a little nervous, for my student card was obtained by lying under oath to a shady expatriate Russian with offices in downtown Athens, but the Indian official doesn't care about that, he just wants to cover his own ass, so he dips into the proper drawer and takes out the appropriate form, which he fills out longhand *in triplicate.* All it says is that the bearer (name, place of birth, date of birth and school) is entitled to half off on a second-class ticket to (Patna) on this (blank) day in the month of (October), year of our (their) Lord (1974).

My copy is to be handed to the guy at the ticket window, but what in God's name is the guy going to do with the two laboriously handwritten copies he's retained? Records are dripping out of drawers, stacked up in mountainous files in the archives, where dusty motes circle in shafts of light like flies above a dungheap. Imagine, three forms for every student who takes the train. No wonder their forests are gone. I suppose it's comforting to know that fifty years from now scholars will be able to go and look it up, to prove that I did indeed pass this way on my way to Patna and that while the wisdom of the age was destroyed in the library fire at Alexandria, every scrap of business ever conducted in this railway terminal in Delhi is intact.

Armed with my note, I run back to fight my way in among the hundreds of Indians clamoring at the ticket window. There's an art to staying in line out here. It's like rebounding in the NBA, the first thing you do is get good position, then you fight to keep it with your elbows and arms, and if somebody turns around to complain, you just point to the guy behind you. No harm, no foul. Let the boys play.

As my breath is being slowly squeezed out, Cheryl walks up, so I hand her the forms and watch her walk directly up to the front of the next line to pay our fares. The Indians, who deep down seem to know that all this pushing and shoving is ridiculous, let the ladies through. It's a strange double standard, but better than no standard at all.

Once we've got our tickets we run out to fill up our insulated canteen with mango milk shakes for the long haul, then hurry back to the station and onto the platform, where a tiny boy comes up to beg money. I avoid his eyes, as if I have more important things on my mind. Fifteen minutes pass and the kid's still standing there, watching us. When the train comes we pick up our packs and push in to find seats near the window on the second-class benches. As the train starts moving, I reach for the canteen, but it's gone. Eighteen hours of unbroken boredom await us with no mango milk shakes to ease the pain.

I think of that kid, with his big eyes on us the whole time we were waiting, and hope to hell he got it. I hope it was him and not some hard-ass vendor who'd dump the contents out before his eyes and sell the plastic container for a few rupees. Maybe the kid caused us to leave it. Maybe he willed it, to get a cool drink for his pathetic little milk-starved belly. I'm haunted by the thought of that kid, but the best I can hope for at this point is that I did some good by accident.

Eighteen hours on a hardwood bench, Delhi to Hapur to Rampur to Sitapur, stopping at every station along the way. Vendors shove in cups of tea in unbaked clay cups to be drained and tossed out on the tracks. No deposit, no return. Lucknow, it's getting dark. Faizabad, Jaunpur, trying to sleep. Varanasi, Dumraon, Arrah, and at the end of the seventeenth hour, as dawn rises with its steamy breath hanging gray above the Ganges, Patna.

On the map it's green, indicating lowlands, but that's misleading. It's only green here when the monsoons fall and all the arable land is washed down the thousands of tributaries through that geographic sieve known as Bangladesh. It's late fall now and it hasn't rained in months. The land is dry, the fields are brown, and the region of Bihar, from here down to Bengal, is undergoing yet another in its endless cycle of famines.

When we step off the train in Patna, the smell of death is in the air. You'd be surprised how easy it is to pick out, even if the worst you've ever experienced is fear. Fear tends to come up suddenly, it lurks in dark alleys and jumps you from behind, but famine never sneaks up, it stretches out its attack for weeks, squatting in the gutter if you happen to be one of the unlucky ones, calling your name.

Famine lies by the side of the road, covered and caked with

mud as your bicycle rickshaw takes you across town. It's a dying man lying naked at the ferry gates, totally ignored. It's a resignation that comes when the children are suffering effects that no subsequent daily ration will cure.

Famine is a cloud, and all who pass within it breathe it. It's a bitter smoke from the funeral pyres at the water's edge. It lodges in the chest and won't be expelled with a cough or washed down with a draught of tea drawn from the Ganges itself, a foul muddy brew which would have us retching were it not for the beggars lined up around us, who would gladly take our cups or lick the sugared spittle from our lips.

One of the beggars, a blind man with milky cataracts across his eyes, starts singing. His voice is a gift in the midst of this gloom that makes our donation seem less like charity than a fair exchange. We spread some rupees, but there are more hands than we have bills. Women who once were exquisitely beautiful reach out piteously until a guard comes and chases them behind a gate.

We're locked in now and our fares are paid. Across the water small barges with bright furled sails bob and turn imperceptibly against the shore. Everything is white gray in a gauze mist, dreamlike and calm. We might be in Egypt on the river Nile. The ferry arrives, passengers stream off, then we climb on to cross the Ganges, leaving Patna behind. Already the horror is fading. That's how it works. Famine doesn't smell half as bad once you've turned your back.

Nepal

THE TRAIN RUNS north from Patna to the Indian border at Raxaul. It's the eighteenth of October, we have one month and two days left. We get stamped out and carry our bags across a buffer strip to wait in line for the entry to Nepal. Once admitted, Cheryl and I book places on the bus north, then discover to our horror that these buses have been designed to accommodate the greatest possible number of this very small race of Nepalese. The back of the seat in front is four inches too close for my knees, so I'll be riding with my legs tucked up under my chin all the way to Katmandu.

Our only relief comes when the bus stops for frequent security checks. The Nepalese government is fighting a war of attrition against certain tribes of armed Tibetans (does this sound familiar?) and is checking the baggage for guns and ammunition. Life is not all fun and games, even in the storybook Kingdom of Nepal.

The lowlands adjacent to India rise quickly into foothills thick with underbrush, forming a natural barrier between Nepal and the ill-fed millions to its south. The first range is steep and uninhabited except for little outposts connected across the valleys by cable lifts. Farther north the canyons open up into spectacular terraced landscapes, chartreuse and green with tawny tips of wheat nearly ripe or just cut down and bundled into sheaths. Two-story Nepalese houses of red clay with thatched roofs are scattered in groups of two or three across the countryside.

The hills widen, the valleys fall deeper down, and the bus continues to climb. The scale is beginning to deceive us. Judging by anything we know, it's large; but when we check again and see that those dots down there are people, we realize that we've badly underestimated the vastness of this piedmont, which stretches out canyon after canyon, awesome and wild. There's no real wilderness as we know it in the American West, people are everywhere and every square inch is cultivated, but for all their numbers, humans seem to rest lightly on the world out here.

The bus drives on past checkpoint after checkpoint, powering further and deeper into a land tossed like the waves of a great ocean. We ride up one side and down the trough of the next, until we slide through a pass, get stopped again and climb out on top of the bus.

Soldiers are all around us, walking back and forth with their bayonets, poking into bags, but there in the distance, behind a valley of crushed green manicured like the fairways of the finest private club in Georgia, lies the jeweled city of Katmandu and just beyond it, the great white ridge of the Himalayas.

In one magnificent vista we have a subtropical valley lying in a protected basin at 4,400 feet and the highest peaks on earth, Gosainthan and Gauri Shankar, Langtang and Melungtse, a gap-toothed row of fangs leading over to Cho-Oyo, Lhotse and Everest, the top of the world at 29,028 feet. Right now the numbers mean nothing. It's the crisp air that takes one's breath away, the impossible blue, the thought of having lived long enough and been lucky enough to have seen the ultimate, a sight that cannot be equaled or surpassed, even in the imagination. You can take your mind's eye and every bit of beauty you've ever hoped to see and fit it all comfortably inside this little scene. We've come all this way, twelve thousand miles on a straight line from Philadelphia (if there were such a thing) and now we know why.

Last winter when Cheryl started talking about going to Nepal I told her to shut up, told her she was crazy. She practically had to drag me out on the road, but as I look past the spires and rooftops of Katmandu to those incredible mountains I realize she was right. She's been right all along, if it weren't for her I'd probably be back in Boston, hammering bangles right now. With all that this trip has meant to me, I'll be hard-pressed to repay her.

There are two cities in Katmandu. The first is modern and spacious, with wide avenues, fancy restaurants, parks, boutiques, high-priced hotels, banks, and the inevitable American Express office, with a huge old tree behind it, filled with hundreds of hanging bats. This is the royal city of the King, supposedly an old Harvard buddy of mine, from Quincy House.

I can't say that I recognize him from his picture on the one-rupee note, but then we never ran with the same crowd, and I doubt that he wore his monarch's regalia into Harvard Square. I think I would have remembered the commodore's hat with the scrambled eggs on the brim, the white cape, and that curious insignia consisting of a Star of David with a sword or cross rising out of the top, a combination of Christian and Hebrew National baloney that is mystifying in this Buddhist stronghold.

The King is nervous these days, as evidenced by the roadblocks on the way in, and with good reason. He's caught in a squeeze between India and China, under pressure from the Chinese (the architects of Nepal's major road system, constructed to give them easy access south) to crack down on the last of those armed Tibetans, who stubbornly refuse to let bygones be bygones.

To prepare for any eventuality, someone very high up is buying insurance, conducting a brisk business on the black market, where small boys run their money-changing operations with virtually no attempt at concealment. They pay up to forty per cent more than the banks for liquid currencies, Deutschmarks, dollars, pounds and francs, with a heavy side traffic in yens.

As we get off the bus in the new city, we latch onto the first boy who speaks up loud and clear in English, saying, "I will pay for your taxi." His taxi turns out to be a rickshaw which he pedals himself, launching the tricycle into the old section, its bell ringing madly past thousands of sheep and goats, bleating in terror.

It's harvest time in the kingdom of Nepal, festival and slaughter time. The streets are hung with banners and lanterns. Big garlands of red, white, yellow and blue blossoms are strung on wooden racks. The statues and idols are daubed with fresh coats of paint. The whole town is decked out, rouged and looking at its best.

In Darbar Square in the center of town, the life-sized monkey-god Hanuman is seated on a stone plinth with a garden umbrella over his head, his body wrapped in a blood-red shroud that obscures his features and turns his whole face and mouth into a howling hole. Demons do a dance of death on the skulls of the unrighteous. Bronze gods with many arms wrap their legs around adoring maidens, sunk up to the hilt on the sanctified lingams, chewing on their ravishers' lips. Little carved couples and *ménages à trois* fornicate, copulate, masturbate and carry on on the cornice-work of a prominent temple, exhorting the townsfolk to do the same, to fill up the earth with their issue, although for much of what they're doing, issue is not the issue at all.

Open sewers line the streets, filled with mud and this year's crop of barefoot bare-assed children, oblivious to the fact in which they figure so prominently, that Nepal's disease rate is among the highest on earth. This is the real Katmandu, a city thriving on a dung heap. Women kneel at dawn, paying homage at their favorite shrines, painting the faces of little bas-relief monkey-gods with orange and red powder, anointing them with oil, balancing rose petals on their shoulders in acts of great delicacy and grace. Just behind them, rickshaws loaded with the carcasses of freshly butchered buffalo drip thick dark blood, and entrails steam like pudding in the early morning mist.

In France I kept hearing well-traveled members of the bourgeoisie complaining that the hippies are ruining Katmandu, but nothing could be further from the truth. It's the rich who are changing things. They're the ones who hang out in the king's sterile half city. It's for them that the great chains will be constructing luxury hotels at the bases of once inviolate mountains, so that tourists too lazy to walk in, even with the help of Sherpas, will be able to sit back in Bell helicopters and get ferried to balconies to sip their gin and tonics.

The rich walk through the old section and see only hippies, because somehow they have this notion that they're the only ones who should be allowed. They want plush red-carpet tours to fairylands of native simplicity. The longhairs aren't ruining Katmandu, they're right down there with the people. Their money goes right into the pockets of the mom-and-pop proprietors. It might seem strange to people who have just stepped off a plane that Katmandu boasts no fewer than a dozen pie shops, where western travelers can chow down on cherry cobbler and listen to the Rolling Stones, but if they had been out on the road long enough they'd understand. We've earned our cake. We'll eat it, too. Most of us have been starving for months, and we've finally reached our reward. Katmandu is a vacation paradise, even for the poor, after the incredible strain of Western Asia.

The people are handsome, friendly and open. The children may be barefoot, but they're not beggars. Everyone gets enough to eat. The men and women aren't walled off from each other as they were in the Moslem countries, and even in repressed Hindu India, but loose and easy. They hold hands on the street. Play games with their eyes. Their daily lives seem touched with the same Tantric spirit that imbues their art with such erotic grace.

Instead of privation, there's a tremendous profusion here. The city is constantly flowering and falling into decay. It springs up overnight with new forms, while restoring and preserving its pagodas and 2,000-year-old temples. The windows are carved into peacocks, women sing as they thresh the wheat in courtyards, and thatched roofs glow in the sun. We spend a delightful week feeding up and idling around, fortifying ourselves for the adventure meant to cap off our travels in Asia, the Himalayan trek.

As exciting as Katmandu can be, we're looking forward to getting out of the city and moving through the world on our own power. We never did make it into the hills of Afghanistan or Pakistan, but this should more than make up for it. Unlike the expeditionary armies which mount their million-dollar assaults, the only provisions Cheryl and I will be carrying are a few jars of peanut butter and some protein supplement for midmorning snacks. Other than that we'll be depending on a compass, a map, and the ability and willingness of villagers to respond to the phrases from our guide book (all the Nepali you ever thought you'd need to know):

Yaha sutna pauncha? Is there any place to sleep here?
Yaha khana pauncha? Is there any place to eat here?

Armed with the above and a trekking permit from His Majesty's Ministry of Home Affairs, we're all set.

We had hoped to do a trek we'd heard about all the way across Asia, the Pokhara-to-Jomosom trek, along the southern and western slopes of Annapurna, a hike of reportedly unequaled beauty, but the Jomosom trek is temporarily off limits because of those Tibetan hill people the King's been fighting, who've been ripping off travelers out beyond the protection of the law. Tribes of brigand-warriors are an old tradition out here. Asian merchants used to travel in large bands to stand up to them. That kind of highway robbery was seen as honorable, as opposed to low-life thievery, for which everyone had contempt. Although it's nice to know that someone is keeping up the old ways, we have to fish around quickly for a new route.

Since we don't have enough time for what would ideally be our first choice, the Everest trek, which demands at least a month, we settle on a little jaunt of over a hundred miles round trip through a region northwest of Katmandu leading from the lowlands around Trisuli Bazaar to the glaciers of the Langtang range. Our disappointment over the change in treks fades quickly as we pore over the map obtained from the Sherpa Society, looking at all the little dotted contour lines, not yet fully aware of what those thousand-foot intervals will do to us as we cross and recross them on our way up and down the ridges.

After stashing all our nonessentials, we report at dawn for the first leg of our ramble, by bus along that Chinese highway to the kickoff point at Trisuli. Cheryl and I give up our seats and convince them to let us ride on the roof, where we settle back on soft bundles of dry goods, propping ourselves up for a birdseye's view of the loveliest country on earth.

Intense gradations of green from the terraced slopes fill our eyes. It's too green, too great, too vast to be believed. We climb up above Katmandu and get our first look at the Langtang range, trying to make sense of the fact that it will take us a full day by bus just to reach our starting point.

The farther we go, the narrower the road becomes. As the afternoon progresses, past checkpoint after checkpoint, the paved surface leaves off and we wind up on dirt, rolling past road crews of women and children who sit all day, reducing rocks to gravel with tiny hammers. The vehicle pitches and sways as it rounds narrow switchbacks undercut by streams which have eroded the roadbeds, leaving just enough room for four wheels, forcing the driver to back up two and three times just to negotiate the corners. Suddenly the roof doesn't seem like such a great place after all, except that by being here we might be able to leap off and save ourselves when the whole thing goes tumbling into the valleys below.

We hang onto the baggage railing as the road becomes even more hazardous. The bus is creeping along at about three miles an hour, bucking like a mule. The hills loom up about us in increasing darkness as word filters back that we're five miles from Trisuli. The last five miles will take more than two hours.

The black night, the hills, and the land falling off to our right have opened up a new void which we can't perceive with any of our five senses, although it scares us numb. The mountains were beautiful to look at from a distance, uplifting, but now that we're out here in them, we suddenly realize how outmatched we are. We've been looking forward to this trek for months, but as the bus labors into the shadow of the mountain all we feel is dread. The scale is more than we bargained for, more than we can comprehend, so unbelievably immense that anyone who doesn't feel himself trembling the first time he enters it, probably doesn't have a soul to lose.

LOG OF THE TREK

Day One

We spend the night on the floor of a dirty hotel, harassed by mosquitoes, forget about breakfast and take off up a long hill running the length of Trisuli Bazaar, to the floor of the valley above. Trisuli, a market town, is in a huge sink, only 1,760 feet above sea level, low enough to collect the runoff from thousands of square miles of mountain drainage.

We hike through the first valley, across a metal bridge that seems farther than the three miles marked on the map. After all the travel, our legs are far from strong. The sun breaks out as we wind through the lowlands, past two-story red-clay huts with straw roofs, across the river basin to the first real hill at Betrawati.

Turning the corner into the upper part of the village, we stumble past four men holding the kicking body of a young water buffalo, its head lying off to one side, eyes open, tongue lolling, blood streaming out the thick neck into a bucket. We just missed the ritual chop, almost heard the thud. Now the blood and those last little hoofbeats raised in resistance. Women and children look on from across the way. We press our hands together and bow, saying "Namaste," the traditional greeting of peace and welcome, aware that we've disturbed them.

The sun is so intense that the lowlands seem to steam. Every so often as we march uphill a waterfall appears and we jump right in. We're not alone on the trail this morning, there's a large party of French alpinists, about fifty of them, kind of a Club Med with crampons. Their women jump into the streams with us and put on a fantastic wet T-shirt show to the great approval of their barefoot porters, who carry fifty-pound baskets supported only by canvas straps across their foreheads. Even without shoes (the most successful of them have thin tennis sneakers) the porters outwalk everyone.

We hike all morning, stopping for protein supplement mixed with iodine-laced water and dried milk, continue through the afternoon, then reach the way station at Ramche just after the sun dips behind the hills. The air gets cold, our sweat dries and our muscles get tight. We've come only fifteen miles on the map and 4,500 feet, but it was up and down all day, and Cheryl and I are both exhausted. The sunset is diffused in yellow crystals of cloud feathered into the sky. Food and lodging cost three rupees. We get hot chocolate from the French and cold comfort on a straw manger.

Day Two

Rain patters on the roof, but we're soon on our way, because we'd like to get ahead of the French. The trail is excellent. Trekking is a major industry in Nepal. In the off season the government hires the porters and locals to work on the paths. You don't need hundred-dollar boots with Vibram soles out here, my little Clark Treks are doing just fine.

The valley is filled with fog, so we can't see the other side, but up close the rocks are alive. Intense greens drift off into gray. Trees thrust silhouettes into empty abysses. We walk all day in a muffled hush. Calm. Quiet. No more jokes from the Gallic joy-boys. We hike thirteen miles with a net rise of less than a thousand feet, but once again we've climbed it five times over. Dhunche is a small town at a crossroads where we find a loft, a meal, and shelter from the storm.

Day Three

Dawn breaks with a clear sky and what we missed the day before is suddenly revealed—the magnificent soft-yellow peaks of the Langtang range in early morning light rise out of the blue depths of glaciers stretching thousands of feet below. Our first order of business is a thousand foot descent to the Trisuli river, then a back-and-forth march up the other side, all in all an hour and a half of hiking and switchbacks with little more than a quarter mile gained.

We approach the first village, Bhargu, where the smoke of breakfast fires hangs over the rooftops. Three men squat on a platform above one house, making their daily offering of *tsampa* (roast barley flour) and butter. White flags flutter in the breeze. We stop in a hut and score some delicious fresh *dahi* (yogurt) with a thick skin, then push on down the river valley, marked at intervals by stone pyramids whose tiers are fronted with flat rocks beautifully carved with prayers, mandalas and Tibetan symbols. The weathering and delicate lichens growing on the sculpted stones give one the feeling that the prayers have been accepted. They're part of the natural world, a fitting tribute to every tourist and shepherd who made it up the last two thousand feet, or is facing the next three thousand down to the valley floor.

We're out of the lowlands now. The Nepalese of Trisuli and Betrawati have been replaced by people who've poured over the passes from the highlands of Tibet. We pause for tea at the Tibetan village of Syabrubensi, across a rope bridge strung over the river. The people are handsome and radiant. We've passed through a dozen countries and all kinds of cultures on our way into these hills, but nowhere have we met a race to compare with the Tibetans. Everywhere in Asia we've been stared at and treated as freaks, curiosities or objects of derision, but these Tibetans don't take us as Westerners, or Easterners or anything in between, they look us in the eyes and take us as we come. We're people. So are they. They don't bristle or get weird when a woman walks by, there's an equality between the sexes in their culture that extends even to the right to sex itself. For all the bandits and marauding tribes that once roamed the Tibetan hills, a woman who traveled needed only fear for her belongings. The bandits had women of their own to satisfy their needs.

Despite the loss of their homeland, the Tibetans are at peace with themselves. One sees the mountains and clouds reflected in their eyes and senses why. Life is difficult out here, but each time they crest a hill they're reminded of its worth. They accept our presence and serve us tea, laughing at our bedraggled state, but with such genuine good humor that they don't make us feel any worse. That laughter is as refreshing as the sweet buttered tea itself. It gives us energy to carry on.

It's only two o'clock, so we decide to push on to Khanjung, just two and a half miles on the map, but straight uphill. Day's end sees us hiking into darkness, really cold in a thick fog and high wind. We come across an old woman with a huge goiter (their diet is completely deficient in iodine), who directs us to a villager who takes on travelers.

We approach him saying, "*Yaha sutna pauncha? Yaha khana pauncha?*" and he holds up three fingers in reply. Three rupees each. With a black market rate of fourteen to the dollar, that makes it something less than a quarter apiece for room and board.

We enter his house and squat on the wood floor under the low roof as our host makes a fire. Smoke soon rises into the rafters, heating the place, but leaving a black residue in the air that contributes in no small way to the high rate of tuberculosis. A few pot-bellied stoves and a bit of iodized salt would do wonders for this country. The Peace Corps volunteer down in Syabrubensi, a terrific young guy with an agricultural degree from the University of Delaware who's revered by the local villagers for the work he's done to help them vary their diets, told us he's tried to obtain iodine and other simple necessaries from the government of Nepal and from our embassy, but that he couldn't get any cooperation and wound up buying the things himself.

I heard another story from a Peace Corps staff member in Katmandu, that the Red Cross had to bribe government officials to bring in a helicopter to use on medical rescue missions. The King is well entrenched, but by 1980 even he will be challenged in the streets by more than 30,000 demonstrators protesting his failure to distribute some of the wealth brought in by tourism. It's pathetic when you consider how very little some of these people need to turn their lives around.

The old man, our host, tends his fire and grins, throwing cups of uncooked rice into a pot, holding up a few red peppers and throwing half as many as he'd like into the *dahl.* When done, the yellow curried lentils will still set our mouths aflame, sending us diving into the rice to turn off the heat. Prices out here may be cheap, but the people aren't. Although our diet on the trail is simple, not once are we served any less than we need to satisfy our hunger.

Day Four

The ill-advised push to Khanjung left us hurting, but we start early again and continue the ascent past another small village, until we turn the corner at the top of the ridge, more than nine thousand feet above sea level and three thousand above the Langtang river, a raging glacial torrent leading directly down the mountain from where we hope to wind up.

The view is extraordinary. A twosome of young Japanese

women, slim and elegant in up-to-date skiwear, high socks and knickers, hike past us with binoculars and cameras while three porters lug their provisions. I'm convinced it's better to go empty-handed into these hills. We're getting closer to the people here than anywhere else we've been, and it couldn't be happening in a better place. The Tibetans have a long tradition of accepting travelers into their midst. The Tibetan monk Thubten Jigme Norbu, brother of the Dalai Lama, explains:

> [This hospitality] is the reason in a city like Lhasa you will find no hotels or restaurants. The pilgrim or trader has only to knock on a door and ask for food and shelter and it will be freely given. Some town dwellers feel that if a guest stays too long, say for a year, they are entitled to ask some recompense; it depends on their means. But even the poorest will open their doors to any who ask.*

Armed only with our faith and protein supplement, we walked off blithely into the hills, but the people are not letting us down. Would we interrupt our routine back home and invite in any Tibetans who showed up in costume at our door? Not likely. Their performance, customary or not, is remarkable.

A morning skirting the shoulder of the mountain takes us to Syarpa, where we've been warned not to bed down because of fleas. Tibetan nomads generally sleep outside, even in the winter. To stay warm, most of them snuggle up to their animals. The big dogs they keep around to scare off intruders are welcome night partners, as are sheep. Although yaks are warm and affectionate (as anyone who's kissed one will readily testify), they tend to kick a lot and are better left in the fields. These people of Syarpa aren't nomads, but they do have fleas, and I wouldn't want to guess as to their nocturnal habits. They have a strange look about them that suggests the possibility of a little inbreeding. Tibetans often practice polyandry, in which one woman marries a whole set of brothers, but

* Thubten Jigme Norbu and Colin Turnbull, *Tibet, Its History, Religion and People.*

these folks may have carried the whole thing one step further.

Cheryl and I walk past a group of small boys tossing coins, entertaining their fathers and uncles, into a house, where we ask for lunch. One of the men drifts in and sits down to look at Cheryl, as an attractive dark-haired teen-ager who may or may not be only slightly plump beneath her gowns prepares our meal. When we've finished and are sitting back with tea, the guy proposes a swap.

"Sure," he says in Tibetan, "why not? You take her"—the plump girl smiles—"and I take her"—he points at Cheryl.

"Hey, Cheryl," I say, "how about it? Wanna trade? This guy says he's in love."

Cheryl gets up and walks out the door, surprisingly unamused. I shrug. He shrugs, and my nubile little teen-ager gives me a wistful smile as I bow out onto the trail. It's too bad, it might have been interesting, and it certainly would have expanded the local gene pool.

The terrain drops off two thousand feet from Syarpa to a dense mountain rain forest. Cheryl's out in front, not talking to me, which I attribute to my roving eye, but when I pull up beside her I realize she's on the verge of tears.

"I can't walk," she says, "it's my leg." We sit down on the side of the path in the cool shadow of tall trees covered with moss. I try to massage her leg, but it doesn't help. The problem is that Cheryl's been wearing these ridiculous Earth Shoes. The selling point of these things is that the heel is a half inch lower than the toes, supposedly recreating the gait of a bare foot in sand. That may be fine if you're back in Harvard Square, running down the beach in your mind, but it doesn't quite make it out here, where the poor girl's been battling the toughest hills in the world with a built-in half-inch disadvantage. Cheryl's tendons are stretched out so badly her legs are inflamed, and intense pains are shooting up the backs of her knees to her thighs.

We're at the bottom of the valley, three miles below the next village. I wrap her legs in ace bandages, hoist her pack on top of my own and start off playing the hero, strong and silent, while under my breath I'm muttering a steady stream of what sounds like prayer, but is really an incantation against the hippie capitalist devils who thought they had a better idea for footwear.

The forest is insanely beautiful, lush and moist at eight thousand feet with the river raging beside us and bizarre trees dripping soft, furry, copper-colored vines. Damp smells rise from the pine needles and bark; everything is overgrown and slippery. We scramble over rocks and huge fallen tree trunks, past waterfalls and calling birds into dense silent interiors, climbing and descending, weaving our way through.

My legs are shaky under the weight, but I'm enjoying this double duty much more than Cheryl, who is intermittently crying with pain and humiliation. I tell her that I don't mind, but that's not the point. She's been looking forward to this trek for a long time and doesn't like the idea that she's pulled up lame.

Late in the afternoon we emerge from the forest into one of the most beautiful mountain valleys on God's earth, 10,500 feet, the village of Ghora Tabela. Clouds ring the peaks on all sides, but the eye of the sky is open and the sun beats down, smiling and warm. We've made it. Nothing could be more glorious than these mountain flowers behind this rock wall, those two white horses in the pasture by that stream. Up above, sharp vertical crevices etched in black rock are dusted with snow. Immense slopes across the way are upholstered with aspen, glowing golden in the late fall.

The light and color are so resplendent we grow dizzy. The air's so thin I'd be floating were it not for the two packs, which grow appreciably lighter as we walk the last quarter mile to the wood structures just above the rise.

A young Westerner hanging out by the side of the road gets up to greet us, introducing himself as Doug, a Canadian. He apologizes for not helping me with the packs, explaining that he's been laid up nearly a week with an attack of pleurisy, an inflammation of the lining of the lungs brought on by extreme exertion in the high altitudes. He does offer, however, to bring us to the lama, to see if he can get us a place to stay.

We follow him past a series of one-room hovels down on the street to a large wooden hall set back off the road. Cheryl and I are nervous as we wait on the porch, because Doug's told us that the lama doesn't accept just anyone. We will have to pass his karmic test. I rid my mind of all evil and focus on the eightfold path, silent, humble and hungry. Cheryl's all set, she's been praying all the way up the hill. Her vibration must have preceded her, for the monk takes one step out of the door, looks down on us and nods. Doug beams and shows us in.

The lamasery consists of one big room with a dozen beds along the walls and a large open space around a square metal stove in the center of the floor. It's warm inside. We plunk down with an involuntary shudder. Cheryl's beat, absolutely incapable of going any further, and after four days of incredibly hard hiking, if I don't get some rest, I'll wind up the same.

Day Five

Last night's dinner was potatoes and cabbage. I thought I died and went to heaven. We had fresh-baked bread, cheese and yak butter from the Swiss-built factory at Kyangin Ghompa, eight miles up the road. We sat around and talked with Doug, then went to bed as the lama, a slight and delightful man, performed his evening devotion, lighting candles and chanting. He was joined by his companions, a half dozen brawny fellows who, we suspect, are ex-soldiers in the Tibetan resistance. The whole evening mellowed out as the flames in the stove died down and went dark.

Around 3 A.M. I wake in my down bag, legs aching in the cold. This isn't just cold, it's a set of teeth that sinks into your knees. It holds on like a Tibetan mastiff and won't let go no matter how you toss and shake, so that from three o'clock until dawn there's nothing to do but wait. Mountain climbers who come up against the killing cold past 18,000 feet don't even try to sleep without drugs. They take a couple of pills to retire and a few more to get going the next day. There's none of this Rocky Mountain organic stuff out here, these are the Himalayas and anybody with a natural brain in his natural head wouldn't even try to climb them. We're not that high—at such an altitude, that is—that we need synthetics, but the cold is creeping down from those heights, seeking its lowest level, which is just under my back about six inches off the floor.

Three o'clock, four. Four-thirty, five. Five-thirty, and although my head's buried in my mummy hood, I hear a quiet rustling in the center of the floor. The lama is up, chanting in a soft voice, shoving kindling in the open grate, lighting a match, saying a prayer for the flame. As the dried leaves begin to crackle, he picks up a broom and gently sweeps the boards, keeping the dust down, chanting the whole time in a little singsong that fills the air. By the time he's been to every corner of the room, the flame is high and the heat is starting to seep out. He lays his broom against the wall, smiles and turns to everyone, fully aware that we're all awake, saying, "OK, people, rise and shine."

He and his men gather for another chant, while Cheryl, Doug and I huddle at the stove. The icy blue outside warms a bit and we step out, stamping our feet, watching the peach rays of early morning light creeping down the mountain tops. I take a cold drink from a stream diverted through a pipe from a nearby source. For the first time since arriving in Asia we can trust the water, we can see where it's coming from, there's nothing between us and the mountain.

We return to the room for a breakfast of hot chocolate, protein supplement, toast and butter, and by the time we're done the lama's boys are already hard at work constructing a trekkers hotel across the road, meant to house travelers such as we in the near future. The men are using modern construction techniques. They are clearly not your run-of-the-mill peasants.

By midmorning I'm down the road, lying out on a large rock

in the warm sun just above the forest, when I get a funny feeling that I'm being watched, look over my shoulder and see a pair of coal black eyes under the bushy eyebrows of a manlike gray langur, about three feet high, looking for all the world like the missing link's younger brother. He scouts me out, hops a rock, says a few words in monkey and is joined by his mate, then his cousin, and soon a whole troupe of these furry white creatures is peering from the brush. We face off silently for about ten minutes until I shift to scratch myself and they scatter. I sense that this whole valley is under the lama's protection. Even the wild beasts know they're welcome here. Himalayan monkeys at 10,500 feet—it's a totally unexpected treat, adding to the magical feeling of this place.

Day Six

Another day in the warm sun, doing nothing. Cheryl's legs are mending.

Day Seven

Up at dawn, we get an hour and a half of hiking in before the sun hits us down on the valley floor, but even with the sun out it never really warms up. The wind is whipping off the ice as we push past the villages of Chomki, Langtang, Mundum and Singdum, where a number of travelers have been robbed. The people of Singdum are a little strange, you can sense something's wrong just by looking at them. It's not all that surprising; at this altitude even the vegetables are stunted.

We're moving up on 12,000 feet, but the mountains still dwarf everything. The word Himalayan is taking on its full meaning now. Tiny streams seen at a distance turn out to be impassable, unthinkable. The boulders are ten times huger than one imagines, larger than anything we've ever seen or dreamed of, strewn among others like them across immense glacial fields, wide curving rivers of rocks hundreds of yards wide, many thousands of feet long. White linen banners on long poles outside the villages flutter in the breeze, each ripple sending a prayer skyward. We follow them up, up a staggering distance, 12,000 feet more, leaning over backwards to see the sky. These mountains are like mountains piled on mountains. The higher one climbs, the larger they loom.

About four o'clock in the afternoon we arrive at our destination, Kyangin Ghompa. *Ghompa* translates as "a dwelling in solitude," an apt description, for in this case Kyangin stands on an open plateau before the last pass leading into Tibet. It's ringed on three sides by high mountains, Langtang Lirung (23,771) directly behind us, with the desolate wastes of Kangya La across the way. Those French alpinists who'd started out with us along the trail can be seen down below, hands on hips, looking up at the forbidding Kangya La pass, which has just been shut down by the first winter snows. Their faithful Sherpas are with them, but despite their reputation for intrepidity, the Sherpas are urging that the French amateurs choose the better part of valor.

"*Sacre bleu!* What miserable fortune!" say the Frenchmen, stomping around, but you know they're relieved and I can't say that I blame them. I have no desire to scale the heights. Neither have I porter, nor boots, nor crampons, nor pickaxe, nor anything to prove. We've made it. The blue-tinged snows of the glacier begin less than fifty yards behind us. We're standing on a rock wall constructed around the compound of a small monastery, three or four buildings with slate roofs, surrounded by prayer flags and little stone stupas. A pair of Australians step out of a woodshed, announcing that they're about to start down, saying we can take their place for the night. No one seems to be around, so we drop our packs inside the door and start down the hill.

The center of the valley floor consists of an airstrip beside a huge yak corral with tiny stone huts for the herders who bring up their animals in the late spring. Next to the corral stands a neatly built Swiss-sponsored yak-cheese factory. Cheryl and I hurry down, get the guardian to open up, and buy ourselves a slab of yak butter and several pounds of a semi-soft cheese something like Danish Havarti, aging in huge rounds. We pay the man, step out the door, tear off pieces of the rich, bland *fromage* and stuff ourselves until we're sick, then wade back, bloated, to lie down by the monastery walls, watching the sun set. A Tibetan nun steps out, looks us over and tells us it will be all right to pass the night, then she disappears and we start arranging things, for it will soon be dark.

A pair of Japanese climbers belonging to a set of tents down in the valley stops by for a chat. They, too, had been looking forward to attempting the pass at Kangya La, but have given up, just like the French. As we're talking, Cheryl and I attempt to get a fire going to warm up the shack, but before long the room is filled with thick black smoke and the Japanese are staggering out, coughing. It's not entirely our fault, the wood is soaked, but I know they're wondering about the two Americans who can't even raise a decent flame.

Eventually we give up on the fire and bed down for the night. It's so damned cold on the floor of this little hut that Cheryl and I wind up lying one on top of the other, holding on through our sleeping bags, but nothing helps. I remind myself of stories I've read about anchorite monks practicing *tumo,* the generation of heat on an ascetic diet of white rice and meditation. There are monks who go naked all winter in Himalayan caves. There are competitions among students, in which they break holes in the river ice, dip sheets into the freezing water, then wrap them around themselves, trying to determine who can dry more sheets in this fashion in a single night. Right now I doubt if I could dry a handkerchief with a blowtorch.

I get up in the middle of the night to look around and find the moon, nearly full, riding the crest of the peaks, illuminating the whole valley with a milk-white glow. Orion is so near and clear you can almost reach out and disarm him.

Day Eight

Cheryl's legs are acting up again in the cold, so she stays back at camp, venturing out just far enough to grab a few photographs, while I spend the morning scrambling across the glacial moraines. One could pass weeks up here. The country offers as much adventure as one has nerve, but I'm satisfied.

Next time we'll trek up to Everest, push up to 19,000 feet. It's nice to have something to look forward to, but I really don't feel that I've missed a thing. We're standing by our hut, thinking those thoughts one thinks when he's about to leave some place that has meant a lot, and that he knows he'll never see again, when the Tibetan nun steps out of her room with the lama to look down at the valley with us.

He's a young man, handsome and tall in a red robe and she's an attractive, trim woman in her early thirties. I suspect that their relationship is not entirely platonic, for abstinence is not required or expected of all Tibetan lamas, but celibate or not, they make a fine couple.

I'm busy trying to come up with some thought or insight to carry away from Kyangin Ghompa, to take down with me from these almost unearthly heights, when the nun steps up, slaps me on the back and says, "What's the matter with you?"

You may be wondering how I know what it is that she's saying, or how I've known what anyone's been saying all along the road. It may have something to do with what the linguistic philosophers call an innate human grammar. I've stood on a street corner in Katmandu, listening to a storyteller entertain a crowd of fifty, and found myself laughing when they laughed, being scared when they were scared, recognizing all the personality types, the miser, the buffoon, the crank—in short, following the story without the slightest idea of details. Language itself is only part of what's happening when someone is talking, and there's a common logic to the way the words come out in any language that lets you know what they mean without even stopping to think. What the nun is telling me now is simple.

"What do you mean, what's the matter with me?" I ask.

"Look at you, all hunched up, your brow all furrowed, working so hard at who-knows-what . . ." she imitates me, standing there, searching for the meaning of the world. "Now look at the lama," she says, "look at him, look at his eyes, how clear they are, how relaxed and proud he is . . ." He's standing behind her, arms crossed, gazing out over his magnificent valley, the rocks which are his flock, the clear air which is the pasture of his mind, then, "Stop slumping!" she says; and she whacks me in the back again. "Be like him . . . *stand up straight!*"

(Pause.)

That's it? I came halfway around the world just to hear some Tibetan nun of questionable morals tell me to stand up straight? That's all? That's the revelation?

Maybe there's something to it. My mother, God knows, has been saying the same thing for years. What is a man profited, after all, if he shall gain the whole world, but his posture's no good? What do I expect? Enlightenment? People have been known to take pilgrimages from one end of Tibet to the other, measuring themselves along the ground, prostrating themselves every inch of the way just to atone for their sins. What should such fellows as I do crawling between earth and heaven?

I look up for something more, but the nun just smiles and nods. You heard me, kid, it's right out in front of you. There's nothing more to say, just stop reaching, throw back your shoulders like the lama and take a look around, you might not pass this way again. Stand up straight, that's all she wrote. The cold air penetrates my lungs. Like the man said, it's all downhill from here.

Day Nine

We hike back to the monastery at Ghora Tabela, spend a warm night, then take off with our Canadian friend Doug, who's hoping his pleurisy will let up enough for him to make the descent. About ten o'clock in the morning three porters hurry past us bearing golden Buddhas in wicker baskets on their backs. Since there is nothing like a temple between here and the glaciers, they have obviously come from Tibet and are smuggling treasures out from under the Chinese.

Cheryl's legs are worse than ever. To ease the pain she has to walk backward down the hills. Two French women from the ersatz expedition trail Doug and me for a few miles, making comments they don't think we understand about our *belles fesses* (pretty little bottoms). We make it all the way down to Syabrubensi, at the confluence of the Langtang and Trisuli rivers, where Cheryl gets a massage from a woman trainer for the French national ski team. Doug's chest is hurting, so we decide to lay up for another day.

Day Ten

Cheryl hobbles over to the hot springs, hot rocks dripping strange colors and slimy yellow moss, where she sits for hours in the shallow pools, soaking. Back in town, we drink tea and eat cookies from the general store. Night falls; it's a full moon. The Peace Corps guy comes out and reports that he's heard it via BBC that Muhammad Ali has beaten George Foreman for the heavyweight crown in Zaire. The moon was just coming out in Africa when Ali rope-a-doped and laid him out in the eighth and now it's here. Same moon, same night, same sky, same earth. Doug walks up to tell us that his chest is killing him and that he has hired a porter, a local man who's hiking down the hill, anyway, and is eager to pick up a little work.

Day Eleven

Our Tibetan porter takes Doug's pack, most of Cheryl's and some of my own. I feel guilty about heaping him up this way, but he says he's fine, and lightening my load, even by a little, makes the hike down considerably more pleasurable. We can hardly keep up with him as it is, and within a few hours have nicknamed him "Iron Man." His short legs pump like pistons up the long hills. He waits for us to catch up, then drives right off again.

Iron Man, in his middle thirties, has soft almond eyes and a leathery face that breaks easily into a beautiful smile. With his help we reach Dhunche by lunch and push on to Thare, where we sleep in a crowded little house with a woman and her two grown daughters. Thanks to our porter, the three days we've allotted from Syabrubensi will be covered in two.

Day Twelve

Last day of the trek. It's hot and humid again as we hit the lowlands, but we are treated to the sight of a pair of young beauties bathing naked in the river. With five miles to go we stop at a *chai* shop, get some tea, and ask for one of the grapefruit they've got stacked up against the wall, huge things the size of yellow bowling balls with pulpy skins three inches thick. You slice the skins with a knife, then peel them off in sections, revealing the fruit.

I don't know whether it's a result of deprivation from the high altitudes, or a quality of these grapefruit themselves, amazing specimens whose cells are yellow spikes an inch long, but the first bite sends a jolt of food energy through my system like nothing I've ever experienced. My fatigue vanishes in an instant and I can't wait to get back onto the trail.

The three of us go bouncing down the road to a small reservoir, where we strip to shorts and jump in for a swim. Several Nepalese gather to laugh as Iron Man sits back, a look of utter satisfaction on his face, "Crazy foreigners," he says with a grin, but I sense he'd like to be right in there with us.

We make it into Trisuli Bazaar for the night, wake early the next morning and hurry down to the bus depot to buy our tickets and find a place on the roof. As we're settling in, an American hippie gets involved in a dispute with Iron Man, telling him in a really insulting manner to move out of his way. He doesn't know that Iron Man could break him like a pane of glass, but the Tibetan doesn't say a word, because down off the mountain he's out of his element. It's with great pleasure that I come to our friend's defense, telling the hippie he can move his own ass or take it up with me. Iron Man looks over and thanks me with his eyes. I settle back on my pack, take out my harp and blow a little country blues as the bus rolls back to Katmandu.

Going Home

WE RUN INTO RICHARD, who has just come in by bus from Delhi, and spend a few days together in Katmandu, shopping and hanging around the pie shops. Checking in at American Express, we find a letter from Marie, who says she'll be arriving in the middle of the month. Richard is planning on the Everest trek, so I sell him my down jacket, then Cheryl and I take off by bus for Pokhara for a short trek around Annapurna and the even more dramatic heights of Machhapuchre.

We spend two days floating around beautiful Lake Phewa, which even in November is a balmy 82 degrees. On the shore, young girls pick poinsettia blossoms from large trees while their brothers splash around the fountains with bright brass water jugs.

We kick back with a bunch of French hippies, grateful that we've learned the language just well enough to hang in on their conversations. The French have a miserable reputation in many places, because many of them seem to get into drugs in a big way and wind up among the inevitable casualties of the road, but I'm usually delighted to bump into them, to practice my tongue, partaking of their terrible cool. One little compliment on my accent is enough to have me eating out of their hands.

Cheryl and I are all set for our mini-trek, but early the first morning, before we're halfway out of town, I get an attack in my stomach and collapse at the side of the road, doubled up with pain. Cheryl helps me down the street to a hotel, where

I lie groaning, convinced I've got appendicitis and that I'll wind up undergoing surgery out here with a rusty knife on a table covered with yak hairs. She goes running out for help and comes back twenty minutes later with a druggist (there doesn't seem to be a doctor), who pokes me in the gut, nods, then walks out, telling her to follow him; then she returns after an eternity with a bottle of sweet, mint-tasting liquid prescribed for cases of extreme dehydration.

It happens to a lot of gringos out here. We get so paranoid about drinking the local water that we subsist solely on Coca-Cola or tea. Since neither of these substances is particularly good for us, we take to drinking less and less, until one day we run dry and double up, convinced we've been poisoned, when it's really what we haven't drunk that's led to our downfall. Dehydration is actually quite serious and the pain is acute. I'm lucky Cheryl was able to find someone who knew what he was doing. Two sips and the knots start to unravel, but we have to give up on the idea of another trek.

We return to Katmandu with one thing left to do. All along we've been saving our money. We've spent less than seventy-five bucks each on transportation all the way from Istanbul to Nepal, but now we're prepared to shell out one third that amount, the staggering sum of twenty-five bucks each, for a one-hour hop on Royal Nepali Airlines, a dawn run up the rim of the giants.

The plane takes off at seven and pierces the cloud cover, exposing the white tips of the Himalayas, gleaming with a crazed intensity. At the first sight I'm jumping out of my seat, heart pounding, pointing out the window as if anyone needed to be told to look. We're in a forty-seat, two-engine aircraft at nineteen thousand feet, but still those colossal heights beam down on us. There's Langtang, where we trekked, Gosainthan at 26,150 feet—we cruise from one impossibly beautiful mountain to the next, down the entire range of the high Himalayas.

When the clouds thin we can see down to the valley floor, rising from intense green through every shade of earth to desolate white. I'm glad we saved this trip for last. Now that we've been out in the hills, we know what it's worth. Just when I think there's no more to be seen, no more I can possibly take in, the stewardess comes back and says if we look to our left, at eleven o'clock, we'll catch our first sight of Mt. Everest.

This is the height toward which all things tend. It's every world record in Guinness rolled into one, personified in one great block of granite. Sagamartha, as the Nepalese call her, queen of the mountains, stands behind her sisters Lhotse, Nhuptse and Ama Dablam, leaving no doubt as to who reigns supreme. There's a force about this pyramidical peak that would tell you it's the ultimate, even if you didn't know. The rock is magnetic, alive, a spiritual loadstone that would pull the plane into a mangled wreck if it strayed too close.

Just as we're pulling up alongside, the stewardess tells Cheryl and me that it's our turn to stroll up into the cockpit. My legs are weak as we pick our way up the aisle and weaker still as we stand in the dome of the nose, pushing its way out toward Bhutan and China, while Everest, unsurpassed and beautiful, stands serene, waiting until we've drunk our fill to smile down on us and say, "It's OK—you can go home now."

There's more, of course. Trips are like books. After the denouement comes the tricky falling action, the working-out of details to establish the tone and bring the weary reader to a final resting place in some uncluttered paragraph full of promise.

As we're waiting in the airport for the plane to leave Nepal, Marie comes rushing up, having just arrived and gotten our message at American Express. She hugs Cheryl and asks us to stay, but we can't. We've been waiting all month for Marie and can't see trading a few days with her now in Katmandu for our one chance to visit Varanasi (Benares), the holy city of India, and Agra, the site of the Taj Mahal. Marie is hurt, but she tells us to ask her parents for some money when we make it back to France, so she can fly home herself.

We spend two days in Varanasi and one contemplative afternoon down the road at Sarnat, where the Buddha first preached, then take the train to Agra for a look at the most famous building on earth. We've all seen the Taj Mahal photographed hundreds of times, from every angle, but nothing can capture the sight of that cream marble glowing as the sun sets through lacy gazebos to the west.

Cheryl and I get one last night's sleep, then wake at dawn for another look at the Taj before the eight o'clock train to Delhi. 'Way back in Europe, the cathedrals were deeply rooted and solid, like the trunks of great trees mired in the mud, the family trees of European man, earthbound as his architecture, like King Claudius:

> My words fly up, my thoughts remain below
> Words without thought never to heaven go.

Next there was Greece and the Parthenon, poised on solid rock, carving out a space and proportion equal to the measure of Mediterranean man, who, cocksure, expected the gods to come from Olympus to visit *him;* and now, finally, the Taj Mahal, levitating, rising into the light, moored by its four minarets and just barely restrained from ascending to the heavens as a prayer.

It's unearthly, so delicate we almost forget the violence with which it was consecrated, when Shah Jahan decided that its architect must die so that he might never duplicate the monument created for the Shah's (presumably) incomparable wife, Mumtaz.

All my speculation and memories swirl about me. The subject expands and becomes fantastical. Folk migrations unite cultures. Mass rapes join one people to the next. Trends, evolutions, whole histories pass in the flutter of an eyelash. All the crossroads are overrun: Athens, Istanbul, Kabul and Lahore. Turks ride east and Mongols west as a profusion of races and tongues arises in the great court of an Aryan shah. Jesters and *dei ex machinis* appear and hover in the wings, displacing theories and armies at will.

We just do make that morning train to Delhi, rent a room to wash up, then head out to the airport as night falls to board a floodlit Air France 747. They seal the door shut on a grand total of thirty-five passengers, most of whom, like us, are flying half fare. We sleep across the rows, or sit up nervously, wondering what's been going on in the so-called real world, as our plane hurtles under the stars, stopping over in Abu Dhabi. The date is November 20, 1974. We left France in late April, that makes seven months all tolled, on the road.

Afterward

There's no country as great as America. I mean, you take our smallest city—Cincinnati, or even Trenton, New Jersey—they're all better than those little countries where there's no TV, no Cokes. Even the ice cream ain't cold.
—Muhammad Ali

RICHARD CAME BACK two months later with a respiratory ailment, but the look in his eyes every time he spoke of his trek, climbing toward Everest past 18,000 feet, left no doubt that it was worth it.

Cheryl and I returned to Boston, where she took a job managing our friend John's store and I began to write, supporting myself, as before, hammering jewelry at night.

Marie proved to be the most intrepid traveler of all. Having gotten enough for air fare home from her parents, she took the money and parlayed it into another six months on the road in Southeast Asia, winding up in Bali and Indonesia. When she finally returned to France, she was ready to take on her longstanding dream of moving to the south, tending a garden and having a baby, which she did.

Looking back on the trip today, it's easy to see how lucky we were. Not only is the open road no longer what it was, but the price of silver and gold has gone crazy and a hack like Capitaine Bijoux would never get invited anywhere. It bothers me to think about what might have happened if I hadn't gotten that push back in 1974, but perhaps it doesn't matter. Maybe I should just listen again to Henry Miller when he says:

> Every discovery is mysterious in that it reveals what is so unexpectedly immediate, so close, so long and intimately known. The wise man has no need to journey forth; it is the fool who seeks the pot of gold at the rainbow's end. But the two are always fated to meet and unite. They meet at the heart of the world, which is the beginning and end of the path.

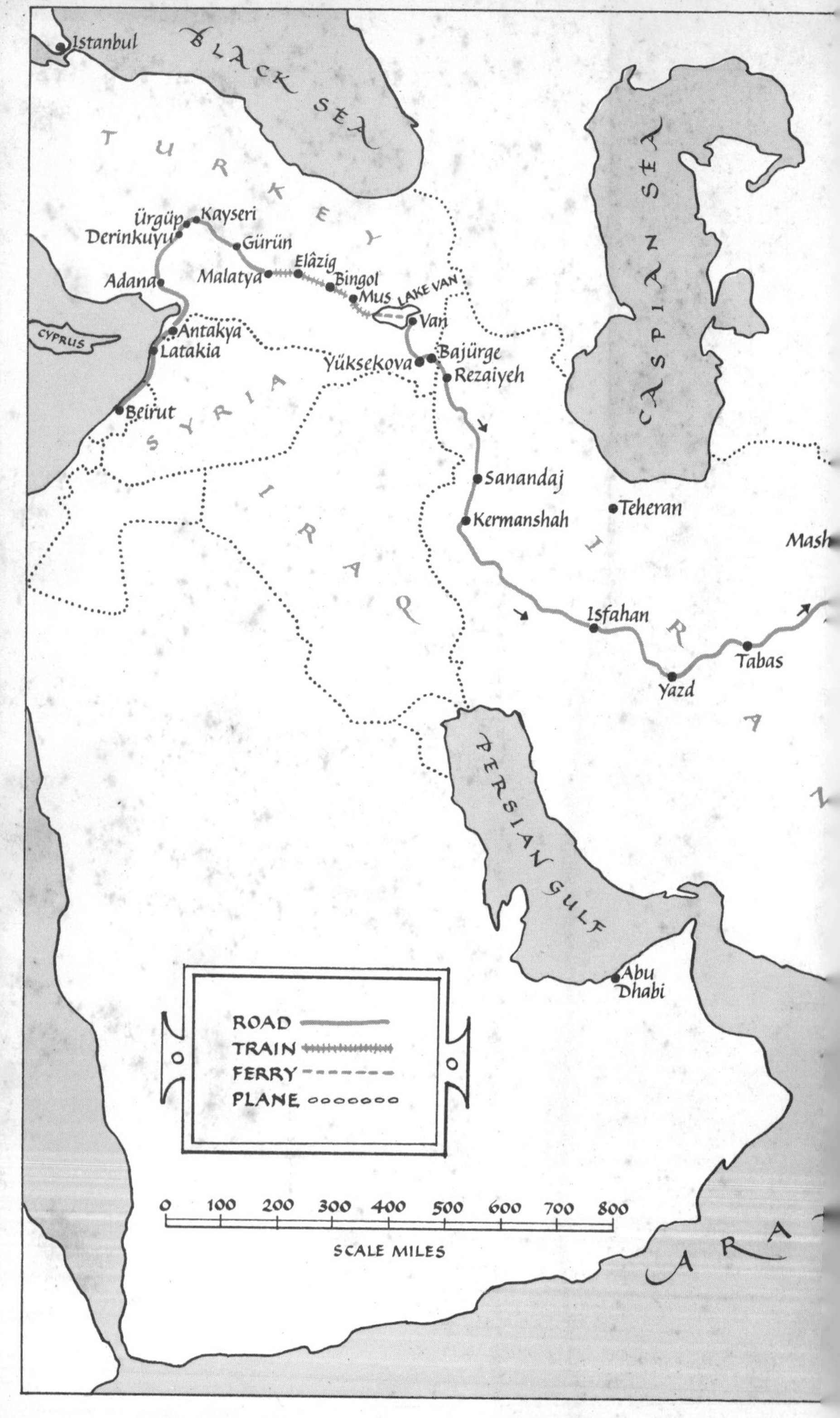

Istanbul
BLACK SEA
TURKEY
CASPIAN SEA
Ürgüp
Kayseri
Derinkuyu
Gürün
Elâzig
Malatya
Bingol
Adana
Mus
LAKE VAN
Van
CYPRUS
Antakya
Latakia
Bajürge
Yüksekova
Rezaiyeh
Beirut
SYRIA
Sanandaj
Teheran
Kermanshah
IRAQ
IRAN
Mash
Isfahan
Tabas
Yazd
PERSIAN GULF
Abu Dhabi
ROAD
TRAIN
FERRY
PLANE
0
100
200
300
400
500
600
700
800
SCALE MILES
ARA